THE
ROYAL
MARINES
AND THE
WAR AT SEA 1939–45

THE
ROYAL MARINES
AND THE
WAR AT SEA 1939–45

MARTIN WATTS

AMBERLEY

MARTIN WATTS joined the New Zealand Shipping Company in 1971 and enjoyed a career, afloat and ashore, in the Merchant Navy before studying history at the Open University and the Polytechnic of North London. Martin was awarded a PhD in 2003 and his thesis 'The Jewish Legion and the First World War' was published by Palgrave Macmillan the following year. Martin is currently Senior Lecturer and Principal Research Fellow at Canterbury Christ Church University, and an Associate Lecturer with the Open University.

First published 2018

Amberley Publishing
The Hill, Stroud
Gloucestershire, GL5 4EP

www.amberley-books.com

Copyright © Martin Watts, 2018

The right of Martin Watts to be identified as the Author of this work has been asserted in accordance with the Copyright, Designs and Patents Act 1988.

Maps courtesy of the United States Military Academy.

ISBN 978 1 4456 6318 0 (paperback)
ISBN 978 1 4456 6319 7 (ebook)

British Library Cataloguing in Publication Data.
A catalogue record for this book is available from the British Library.

Typesetting and Origination by Amberley Publishing.
Printed in the UK.

CONTENTS

	Introduction	7
	Acknowledgements	9
1	Her Majesty's Royal Marines	10
2	Nobby Joins the Fleet	21
3	Peacetime Deployment	35
4	To War	46
5	Mediterranean	66
6	HMS *Jamaica*	105
7	Blockade, Ice and Battle	136
8	Return to the Frozen North	152
9	More Convoys, Invasion, and the End of Tirpitz	179
10	Manpower, Pacific and Victory	199
11	Conclusions	231
12	Epilogue	237
	Notes	240
	Bibliography	247
	Index	251

INTRODUCTION

As a working-class boy brought up in London in the late 1950s
and '60s, I found myself, just like millions of others, becoming
fascinated about the Second World War. My role models were
firmly fixed in the generation that served, both within and
without the Armed Forces, especially members of my extended
family and my teachers. The constant output of British war films
though this period had a prolonged cultural effect, and weekly
reading of comics such as *The Victor* (first published in 1961)
and the graphically illustrated *Commando* series, reinforced the
stereotyped history with which I entered adulthood. Indeed, the
adoption of the title 'Commando' firmly fixed in one's mind not
only the development of this elite fighting force in the war, but
the fact that the first Commandos were Army Commandos and
they were followed by the Royal Marines. By 1960, Royal Marine
Commandos had become the *raison d'être* of the Royal Marines.

This begged a question about the Royal Marines' involvement
in the war, particularly about those who were not destined to
train as Commandos. Fortunately, my great uncle, Albert Elliott,
had served as a Royal Marine between 1926 and 1950, and had
spent almost the entire war afloat, serving in every major theatre
of war. A native and lifelong resident of Devonport, Uncle Nobby,

then serving as a dockyard policeman, had taken our family on tours of the dockyard when we holidayed in Devon in the 1960s. My brother Nigel and I marvelled at the aircraft carriers, cruisers, destroyers and frigates that filled the berths and dry docks. Later, in 1971, as a deck cadet with the New Zealand Shipping Company, I was sent to navigation school in Plymouth, an experience that was repeated after further sea service, and I relished the Sundays spent with Uncle Nobby and Aunt Rose, both for the roasts, cream teas, and the retelling of stories from Nobby's long service.

Years passed and today Nobby and Rose are sadly no longer with us. In the meantime, I have become a professional historian and university lecturer and, with the aid of Nobby's papers, the help of the family and my own research, I now wish to tell the story of the Royal Marines and the war at sea.

Dr Martin Watts
Maidstone, 2018

Sergeant Major
Nobby Elliott.

ACKNOWLEDGEMENTS

Firstly, I wish to acknowledge the assistance provided by members of Nobby's immediate family in granting permission to access and use his papers and records. Thanks, then, to Mrs Mary Lowman (daughter), the late Sydney Elliott (son and former Fleet Chief Petty Officer Royal Navy) and Paul Elliott (grandson and former Royal Marine Commando). I am also grateful to the late Miss Doris Pullinger, Nobby's sister-in-law, who provided much valuable information about the family and Rose's early life. Secondly, like all historians, I owe a debt of gratitude to the professional archivists, librarians and staff who make our work possible. During this project, I have been ably assisted by curators and staff at the Royal Naval Museum, Portsmouth; the Royal Marines Museum, Eastney; the National Maritime Museum, Greenwich; the Imperial War Museum, London; and the National Archives at Kew. I would also like to thank Professor Kevin Ruane, a valued colleague at Canterbury Christ Church University, for sharing research on the British Pacific Fleet. Thanks also to my editors Cathy Stagg and Matilda Richards at Amberley Books.

I remain completely responsible for the contents of this book, and have sought acknowledgements where due. All errors and omissions are mine alone.

I

HER MAJESTY'S ROYAL MARINES

As a Corps and an integral part of the Royal Navy, the Royal Marines celebrated their tercentenary as long ago as 1964. Longevity, however, is no guarantor of survival, and the Corps had to face several existential threats over its long history, and its ultimate survival has been due in no small measure to its adaptability in both peace and war. The amphibious nature of its duties has, on various occasions, led to arguments both in favour of disbandment and continued operation. Within this overall context, therefore, it is no surprise to note that in the aftermath of the First World War the very purpose and future employment of the Corps was called into question.

The Corps had expanded to its largest-ever size during the war, so that by the time of the Armistice in November 1918, its strength had reached about 55,000 officers and men. At this time, Royal Marines served in two branches, the Royal Marine Light Infantry, where the lowest rank was Private, and the Royal Marine Artillery, where the equivalent rank was Gunner. Both branches served at sea in cruisers, battlecruisers and battleships, and in various small boat roles. The majority of Royal Marines also played their full part as members of the Royal Naval Division, which served alongside the British Army in campaigns in France, Flanders and the Mediterranean. This Division, known as the 63rd (Royal Naval Division), mainly consisted of newly enlisted volunteers and naval reservists for whom no billet at sea was available. This meant that the smaller cadre of pre-war regular, fully trained marines were largely to be found on board larger warships, where they provided the Royal Navy with an amphibious and boarding capability, and manned a share of the ship's main and secondary armament. The extent of this commitment is demonstrated by noting that a typical Royal Marines complement on board, for example, a Queen Elizabeth class battleship, consisted of three officers (one Captain and two Lieutenants), one Commissioned Gunner RM, sixteen NCOs, two buglers and 136 marines. These super dreadnoughts, which saw service in both world wars, also carried fifteen musicians, two marine butchers and one marine attendant (equivalent to a batman in the British Army), making a total of 176 men.[1] The musicians, commanded by a bandmaster, provided a band for ceremonial duties and were often employed in action in the Transmitting Station (TS), where the data required for the aiming and firing of the ship's armament, received from gunnery control towers and spotting tops, was processed. Situated under a heavily armoured deck, towards the bottom of the ship, the TS used a mechanical computer, the Admiralty Fire Control Table, to calculate the elevation and training angles required to enable the guns to hit a moving target. Used to working as a team and equipped with manual dexterity and an elementary education, it can be seen why it was thought that bandsmen would be particularly suited to this task.

The Royal Navy's use of marines in the days of sail had involved duties as marksmen and, to coin a phrase, amphibious infantry, but these sea soldiers were also employed to maintain discipline on board and, in extreme circumstances, to literally protect the Captain and Officers from a hostile or mutinous crew. This explains the tradition of placing the marines mess deck, officially known as 'barracks', between the officers' quarters and the seamen's accommodation, a practice further demonstrated by the posting of marine sentries outside the Captain's cabin and in front of the office of the First

Sea Lord in the Admiralty in London. Incidentally, the Sergeant's Mess was known as the 'Horse Box', separated by a door from the barracks, and boy buglers also slept there in order to be afforded some protection from possible bullying.[2] It is also worth mentioning here that Royal Marines were sworn men while the Officers and ratings of the Royal Navy were not, this distinction being due to the fact that the navy was created and maintained under royal prerogative, while the army and marines were subject to the Army Act under the auspices of Parliament. Thus, while afloat, marines were subject to the Naval Discipline Act but, once ashore, they came under the Army Act.

With the development of the late Victorian and Edwardian navy, involving a technical revolution in education, training, propulsion and armament, marines and sailors had to become technical team workers as never before. The idea, therefore, of a ship's marines being used to enforce discipline among their own shipmates ran counter to maintaining a high level of fighting efficiency produced by the deployment of a highly trained ship's company. This is not to say that there was no competition between marines and sailors; indeed, with the Royal Navy's emphasis on the speed of loading and firing of main armaments, healthy competition was encouraged, with Royal Marine turrets (usually Y turret in ships equipped with four turrets, or Q – the centre – turret in ships with five) gaining a reputation for efficiency and speed. As the fleet modernised, it must be recognised that the number of pre-dreadnought and dreadnought-type battleships increased rapidly, and this placed excessive demands on the navy's cadre of trained seaman gunners, which was relieved to some extent by the availability of marine gunners, and is the reason why the Admiralty sought to emphasise this capability. Maintaining gunnery manpower throughout the First World War was the Admiralty's priority.

Nothing illustrates this more forcibly than the only Grand Fleet action of the war, when it confronted the German High Seas Fleet off the coast of Jutland in the afternoon of 31 May 1916.

With a fleet of 151 warships whose capital ships, made up of twenty-eight dreadnought and super dreadnought battleships, plus nine similarly armed but less heavily armoured battlecruisers, amounted to thirty-seven, it can be reckoned that the Royal Navy depended upon the Royal Marines to man more than a fifth of its main battle armament. In line with the earlier quoted figures covering the marine complement of a capital ship, this meant that in excess of 4,000 marines were engaged in this activity, not forgetting that at least a further 1,500 were carried in the accompanying heavy and light cruiser squadrons. The typical capital ship gun turret, with a pair of guns of a calibre between 12.5- and 15-inches, consisted of an above deck gun house with working chambers, shell rooms and magazines below, and employed between sixty and ninety men depending on the class of vessel. It is important to note that members of both the Royal Marine Artillery and Royal Marine Light infantry worked together in the operation of the turret, with those responsible for the specialist gunnery roles, such as gun layer and trainer, having received the same training and qualification as their naval counterparts and shipmates. In many ships, the Royal Marines also manned a share of the secondary armament, ranging from smaller calibre guns in fixed mountings to automatic weapons. During the battle the Royal Navy lost none of its battleships, but the battlecruiser fleet, with its lighter deck armour protection, suffered grievously at the hands of the modern dreadnoughts of the opposing High Seas Fleet. Three battlecruisers, HMS *Invincible*, HMS *Indefatigable* and HMS *Queen Mary*, representing one third of this type engaged, were lost following magazine explosions caused by the penetration of German shells, resulting in the death of 3,320 sailors, a figure that accounts for more than 50 per cent of the navy's total losses during the battle. It could have been worse as Vice Admiral Beatty's own flagship, HMS *Lion,* was also struck by a heavy German shell that exploded in the gun house of Q turret, situated amidships between its two funnels. Contemporary photographs show that the explosion removed over half of Q turret's roof, and the resultant fire threatened the magazine below, thus exposing the ship to the same catastrophic fate as its companions. This was averted, however, by the brave action of the officer commanding the turret, Major Francis Harvey RMLI, whose heroism was subsequently recorded in his citation for the award of a posthumous Victoria Cross:

> While mortally wounded and almost the only survivor after the explosion of an enemy shell in 'Q' gun house, with great presence of mind and devotion to duty ordered the magazine to be flooded, thereby saving the ship. He died shortly thereafter.[3]

Major Harvey was buried at sea and, according to the Imperial War Museum's Lives of the First World War project, the *Lion* sustained another fourteen hits, resulting in the further loss of 100 of its crew, 'of which around half were marines'. Aged 43 at the time of his death, Major Harvey originally came from Sydenham and he is commemorated in the Chatham Royal Naval Memorial.

In addition to Major Harvey's award, officers and men of the Royal Marines received another four Victoria Crosses in the First World War, and these demonstrate the wider scope of the deployment of the Corps. Lance-Corporal Walter Parker RMLI won his when serving as leader of a stretcher-bearer party in Gallipoli on 1 May 1915, while Major Frederick Lumsden RMA was similarly decorated when rescuing, under fire, six captured enemy field guns near Francilly, France, on the night of 3/4 April 1917. The remaining two VCs were awarded to Captain Edward Bamford RMLI and Sergeant Norman Finch RMA for their gallant efforts during the raid on Zeebrugge on St George's Day, 23 April 1918. All four survived the action that witnessed their decoration and, except for Major Lumsden, they also survived the war. Lumsden, by then a Brigadier commanding the 14th Infantry Brigade with a VC, CB, DSO and three bars, was killed near Arras on 4 June 1918.

The end of hostilities in 1918, with demobilisation and the war's dramatic effect on the nation's economy, meant that the Royal Marines were, in 1919, reduced by 40,000 men to a Corps with a strength of just 15,000.

This severe reduction should be seen against the background of what has come to be known as the 'Geddes Axe', named after the chairman, Sir Alexander Geddes, of the newly established Committee on National Expenditure. With the resumption of peace and with the Armed Forces having the largest share of public expenditure, the committee had a strong case for severe cuts in defence estimates. This was politically supported by the government decision, in 1919, to instigate the ten-year rule, whereby the navy, army and air force were told to plan on the basis that there would be no major war for ten years. At first glance this may have seemed reasonable after the cataclysmic shock of the First World War and its effect upon the British economy, and it did seem to offer the armed services an opportunity to be modernised, albeit modestly, by spreading expenditure over the next decade. For the navy, however, this was not the case, as it required a large industrial infrastructure to support the building and outfitting of ships. This infrastructure was threatened by the smaller order book, which led to a reduction in capacity and the loss of some of the specialist companies and skilled staff, whose sustainability was key to any modernisation, let alone future expansion of the fleet.

A further blow to the navy was the Washington Naval Conference of 1921–22, called by the United States to introduce international disarmament, thus reducing the possibility of a future arms race, such as that which had occurred between the United Kingdom and Germany in the run-up to the First World War. If agreement could be reached then not only would fleet sizes and rivalries be reduced, but also demands on the public purse and strain on economies would be lessened. The conference did produce an agreement between the five major (and victorious) naval powers, the United Kingdom, USA,

Japan, France and Italy, whereby the UK and US would have parity in numbers of battleships, followed by a lower number for Japan, France and Italy. Furthermore, the agreement set out that no major warships could be built for ten years, thus chiming with the UK's ten-year rule, and maximums were agreed for the size and armament of battleships, aircraft carriers and cruisers. While the intention was to agree similar treaties with regard to air and land forces, these never materialised, thus disproportionately penalising the UK as a predominantly naval power. Indeed, the effect of the Washington Treaty was to reduce the Royal Navy – which had by far the largest fleet, by almost three-quarters – to match the Americans. This led to the instigation of a massive programme of decommissioning and scrapping of warships, with a concomitant effect on shipborne manpower including, of course, the Royal Marines. This situation inevitably led to a broader consideration of the future of the Corps by the Admiralty, which simultaneously came under pressure from the Treasury to abolish the Royal Marines altogether. In some respects this proposal was not unreasonable, if it was to be believed that the age of the battleship was passing, in favour of naval aviation and submarine warfare. There were, however, few such visionaries at the top of the Royal Navy, and the retention of battleships and the need for cruisers to protect trade and police the Empire, meant their Lordships were keen to retain a cadre of trained Royal Marine gunners and infantry. The Admiralty finally responded to the constraints on manpower and money by amalgamating the two Royal Marine branches and, in an Admiralty Order issued in June 1923, they were replaced by a single Royal Marines corps, and 'Gunners' and 'Privates' became Marines, receiving training as infantry and seaman gunners.[4] The effect of the amalgamation was to reduce numbers by a third, from 15,000 to 10,000 which, unsurprisingly, led to a further examination of the role and purpose of the Corps.

This was carried out by a committee under the leadership of Admiral Sir Charles Madden (a future First Sea Lord) which, after six months deliberation, delivered a report to the Admiralty in August 1924. Among its recommendations the Madden Committee, acknowledging the work carried out by the United States Marine Corps in identifying its own future role, confirmed that on-board detachments, operating armament and providing a small assault force, should be retained. However, the Committee also proposed the development of a brigade-sized force that could be deployed to acquire and protect temporary naval bases that the Royal Navy would need in time of war. This latter recommendation, although accepted in principle and confirmed in the 1927 Official Instructions for Royal Marine Divisions, was destined not to be implemented until the Second World War, because the economic and political decisions mentioned above meant there was simply no financial means to make it a reality.[5] In practical terms, the now 10,000-strong Corps were divided into three detachments, with one in each of the Royal Navy depots (properly known as Divisions) in Chatham, Plymouth and Portsmouth. Warships were allocated to a Division from which they drew their crews and maintenance. Like their sailor counterparts, marines were allocated to ships (cruiser and heavier) and could expect to serve a full two to two-and-a-half-year commission, involving service virtually anywhere in the world.

A further effect of the amalgamation and the associated reduction in manpower was that some men had to be selected for discharge, in a process that would be known today as voluntary redundancy. This legal process consisted of the Admiralty, following the provisions of the Naval and Marine Pay and Pensions Act 1865, using Orders in Council, approved by the King, to vary pay and conditions as they saw fit. In respect of the proposed reductions in manpower, two Orders in Council were issued, the first of which, dated 13 October 1922, detailed the compensation that would be paid to volunteers for discharge:

Your Majesty was pleased to sanction the payment of pensions, gratuities [*sic*], and bonuses to men selected for discharge in consequence of the reduction of Your Majesty's Naval or Marine Force subsequently to the 12th May 1922, the time to count for pension purposes being reckoned up to 3 months after that date ... or to the date of discharge in the case of men detained beyond that date through causes not under their control...[6]

The second Order, promulgated on 30 July 1923, effectively put the scheme into operation, as shown in the following extract:

AND WHEREAS in consequence of the amalgamation of the Royal Marine Artillery and Royal Marine Light Infantry, involving a further reduction in the Royal Marine Force, we have found it necessary to invite applications from Royal Marines for discharge from that force...[7]

At the time, while not seeming to be overly generous, these terms did attract volunteers in an age when statutory employment rights were almost non-existent, and are a further indication of the financial plight of the nation and its effect on service expenditure. Some retired marines were able to take up posts in the newly formed Royal Marine Police which, tasked with policing Britain's naval bases, specifically recruited recently retired men whose training and experience made them ideally suited to this role.

For those remaining in the service, economic pressure was also to be exerted upon their pay and conditions. New rates of pay had been introduced in 1919–20, in the aftermath of the war, but, in an indication of what was to come, pay reductions began to be introduced from 1924. Using the process described above in relation to redundancy, the Admiralty reduced Officers pay by 5½ per cent, with effect from 1 July 1924. The Admiralty sought to explain the reduction:

As some misconception appears to exist as to the method by which the rate of reduction has been fixed... the rate of approximately 5½ per cent decided upon has been arrived at as follows: –

In 1919, when new rates of pay were fixed, it was decided that 20 per cent of those rates should be considered as due to the then high cost of living and should be subject after five years to change, either upwards or downwards, according as the cost of living rose or fell.[8]

Using Ministry of Labour index figures, the Admiralty calculated that the 'excess cost of living has actually fallen by approximately 27½ per cent', and applied this percentage to the 20 per cent cost of living allowance mentioned above, thus arriving at the figure of 5½ per cent.[9] The Admiralty went on to add that rates of pay would be reviewed again on or after 1 July 1927 and indeed they were, with another reduction of officer pay imposed.

Although not affected by this specific review, the pay of naval ratings and their marine counterparts was also revised in 1925. In this case, the Admiralty decided to introduce new pay scales for new entrants (both officers and enlisted men) with effect from 1 October 1925. The new rates were 75 per cent of the old, and thus produced an unprecedented situation whereby sailors and marines, serving together, were subject to a two-tier pay system. This had two effects. Firstly, having shipmates on different pay scales was hardly likely to improve the morale and teamwork that have always been essential to operational efficiency. Secondly, the pre-1925 ratings and marines who were in receipt of the 'generous' settlement that had been made in 1919 were more likely to enter into new financial arrangements, such as taking advantage of hire purchase commitments. Both effects were to come to an unhappy culmination with the Invergordon mutiny of September 1931, following an attempt by the Admiralty to reduce the pay of those on 1919 rates to the 1925 rate; an effective reduction of 25 per cent. The resulting unpleasantness in some ships of the Atlantic Fleet (shortly afterwards renamed the Home Fleet), based at Invergordon, saw a number of Royal Marines join in the protest, thus dispelling the notion of the marines acting as an internal police force. Within a few hours of the 'strike', which involved about 1,000 sailors and marines on 15 September 1931, the Admiralty made several concessions, including the extension of marriage allowances to those under 25 years of age and cancelling the reduction for those in the lower ranks. This had the effect of limiting the pay cut to around 10 per cent overall, which was accepted by the sailors and marines, as evidenced by their obeying of orders to proceed to sea late on the same day and return to their home ports.

While pay comparisons across different sectors of the economy are notoriously difficult to make, particularly when there are a range of allowances available for certain categories, it is perhaps worth examining the 1919 rates and comparing them to average wages in industry and transport. For example, a Staff Sergeant RM on appointment had a weekly wage of £2 16s per week,[10] a rate of pay that exceeded, by 6 shillings, the average wage of privately employed ship joiners, shipwrights and engine drivers, who appear at the top of government wage statistics.[11] This comparison lends weight to those who considered the 1919 settlement had to be rowed back, as the country entered the Great Depression and Ramsay MacDonald's government decided to slash public expenditure.

For the Royal Marines, as for the other armed services and the public sector in general, the economic consequences of the First World War resulted in severe financial and material cutbacks, compounded by the unfavourable outcome of the Washington Naval Treaty. This is the inauspicious background against which, on 27 August 1926, Albert Thomas Elliott, aged 14 years and 9 months, joined the Royal Marines as a Boy Bugler.

2

NOBBY JOINS THE FLEET

The 14-year-old recruit, Albert Elliott, known to his shipmates, family and friends as 'Nobby', was born in St Aubyn, Devonport, on 12 November 1911. His service number was 100, confirming his membership of the Plymouth Division and with the 'X' denoting the fact that he was engaged under the terms of the 1925 pay scale, initially receiving 2s and 9d per day (about 27.5p in today's decimalised currency). Described as being of Baptist background, 5 feet tall and having blue eyes and dark brown hair, Nobby came, unsurprisingly, from a naval family.[1] Nobby's father, William Moses Smerdon Elliott, had been born in Torpoint, Cornwall, just across the River Tamar from Devonport, on 21 September 1878. He initially worked as a labourer then as a bricklayer. On 17 May 1898, aged 19, William enlisted in the Royal Navy as a stoker, joining the Plymouth shore-based training establishment, HMS Vivid.[2] Initially signing up for twelve years, William eventually served until December 1919, having qualified and risen to the rank of Stoker Petty Officer in April 1911. In 1903 William had married Mary Maria Caplin, and the couple had two sons, William Joseph, born 10 January 1907, followed by Albert (Nobby). Unfortunately, Mary died in 1913, at the age of 30, leaving William Snr with the challenging responsibility of arranging care for his two young sons while he continued his career in the navy. During this period, William was serving on board HMS *Blake,* a protected cruiser that had previously been the flagship of the North American and West Indies squadron, and was now a converted depot ship, in which capacity she hosted the 11th destroyer flotilla of the Grand Fleet, based at Scapa Flow. To overcome the difficulties presented by having two boys several hundred miles away from their father's ship, William arranged for them to be looked after by a local landlady in Scotland, Lilian Martin. According to family recollections, when William's service took him back to Devonport, Lilian and the boys went with him, and there, in the second quarter of 1919, William married Lillian and they later had a daughter, a stepsister to William Jnr and Nobby.[3,4] It remains unclear how the acquisition of a stepmother suited the two brothers but, like many children of a service family living in a traditionally strong recruitment area, both joined the armed services (William joined the Army) as soon as they were old enough.

Nobby's father's service during the First World War included participation in the Battle of the Falklands in December 1914. Upon the outbreak of war in August 1914, William was a Stoker Petty Officer aboard HMS *Carnarvon,* a 10,850-ton armoured cruiser built between 1902 and 1905. One of six Devonshire class vessels, *Carnarvon* was more than 470 feet long and had main armament consisting of four turrets, each housing single guns of 7.5-inch calibre, with an effective range of almost 8 miles. As was fairly typical at the time of her construction, *Carnarvon's* 6-inch secondary armament was housed in casemates on the main deck, where they were exposed to all but the slightest seas, thus reducing their overall effectiveness. This was rectified later in the war by the removal of these guns to the upper deck and the plating over of the casemate openings. *Carnarvon's* two triple expansion engines generated 21,000 horsepower, giving a maximum speed of 22 knots, and her wartime complement consisted of some

610 officers and men.[5] On 5 August 1914 *Carnarvon* was in Gibraltar as the flagship of Rear Admiral Stoddart, from where she immediately proceeded to the Cape Verde Islands on a patrol looking for German merchant shipping. On 22 August *Carnarvon* took SS *Professor Woermann* as a prize, and delivered her to the port of Freetown, Sierra Leone. *Carnarvon* then took up patrol off the South American coast, until ordered to join the squadron of Vice Admiral Sturdee, then en route to the Falkland Islands. Sturdee's squadron had been ordered south in pursuit of the German Vice Admiral von Spee's East Asia squadron, which, having bombarded Tahiti, had proceeded towards the South American coast on its commerce raiding mission. On 1 November 1914, the East Asia squadron encountered a weak British cruiser squadron, commanded by Rear Admiral Cradock, off Coronel on the Chilean coast. In this short but savage engagement, two British cruisers, the flagship HMS *Good Hope* and HMS *Monmouth,* were sunk with the loss of all 1,600 men on board, including Rear Admiral Cradock, while the German fleet escaped almost completely unscathed. While the East Asia fleet was equipped with modern warships and crews that had been trained to a high degree of efficiency, the old cruisers in Cradock's squadron had not had a proper opportunity to work up their gunnery skills, and his crews had many reservists on board, particularly in *Good Hope* and *Monmouth*. Taking advantage of failing light and poor weather, the capable and well-drilled German gunnery took swift and decisive action to bring the battle to a close. Despite this, however, Vice Admiral von Spee knew that his fleet was isolated, with its base in Tsing Tao now having been overrun by the combined forces of Britain and Japan, and that it was only a matter of time before the British Admiralty would despatch a more powerful force to hunt him down. Vice Admiral Sturdee and his ships arrived at Port Stanley in the Falkland Islands, where he ordered every vessel to refuel from the colliers that were maintained there, before resuming the search for von

Spee, whom the Admiralty believed would be rounding Cape Horn in an attempt to make German home waters. It is easy, therefore, to imagine Vice Admiral Sturdee's grateful surprise – and Vice Admiral von Spee's shock – when, on the morning of 8 December, Vice Admiral von Spee's squadron hove into view, apparently intent upon destroying the radio station at Port Stanley before resuming their voyage home. As many of his ships were still coaling, it took a couple of hours before Vice Admiral Sturdee could order a general chase. Having two modern, fast battlecruisers, HMS *Inflexible* and HMS *Invincible* in the van, the British squadron was soon able to catch and engage the German ships while keeping themselves out of range of their opponent's guns. In the inevitable action that followed, Vice Admiral von Spee's flagship, *Scharnhorst*, was sunk first, swiftly followed by three others. German losses amounted to more than 2,000, including Vice Admiral von Spee and both of his sons, while ten British deaths were incurred in this decisive and confidence-building victory. As for *Carnarvon,* her relative slow speed meant she did not engage with the enemy until later in the afternoon, finally engaging *Gneisenau* until the ceasefire was ordered at 1750. *Carnarvon* picked up twenty survivors from *Gneisenau* after the German captain, in acknowledging the overwhelming damage that had been inflicted upon his command, ordered her to be scuttled, the hull finally disappearing beneath the waves at 1800. William remained on board until 15 August 1915, during which time *Carnarvon* assisted the search for the German cruiser *Dresden*, after which she ran aground off Brazil and was temporarily repaired in Rio, then permanently repaired in Montreal before escorting British submarines from Halifax to Plymouth. After six months ashore in HMS *Vivid*, William joined HMS *Godetia* on 10 March 1916, a sea-going appointment that would take him to the end of the war. *Godetia* was brand new and one of thirty-six wartime-built Arabis class sloops, with a tonnage of 1,350 and fitted with minesweeping capability.[6]

Following on from his father, Nobby joined the marines at a time when they were recruiting about 700 men a year as replacements for natural turnover. His career began with a year ashore in Plymouth, undergoing basic training as a boy bugler. Two months after his enlistment Nobby passed his 3rd class School Certificate, which highlights the importance of education in the armed services for their young recruits, many of whom had failed to benefit from the elementary public education that had been introduced in 1870 and then uprated through the introduction of Local Education Authorities in the Education Act 1902. The new Act was designed to create a better educated workforce for a society that, while holding a leading position in industry and manufacture, was some fifty years adrift of public education provided in parts of Europe and the United States of America. Given that warships, especially dreadnoughts and their successors, represented the then pinnacle of design, technology and complex manufacture, it was clear the Royal Navy took its responsibilities for general education and technical training seriously.[7] In addition to general musical

In peace or war, musicians studied at the Royal Naval School, Deal, before joining their ships and depots. Here is a class of Royal Marines, each man with his saxophone.

duties, boy buglers were used (and continued to be used for many years) to sound off orders through a ship's speaker system, calling hands to action and to many more evolutions, and were a standard feature on every ship with a Royal Marine detachment.

In October 1927 Nobby proceeded to Portsmouth for six weeks of turret training on board HMS *Erebus,* a First World War monitor of shallow draught, equipped with a single turret housing a pair of 15-inch guns. *Erebus* had won a battle honour at Zeebrugge in 1918 when she acted as a blockship in the raid on that port and Ostend. Nobby's turret training, which introduced him to the strict discipline and routine of handling ammunition and operating the largest and most complex gunnery type then available, helped to prepare him for his first sea-going commission.[8] On 24 February 1928, aged 16 years and 3 months, Nobby joined HMS *Frobisher,* a post-war built Hawkins class cruiser. These cruisers were developed as a result of wartime experience with the pursuit of German raiders, hence their speed and more powerful – when compared to most cruisers of their size – main armament. Built at Devonport and completed in September 1924, *Frobisher* had a tonnage of 9,750, was just over 600 feet in length with a maximum speed of 30 knots, and a crew of 712.[9] Included in this complement was the Royal Marine detachment consisting of two officers, a Captain and Lieutenant, a Colour Sergeant (as senior NCO on board also known as Sergeant Major, a practice peculiar to the marines), ten other NCOs, two buglers and fifty-four marines. In addition, there was a marine band of fifteen, including a Bandmaster, two marine butchers and one marine attendant, who was assigned to the marine CO. *Frobisher* was equipped with a main armament of seven 7.5-inch guns in single mounts, with a further twelve single guns of lesser calibres. In meeting the requirement to man a share of the ship's armament, the marine detachment included three gun layers, one range taker and thirteen quarters' rated men who were trained in their specialist skills alongside their naval rating counterparts. Quarters men acted as gun trainers and supervised the workings of the shell room and magazine, the term 'Quarters' being a reference to chief gunner's assistants in the days of sail who were usually placed in charge of a group of four guns. The marine band had their action station in *Frobisher's* main transmitting station, in line with the practice mentioned earlier. Not long before Nobby joined her, the *Frobisher* had undergone a major refit in which one of the secondary guns was moved to allow for the installation of a crane and catapult, thus giving the ship an aircraft operating capability, reflecting the evolving use of aircraft for advanced reconnaissance at sea. With Nobby on board, *Frobisher* sailed for duty with the 1st Cruiser Squadron of the Mediterranean Fleet, giving the young marine

Gun crew in action: Royal Marines training for gunnery, one of their principal wartime duties. This picture was taken at a shore establishment.

his introduction to foreign parts and the delights of, among other places, Alexandria and Malta. This peacetime commission, comprising fleet manoeuvres and 'showing the flag', came to an end when the *Frobisher* returned to Plymouth in early September 1929. The crew was dispersed and the ship was docked for a further refit that would see her fully converted to oil from coal, and Nobby went ashore for a year's training in Plymouth and Deal. The depot in Deal was mainly used for initial training in seamanship, field craft and weapon handling; this was needed by Nobby as he approached the end of his boy service and re-engagement as a marine on reaching his 18th birthday.

At the time training was under review and a new Royal Marine Training Manual was being prepared to incorporate the organisation and role of the Corps, following the 1923 amalgamation and the Madden Report. The publication of the manual in 1932 reflected the results of this review and the ongoing development of training during the post reduction period. The preamble to the operating content of the training manual defined the status of, and summarised the post-First World War evolution of, the Corps:

The corps of Royal Marines is a military body specially organised and trained for service in the Fleet as well as on shore. It forms part of the Regular Forces of the Crown, with the sanction of Parliament, renewed annually in the Army Act.

Its function in war and peace is to provide detachments which, while fully capable of manning their share of the gun armament of ships, are specially trained to provide a striking force drawn either from the Royal Marine Divisions or from the Fleet ... for amphibious operations such as raids on the enemy coast-line and bases, or the seizure and defence of temporary bases for the use of our own Fleet.[10]

Just like the Madden Committee, the selection of these duties was a continuation of the role actually taken by the marines in operations from the 1840s to the end of the First World War. Various small-scale landing parties had been employed in the Indian Mutiny in 1857, in New Zealand in 1864, and later in East Africa and the Arabian Gulf. Attacks on enemy coasts had been carried out during the China wars, the Boxer Rising, West Africa and then at the Dardanelles and Zeebrugge in the First World War, as described earlier. The war also saw Royal Marines used to defend naval bases at Cromarty, Scapa Flow, Murmansk and the Aegean Islands. While the employment and purpose of the Corps now appeared to be more secure, the reduction in manpower, as noted earlier, meant the formation of full divisions would not be possible until rearmament and the commencement of hostilities in 1939. Nevertheless, the requirement to be trained to fulfil the operations described above was fully embraced in the 1932 manual. This confirmed the need for marines to be trained in both military and naval disciplines, with a small number of specialists receiving instruction in land artillery. The latter was carried out by the School of Land Artillery and involved the use of coastal guns, mobile and anti-aircraft artillery. For the co-ordination of naval bombardments from shore, selected marines were trained to act as shore observers and liaison officers. Infantry training prior to qualification and embarkation was carried out at Deal and with the Army School of Infantry. Once embarked, however, the manual laid down planning guidance for tactical training in the field, listing a six-day programme covering landing and encampment, fire and movement, reconnaissance and night attack, protection and field craft, tactical and night exercises, and withdrawal. In 1930, conditions in the Mediterranean Fleet were such that senior officers were able to build upon this training and prepare a striking force consisting of two battalions drawn from shipboard detachments. Again, however, this only served to reveal that such a deployment could only be undertaken at the expense of a significant reduction of trained ships' gun crews, and this presented a risk that admirals would be reluctant to take, as the protection of the fleet was paramount. Indeed, as far as naval gunnery was concerned, programmes of turret drill were continued alongside pre-embarkation refresher courses in all aspects of this discipline, with the objective of ensuring that skills were kept up to date and marines were fully prepared to take up their duties on joining their ships.[11]

As the training manual was being prepared, the British government hosted another major international naval conference in London, involving Britain, France, Italy, Japan and the United States. It was signed on 22 April 1930 and was to have a profound effect upon the Royal Navy. In the words of Corelli Barnett, the distinguished military and naval historian:

> This naval conference, held in London in 1930, completed the demolition work on British sea power begun at Washington in 1922 and continued piecemeal by Conservative and Labour Chancellors of the Exchequer thereafter.[12]

Indeed, the Admiralty's difficulties were compounded by the fact that in 1928 the Conservative Chancellor of the Exchequer (and former and future First Lord of the Admiralty) Sir Winston Churchill had made the ten-year rule permanent. This meant the armed services could never reach fulfilment of their ten-year plans, thus saving the Treasury money that would otherwise have been spent on modernisation. Under the limitations imposed by the earlier Washington conference, the Royal Navy had been able to commission only two capital ships in the 1920s, HMS *Nelson* and HMS *Rodney*. In taking account of the tonnage restrictions imposed by the treaty, these two ships incorporated nine 16-inch guns in three triple turrets all forward of the bridge superstructure which was, therefore, situated towards the aft end of each vessel. The incorporation of heavy armour protection had the effect of reducing the speed of these battleships to 23 knots, a compromise that was to limit their effectiveness. All in all, their unusual appearance represented the physical embodiment of the need to comply with the requirements of the treaty, while making a gesture towards the modernisation of the British battle fleet. It is not, however, the situation regarding the limitations on capital ships that was foremost in the mind of the Admiralty. With treaty parity with the United States (fifteen vessels each) and the maintenance of at least twice as many of these ship types when compared with Japan (nine), France (five), and Italy (five), there was little choice but for the Admiralty to accept the new status quo. When it came to the restrictions on cruisers, however, the Admiralty was both exercised and vexed by what would be agreed in London. The basis for their Lordships' consternation centred on the number and quality of cruisers allowed, the former arising from the trade and imperial protection responsibilities that the Royal Navy was expected to maintain. Given the geographical size of the British Empire and the dominant role the British Merchant Navy fulfilled in world trade, these responsibilities were far in excess of those expected of the other treaty fleets. Ahead of the signing of the Treaty of London, on 17 January 1930, the First Sea Lord, now Admiral of the Fleet, Sir Charles Madden, wrote a long memorandum to the British government, expressing the Royal Navy's concerns and reservations. The London Treaty, to all intents and purposes, was an extension of Washington from which the Royal Navy, in acceptance of the maximum tonnage of 10,000 tons with 8-inch guns, argued for two types of cruiser, specifying a tactical role for light cruisers equipped with 6-inch guns, and noting that, within overall tonnage limits, more cruisers in total could be built.

Madden had used this argument to partly counter America's insistence upon the larger type, who wished to build because, according to Madden:

(i) The gun must be of the maximum size of 8 inches to meet a supposed menace from our (*Britain's*) greater merchant fleet, and in order that they may never be outgunned by an enemy cruiser.

(ii) The ship must be of maximum size of 10,000 tons so that cruisers can operate at great distances and to counter balance a lack of (*American*) overseas bases.

Madden dismissed the first American claim as modern 6-inch cruisers had more than sufficient power to deal with any merchant vessel and argued that if America could agree to building these ships, an increased range that equalled or exceeded that of the 10,000-ton class would result. In other words, more cruisers of smaller size could be built within the overall tonnage limits contained in the treaty.[13] This latter point demonstrates the cruiser quandary that the Royal Navy now found itself in. Before the conference the Admiralty had produced a map, 'British Empire Cruiser Peace Distribution', which detailed the locations of cruisers and their deployment around the world. Thus, five cruisers were required for the Atlantic fleet, nine for the Mediterranean, six for China Station, five for the Americas, three for the Indian Ocean, two each for Africa and New Zealand, and four on duty with the Royal Australian Navy. With eighteen allocated to reserve, this amounted to a total of fifty-four vessels. Considering planning for a likely wartime scenario, Madden then argued:

For security in the west, the distribution above has to be modified. When it is realised that the protection of British food supplies along the Atlantic routes, on the flank of a possible enemy, may involve on any one day over thirty convoys being at sea, not including arrangements for the Mediterranean and the North Sea, and when it is remembered that at any one time about twenty five per cent of the thirty five trade route cruisers will be refitting or refuelling, the number seventy, after provision has been made for battle fleet requirement, cannot be considered anything but a minimum figure.[14]

While the Admiralty clung fiercely to this argument it had, in the end, realised that this did not take into account the position of the United States and had to accept the treaty imposition of fifty cruisers. Madden made it clear that the Royal Navy viewed this limit as being temporary in that further naval conferences were to follow, with London again being the venue in 1935. The Admiralty also stipulated that within the number of new builds permitted under the treaty, relating to replacement of older ships, within the overall tonnage limit, the Royal Navy required a high proportion of vessels that were capable of 'extended operations' and be 'habitable in all climates.' Both remarks acknowledge that many vessels of the existing cruiser fleet had been built during the First World War for duty in the North Sea, and were therefore not suitable for what the Admiralty determined as the minimum requirements for defence. The Admiralty did not give up its fight, however, as Britain took the initiative in the next round of disarmament talks in Geneva between 1932 and 1934. This round collapsed without agreement and, against a worrying international background, the ten-year rule was stopped in its tracks, and Britain started to rearm.[15] Nevertheless, the damage had been done, as the combination of restriction of numbers and overall tonnage agreed in London meant the Royal Navy would enter the Second World War with a number of relatively under-armed cruisers, and a fleet that would be almost impossibly stretched across the globe. This was not, however, the end of Britain's endeavours to reach some international agreement that would help to limit the decline in naval superiority. To this end, and following the collapse of the Geneva talks, Britain reached an Anglo-German Naval Agreement with Germany on 18 June 1935.

Much to the annoyance of France and Italy, who had not been consulted, Britain agreed to a ratio of 35:100 in relation to German and British fleet sizes, with the Admiralty taking the view that a regulated German fleet of this proportion would be easier to deal with in the event of war. There were two major flaws in this argument. Firstly, to allow Germany to build a fleet that equalled 35 per cent of the Royal Navy would be in breach of the strict tonnage limits imposed by the Treaty of Versailles, hardly reassuring to the United States, and, more importantly, Britain's allies in Europe. Secondly, was Chancellor Hitler to be trusted with keeping to this plan? Already Germany had commissioned the vessels that came to be known as pocket battleships and which, because of their size, endurance and speed, were a specific threat to merchant shipping at a time, as we have seen, when the Royal Navy did not have enough cruisers for global trade protection. In the end it all came to nought, as Hitler renounced the agreement on 28 April 1939.

3

PEACETIME DEPLOYMENT

During the period of the London Naval Conference, Marine Nobby Elliott was coming to the end of his time at Deal, before moving on to Portsmouth and Plymouth to complete his training. Towards the end of this period, in June 1931, Nobby obtained his Quarters rate qualification with a 'satisfactory pass of 74 per cent' that was followed by his drafting into HMS *Malaya*, on 2 September 1931, for a two-year commission. *Malaya* was a Queen Elizabeth (QE) class battleship, which had been paid for by the Federation of Malay States and, along with her four sisters (HMS *Warspite,* HMS *Queen Elizabeth,* HMS *Valiant* and HMS *Barham*) she saw service in both world wars. While all these ships incurred casualties and damage during their wartime careers, only the *Barham* was lost when one of her main magazines blew up after she was struck by torpedoes from U-331 in the Mediterranean between Crete and Cyrenaica. *Barham* had rolled over on to her side when the explosion, which was filmed and is frequently shown in television documentaries, occurred – and it makes for a shocking sight. It is poignant to record that *Barham* was the only one of the QEs that was not fully modernised between the wars, but it is difficult to state with any confidence whether this would have saved her. In any event, the slight delay between rolling over and blowing up permitted 450 men to survive, but 861 of their shipmates were lost. The overall war record of the Queen Elizabeth class is therefore testimony both to the strength of their initial construction, the value of their inter-war refits when they were effectively rebuilt twice, and the operational efficiency of their crews. *Malaya* was completed on 1 February 1916 at Armstrong's shipyard, Elswick (on the Tyne), and displaced 33,500 tons, with a main armament of eight 15-inch guns in a conventional layout of four twin turrets. She was powered by geared turbines supplied by twenty-four boilers, generating 75,000 horsepower for a maximum speed, delivered through four shafts, of 25 knots. Designed as a class of fast, super dreadnought, heavily armoured and with the speed to match or exceed any heavy opponent, the Queen Elizabeth class can be rightly regarded as one of the Royal Navy's most successful designs. The ship's company in peacetime comprised 951 officers and men, of which the Royal Marine detachment numbered 176, including the manning of X turret and the Transmitting Station. In 1931 *Malaya* was part of the second battle squadron, Atlantic Fleet, and acted as the Royal Guard Ship at Cowes Week in both 1931 and 1932, so this commission was to see Nobby fully integrated into the crew of a large and complex warship, employed in normal ship husbandry and maintenance routines, as well as in the working drills of the main armament. No doubt *Malaya's* home duties offered the opportunity to exercise the band in its musical role, and added ceremonial to offset any possible boredom.[1] By the time Nobby joined *Malaya,* the ship needed further updating and this work, involving an increase in aircraft operating capability and the installation of further anti-aircraft armament, was to be carried out after he left her in September 1933. These modifications are testimony to the Admiralty's belated recognition of the effect of airpower in terms of both attack and defence, a capability that would be sorely tested in the coming war.

Nobby, after nine months in barracks in Plymouth, then joined HMS *Capetown* on 17 July 1934 for another two-year commission, this time with the 5th Cruiser Squadron based on the China Station. *Capetown* was a 'C' class light cruiser, laid down in February 1918, completed on 10 April 1922 with a full load displacement of some 5,300 tons. Armed with five single-mounted 6-inch guns and four pairs of torpedoes, this 450-foot-long ship drew just over 14 feet and had engines that developed 40,000 horsepower, providing a maximum speed of 29.5 knots. Relatively fast and agile, this class of cruiser had a more elevated bow than preceding classes, as experience during the First World War had shown that the earlier design made the ship very wet forward, and this small modification corrected this hindrance to gunnery and seakeeping. *Capetown* carried a crew of 334, including a marine detachment of around forty men, and was the only one of this class of five vessels that never converted to an anti-aircraft role.[2] There will be more detail on this later when Nobby joined one of the converted ships, HMS *Carlisle*, and went to war in her at the beginning of 1940. Having been placed in reserve in 1929, *Capetown* came out of refit prior to recommissioning. Before sailing for the China Station, she called in at Portsmouth to take part in the 1934 Navy Week, and the ship was opened to the visiting public who eagerly attended these events in great numbers. This was particularly significant for Nobby, as one Rose Watts (the author's great-aunt), from the World's End in Chelsea, took advantage of a discounted travel offer in her daily newspaper to visit Navy Week with a girlfriend. Rose visited *Capetown* and family legend has it that Nobby was in the welcoming party, at the head of the gangway, resplendent in his best blue dress uniform with white covered peak cap, and the rest, as they say, is history! Before renewing their acquaintance, however, *Capetown*, with Nobby and his shipmates, departed for China, and would not return until 5 July 1936, almost two years to the day later.

Capetown duly departed for Hong Kong sailing via the Suez Canal, Aden and Singapore, displaying the endurance and suitability of this light cruiser for trade protection and patrol work. After joining her squadron, the ship was actively employed on trade protection duties looking after the interests of the many British-flagged merchant vessels operating in the busy seaways off the coast of China. In 1935, the ship conducted speed trials off the entrance to the Yangzte River, at Yangzte Kiang, before proceeding up the river itself to places (using the names used at the time by the Royal Navy) including Kiukang, Walo and Woosong. *Capetown's* Royal Marines were landed at each of these points to conduct patrols, thus reflecting the growing tensions caused by the Japanese invasion of Manchuria in 1931, and the failure of the League of Nations to deal with it. She then returned to Hanking to act as a Guard Ship to provide cover and protection for local British interests and citizens, before resuming squadron duties at Hong Kong.[3] Originally it had been intended that *Capetown* would serve in this commission for two and a half years but, for reasons that have yet to be discovered, she was recalled six months early, and departed Hong Kong on 25 April 1936. Arriving back in Devonport in early June, she decommissioned and paid off on 5 July 1936, just in time for Nobby and Rose to be married in St Mark's Church, Ford, Plymouth on the 14th.[4]

Nobby took the leave due to him and was then based in Plymouth, which meant the happy couple were able to be together until 4 September, when he was drafted into HMS *Rodney*. This was the sister battleship of the aforementioned HMS *Nelson*, with its large marine detachment centred on the manning of one of the three massive triple 16-inch turrets that gave these ships their distinctive appearance. Launched towards the end of 1925 and completed on 1 November 1927, *Rodney* and her sister ship were refitted in the 1930s and *Rodney* became the first battleship to be fitted with radar (Type 79Y) in 1938. She went on to serve in the Second World War in the Atlantic and Mediterranean, and participated in the sinking of the *Bismarck* and in Operations *Torch* and *Overlord*.

Nobby joined her as part of a draft of twenty-eight Royal Marines, completing the ship's detachment before departure from Devonport on 8 September. *Rodney* was due to join the Home Fleet, the new name given to the Atlantic Fleet after the Invergordon mutiny in 1931, and departed for the fleet's anchorage and base at Scapa Flow, in the Orkneys, where she arrived on 21 September, having called in at Fleetwood and Loch Ewe en route. The five days she spent at Fleetwood were used on what might be called public relations duties, opening up the ship to the public of the north of England and Wales. After a brief period in Scapa Flow, *Rodney* returned, via the North Sea, to Spithead and then Devonport, in time for Christmas and New Year 1936/37, thus completing a circumnavigation of Great Britain as she did so. Nobby's time on *Rodney* was relatively short, about seven months, and he left the ship on 8 April 1937 for training ashore. Over the next three months, Nobby passed the naval Quarters Gunner or gun layer's course, with a rating of 'Pass 1', and he was duly promoted to Corporal on 13 July 1937, collecting pay of 4s 11d per day, plus an additional 3d per day in recognition of his new qualification. Nobby was now ready to rejoin the fleet in the role in which he would be employed in the Second World War.[5]

The period 1936–37 was critical to the future of the Royal Navy and its part in the coming global conflict and, as remarked upon in the previous chapter, the breakdown of international disarmament talks had led to the cancellation of the ten-year rule and the political acceptance of rearming, the latter manifesting itself in the General Election of November 1935. The Admiralty's concerns at the fifty-cruiser limit, which it regarded as temporary, was compounded by the fact that the London Naval Treaty of 1930 also banned the construction of capital warships through to the end of 1936, effectively wasting a year. Nor was Britain able to build a fleet to the scale now identified by the Admiralty to meet Atlantic, Mediterranean and global trade protection requirements, as well as creating a naval deterrent in the Pacific. Cabinet papers reveal the demands of the Admiralty for this 'New Standard Navy' and the government's response, which had to point out the fragility of the economy, lack of manufacturing capacity and other priority calls on defence expenditure, headed by the air defence needs of the Royal Air Force.[6] As a consequence of these 'discussions' the Admiralty requirement for a fleet consisting of 20 battleships, 15 aircraft carriers, 100 cruisers, 200 destroyers and 82 submarines, was reduced by the government to 15, 8, 70, 144 and 55 respectively, to be operational by 1940. Obviously this number included many ships already in service, especially those that had undergone major refits between the wars, but the overall effect of new building and further refitting was designed to give the Admiralty a fleet not to the larger scale it desired, but a more modern force better equipped to fight a new war. The only exception to the overall limit on numbers was, again, cruisers, and it will be recalled that the seventy now permitted represented what the Admiralty had previously identified as a bare minimum. In the end, the 1940 target proved impossible as delays in construction, resulting from shrunken shipyard capacity and skills and the need to source some material and weapons from abroad meant deliveries of capital ships fell behind schedule. This situation also meant that in critical areas such as gun control, Britain's industry was found lacking in specialised capacity. Again, Cabinet papers show that the cruisers due for delivery in 1937 were to lack the essential control mechanism for their high angle anti-aircraft armament.[7] As far as new battleships were concerned, apart from the previously described building of the *Nelson* and the *Rodney*, the navy began work on the design for a new class to be built from 1931, following the expiration of the Washington Treaty. The London Treaty extended this to 1936 and so, drawing on the earlier design work and complying with treaty limits of 35,000 tons and a maximum main gun calibre of 14 inches, the King George V (KGV) class was ordered. Five were built with HMS *King George V* commissioned in 1940, HMS *Prince of Wales* and HMS *Duke of York* in 1941 and HMS *Anson* and HMS *Howe* in 1942; by the time of their completion their tonnage exceeded 40,000 tons displacement and they were capable of a high speed of 28.5 knots.

All the KGVs were heavily involved in the Second World War and proved their worth because, despite the unusual configuration of their main armament, involving two quadruple and a twin turret (due once more to manufacturing challenges and treaty considerations), their seaworthiness and stability as a gun platform made them effective and reliable. The only loss of the class was that of the *Prince of Wales* when, as part of Force Z, she was sunk off the coast of Malaya on 10 December 1941 by Japanese aircraft, sharing the fate of her consort HMS *Repulse*. Force Z was operating without adequate air cover having lost its aircraft carrier, HMS *Indomitable*, to a grounding in the West Indies while on its way to rendezvous with the remainder of the force. *Prince of Wales* was under attack and heavily bombed from 1130 until 1320, when she capsized and sank with the loss of

An aerial
view of HMS
King George V.

more than 320 of her crew, including Admiral Phillips and Captain Leach.[8] Poignantly, Captain Leach's son Henry had been appointed to the *Prince of Wales* as a midshipman; however, when his father took over command he was transferred to the cruiser HMS *Mauritius*. Father and son dined together in Singapore two days before the *Prince of Wales* was lost and Henry searched in vain among the survivors for his father. Henry went on to become, as Admiral Sir Henry, the First Sea Lord 1979–1982, in which capacity, and against the threat of cutbacks in naval expenditure, he convinced the Prime Minister, Margaret Thatcher, that the navy could send a task force to the Falkland Islands, and that this was something Britain should do if it wished to preserve its reputation as protector of freedom. Following the decision to go ahead, the task force was despatched on 5 April, an incredible three days after the invasion and occupation of the islands by Argentinian forces. The result of this action was that the islands were liberated on 14 June, with the surrender of the occupying forces. Perhaps this was the last major example of British projection of sea power and the role of the Royal Navy in defending British interests.

Having thus far briefly examined the battleships of the Queen Elizabeth, Nelson and KGV classes, it is necessary to look at the five ships of the 'R' class, which represented the remainder of the battleship fleet available in 1939–1945. This class, which is sometimes referred to as the 'Revenge' or 'Royal Sovereign Class', was, despite being built after the Queen Elizabeth's, both smaller and slower than its predecessor, being some 20 feet shorter and capable of only 21 knots. While this made the 'Rs' cheaper, they still carried eight 15-inch guns in four twin turrets in the same configuration as the QEs. Further compromises were also made in their design. For example, Admiralty concerns over the QEs' reliance on imported oil as their only fuel meant that the Rs were fitted with dual coal and oil capability. Furthermore, to reduce rolling and provide a more stable gun platform, the stability of this class was set at the lower levels of acceptability, and it can be argued that this severely compromised the scope for upgrade of design, and probably explains why these ships were not subject, unlike their contemporaries, to major refit between the wars. Originally eight ships of this class were ordered, with one cancelled, and two completed as less heavily armed battlecruisers, HMS *Renown* and the ill-fated HMS *Repulse*. Of the five that came into service only HMS *Revenge* and HMS *Royal Oak* were commissioned in time to participate in the Battle of Jutland, while HMS *Ramillies*, HMS *Royal Sovereign* and HMS *Resolution* came into service later in 1916 or 1917. As indicated above, by the time of the Second World War, these ships were obsolete and were only 'saved' by the outbreak of hostilities. During the war, they were mainly employed in secondary roles such as convoy escort and shore bombardment, thereby relieving faster and more modern battleships for fleet operations.

Corporal Elliott's first posting as gun layer was to HMS *Royal Oak* in Devonport on 23 November 1937, confirmed by an entry in the ship's log: 'exchanged 1 Cpl and 1 RM with barracks'. The same

The mighty guns of HMS *Hood*: Like all battlecruisers, the *Hood* was well armed but too lightly armoured and so vulnerable to high, plunging shot – as the Admiralty later found out to their cost.

log records '25 November 1937 Flag half-mast at 1040 HMS Apollo arrived from West Indies with body of J. Ramsay MacDonald.'[9] The former Prime Minister had been taking a cruise for health reasons on board the liner *Reina del Pacifico*, when he suddenly died at sea on 9 November. Earlier in the year *Royal Oak*, which was the last and largest ever battleship to be built at Devonport Dockyard, had been engaged in events of the Spanish Civil War. Undertaking what were known as non-intervention patrols, she had been attacked, in error, by three aircraft of the Republican Air Force, while sailing east of Gibraltar. When later patrolling off Valencia she was hit, again by accident, by a Republican anti-aircraft shell during an air attack on the city by Nationalist forces. In January 1938, *Royal Oak* joined the Home Fleet at Portsmouth as flagship of the 2nd Battle Squadron, taking part in spring and summer exercises and manoeuvres in the Atlantic and home waters, interspersed with a series of port visits to show the flag. The 2nd Battle Squadron was commanded by Rear Admiral Lancelot Holland who, as Vice Admiral, was later lost with all but three of his 1,417 shipmates when HMS *Hood* was sunk by *Bismarck* in the Battle of the Denmark Strait, on 24 May 1941.

On 24 November 1938, exactly one year after Nobby had joined, *Royal Oak* was selected to carry the body of Queen Maud of Norway, who had died while in London, accompanied by her husband King Haakon VII, to her State funeral in Oslo. Queen Maud had been born in Britain and the Norwegian royal family retained strong links with the United Kingdom, links that were to be further strengthened by the arrival in London of the king and Norwegian government-in-exile following the German occupation of Norway in May 1940. *Royal Oak* paid off in December 1938 and was recommissioned in June 1939, in preparation for service in the Mediterranean. In what was to prove a fortuitous move, Nobby was suddenly drafted ashore on 7 June 1939, with eight of his colleagues, and this party was sent to the Royal Marine

Barracks in Eastney, Portsmouth. Almost immediately the *Royal Oak's* Mediterranean deployment was cancelled and she was sent to Scapa Flow, as the Royal Navy responded to increasing international tension and the likelihood of war with Germany, following the Nazi occupation of the rump of Czechoslovakia. After the commencement of hostilities in September, *Royal Oak* took part in a sweep looking for the German battlecruiser *Gneisenau* in the North Sea, but her poor condition and low speed, by now reduced to about 20 knots, meant that she could not keep up with the fleet. The Commander-in-Chief Home Fleet, Sir Charles Forbes, and the Admiralty were concerned about the safety of the Scapa Flow anchorage, which had fallen into disrepair during the years between the wars. As it was estimated that at least four to five months were necessary for the strengthening of these defences, many ships were dispersed to other ports, the main part of the Home Fleet being based in the Clyde. The *Royal Oak* remained at Scapa Flow, and her primary and secondary armament became an integral part of the local defence, especially against attack from the air. On the night of 13 October 1939, the feared German attack did come to Scapa Flow, but from below rather than above the waves. U-47, commanded by Günther Prien, weaved her way through the anchorage in a considerable feat of navigation and, at 2358 hours, fired off four torpedoes, one of which hit the forward part of *Royal Oak*. This was followed by a further salvo of three torpedoes at 0016 on 14 October, all of which hit the same ship. These tremendous explosions tore great holes in the *Royal Oak,* which caused extensive damage and heavy flooding, resulting in her sinking in less than fifteen minutes. The human cost was heavy, with 833 men lost out of a crew of about 1,000.[10] Nobby and his eight fellow marines had indeed been lucky with their posting but they experienced, for the first time, the grief and shock of losing so many former shipmates.

4

TO WAR

With rearmament and the retreat from appeasement, in the face of German's aggressive foreign policy, we have seen how the Royal Navy entered the period 1938–39 with several recently commissioned new cruisers and with five KGV class battleships being built for delivery between 1939 and 1942. In preparation for the manning of these vessels, and allowing for the time to train skilled gun crews, the Admiralty again prioritised the employment of Royal Marines in their traditional shipboard role. This gunnery function was therefore given more importance than the previously envisaged additional wartime requirement for a Royal Marine Brigade for amphibious operations and a naval base defence force. While several ships' detachments could be employed locally in small-scale amphibious tasks, the Admiralty did manage to make available about 1,500 marines for an initial Mobile Naval Base Defence Organisation. Putting this number in perspective, however, is the fact that the new cruisers required a total of 1,500 marines and the KGVs required another 1,750. The former included a number of marines made available from the decommissioning of several older cruisers, whereas the latter represented an additional demand for men, and neither figure takes into account factors such as ongoing training, leave, sickness and replacements. It appeared, too, that with the Corps Adjutant General reporting to the Second Sea Lord, who had overall responsibility for personnel, the Corps itself was keen to retain its shipboard duties, although it had little choice given the navy's priorities. The background to the predictable unreadiness of the Corps to fulfil all its functions can be found in Cabinet papers. In January 1938 the Committee of Imperial Defence (CID) looked at the question of raising an amphibious strike force, and agreed that the Royal Marines were 'the experts in this field'. However, correspondence between the Deputy Chief of the Naval Staff, Vice Admiral James, and the Deputy Secretary of the Committee, Colonel Ismay, revealed that the navy was

> ... concerned about this business, because we find here we cannot keep our mobile naval base at short notice without enlisting a large number of Marines, for whom we cannot show a good purpose in peacetime.[1]

In fact, the Royal Marine establishment only reached around 13,000 by the end of 1938, and the Corps, unlike the army and navy, had a very small number of reserves on which it could call. The necessary expansion for war was not undertaken until after the passing of the Military Training Act by Parliament in May 1939. This initial bill provided for the registration and subsequent calling up for six months' training of single men aged between 20 and 22. The marines could not take quick advantage of this situation as the new training facility at Lympstone, near Exmouth in Devon, was still under construction; when complete it would provide, along with the depot at Deal, much expanded training facilities for the anticipated conscript intakes. On the outbreak of war, 3 September 1939, Parliament immediately replaced the Military Training Act with the National Service (Armed Forces) Act, which broadened conscription to all medically fit men between the ages of 18 and 41, making provision for conscientious objection and granting exemption to those employed in key industries.[2]

Faced with an expansion of manpower, the Admiralty had to consider ways in which the experience of its 10,000 pre-war regulars could best be used and distributed around the fleet. One of these measures, which clearly demonstrates the thinking behind the solution to this problem, was a relaxation of the educational requirement for promotion to Sergeant, as promulgated by Admiralty Notice 3583 on 23 November 1939:

> Approval has been given, as a temporary measure, for the educational qualification for promotion to Sergeant and above ... be waived for the duration of the present emergency. The educational qualification for promotion to warrant rank will remain unchanged.[3]

The effect of this action was to release, for promotion, Corporals who were technically but not educationally qualified, so that they could take up the additional senior supervisory roles created in the fleet. Before the waiver was introduced, Corporals required a second-class school certificate for advancement to Sergeant and then Colour Sergeant, with the requirement for higher rank, up to and including Warrant Officer, needing a first-class certificate. By keeping the higher standard for advancement to warrant rank, the Admiralty sought to limit the effect of dilution upon the overall standard of conduct and operational efficiency. Interestingly, the navy had also introduced a similar waiver for the seaman and cook branches, where such a measure was even more necessary. This was because of the larger expansion of naval manpower to meet the rising demand for escort crews, in ship types that were too small to carry marines. Other personnel adjustments or reforms were introduced around this time with perhaps the most remarkable involving the matter of the new Service Dependants' Allowance.

Previously, from October 1920, marriage allowances had been paid to the 'lawful' wives and children of all ranks, replacing a system of separation allowances. To qualify for a marriage allowance sailors or marines had to be legally married and living with their wife and children, apart from when they were required to serve away from home. They were also required to make a monthly allotment to their dependants from their pay, with a set minimum proportion, and the combination of allotment and marriage allowance was designed to maintain the family. If the family was living in married quarters, then a deduction was made from the allowance, reflecting the cost of the accommodation, but never at a level that exceeded the allowance. Children's allowance was included and payable until the child reached the age at which full-time education ended.

The new scheme of Service Dependants Allowance, which continued the payment and structure of the Marriage Allowance, was introduced on 25 September 1939, just three weeks after the declaration of war against Germany, and represented a major reform in the recognition of individual family arrangements. It was introduced by the government and applied to all the armed services. The most significant and surprising element of the new allowance involved the position of what has been called the common-law wife (despite their lack of any legal status) and illegitimate children. Considering the then social stigma surrounding unmarried mothers and their offspring, it was a revelation to see that the government through, in this instance, the Admiralty, now proposed to pay these dependants marriage and child allowances on the same scale as those that fell under the 'lawful' category. The child allowances in this instance were subject to the proviso that the children must have been fathered by the rating or marine concerned. The allowance was also extended to 'cover wife and children where estranged, grandchildren, stepchildren, siblings, half-siblings, foster parents', although only one allowance per man, subject to the allotment qualification mentioned earlier, could be paid. To keep costs under control, a ceiling was introduced for household income, meaning that no allowance was available if any household income, not taking into account the dependants' allowance and allotment, exceeded 15s per week per member of household.[4] The fact that this allowance recognised the many and varied familial circumstances of those that served, or perhaps more significantly, those that were soon to join, reveals the government as being able to adopt a progressive and realistic approach to personnel management. With conscription and a long war now underway, it offered better financial security for those serving at sea or otherwise away from home, encouraged responsible allotment payments and treated dependants with a degree of unprecedented equality. Furthermore, in many cases it may well have helped to reduce the gap between service and civilian pay, something the government was only too aware of. As far as Nobby was concerned, he was in receipt of the marriage allowance covering both his wife and, since the spring of 1938, their son, Sydney.

After leaving *Royal Oak* for Eastney barracks on 7 June 1939, Nobby spent just over seven months based ashore before being drafted to an anti-aircraft cruiser, HMS *Carlisle* in Devonport, thus commencing what proved to be an extremely busy and dangerous two years on this converted 'C' class cruiser. It will be recalled that Nobby previously served the years 1934–36 in HMS *Capetown*, which was the only one of the five ships of this class not to be converted for anti-aircraft purposes. Constructed at Fairfield's yard on the River Clyde and completed on 1 November 1918, *Carlisle*, like her sisters, did not see any action in the First World War. She was originally equipped with five single-mounted Mark XII breech loading 6-inch guns, two 3-inch anti-aircraft guns and four 3-pdr guns and, unlike the previously described *Capetown*, did not have any torpedo tubes.[5] *Carlisle* was manned by Chatham Division and spent the next ten years on the China Station, with two periods for refit at her home base. In August 1929, she was switched to Devonport Division and recommissioned in September for service in the South Atlantic and in the South African Station, based in Simon's Town, the large naval harbour close to Cape Town. She remained on this station until March 1937, with periodic returns to the United Kingdom for refitting and crew change. By September 1937 she was decommissioned and laid up in Devonport as part of the reserve fleet, but her status was about to undergo a dramatic change, as the decision was made, in early November, to have her converted to an anti-aircraft ship. As *Carlisle* waited for a suitable berth for conversion in Devonport, she was reactivated and spent several weeks as a boys' training ship before entering dry dock.

The Admiralty, in recognising the need for greater anti-aircraft capability and protection for the fleet, had commissioned, in 1935, the first purpose-built class of anti-aircraft light cruisers, named after the lead ship, HMS *Dido*. Eleven ships of this class were built, with a full load displacement of 6,900 tons and a maximum speed of just over 32 knots. They carried a crew of 487 and were much needed by the fleet when they entered service between May 1940 and August 1942. These vessels had an unusual appearance with five twin 5.25-inch low angle/high angle turrets, three placed forward of the bridge on three levels and two aft, and it was the development of these guns and an improved high angle control system that made it possible for the Dido's to fulfil their designated role.[6] Shortages of material and pressure on shipbuilding capacity, however, meant several of the Dido's were completed without their full complement of twin 5.25 turrets. To illustrate how these shortages were manifested, it must be noted that these guns were also fitted to the KGV class battleships, their dual capability giving essential protection from air attack, and the Admiralty gave, understandably and rightly, priority of supply to the bigger ships. Despite the welcome addition of the Dido class, it was clear that their numbers were woefully inadequate in dealing with the developing threat of attack from the air, and this was why four 'C' class cruisers, including the *Carlisle*, were converted to the AA role.

The first to undergo this major refit was HMS *Cairo* in Chatham Dockyard, where the work was completed in May 1939. She subsequently participated in the Norwegian campaign and North Atlantic convoy duty before joining Force H in Gibraltar in 1942, and becoming part of the large escort afforded to the major Malta supply convoy, designated Operation *Pedestal*, between 11 and 12 August. Under constant air and submarine attack the escort, consisting of more than thirty warships, including two battleships and three aircraft carriers, could not prevent the loss of nine of the merchantmen, and the gallant arrival in Valletta of the tanker *Ohio*, almost awash, has passed into Maltese and naval legend. *Ohio*'s master, Captain Mason, earned a highly deserved George Cross for bringing his ship to port after the most horrendous voyage. *Ohio* was torpedoed and badly damaged on the night of 11 August in an attack by the Italian submarine *Axum*, before limping on to Malta. In the same attack, the *Axum* also torpedoed the cruiser *Nigeria* and scored two hits on the *Cairo*, crippling the former and forcing her to turn back to Gibraltar, accompanied by two destroyers that had perforce to leave the escort. *Cairo* suffered fatal damage with her stern blown off and her crew abandoned ship; she was sunk the next day by HMS *Pathfinder*. *Cairo* lost twenty-four of her crew, twelve of whom were Royal Marines.[7]

Also converted at Chatham was HMS *Calcutta*, and work on her was completed in July 1939, just prior to the outbreak of war. She was deployed in the Norwegian campaign and in Operation *Dynamo*, the evacuation of the army from the beaches and mole in Dunkirk. Joining Force H in Gibraltar in the late summer of 1940, *Calcutta* escorted early convoys to Malta and took part in the bombardment of Benghazi as part of the 3rd Cruiser Squadron. In the spring of 1941 she saw further action during the landing and subsequent evacuation of Greece, which was soon followed by the evacuation of British and Allied forces from the island of Crete, in company with *Carlisle* and other warships. On 1 June, during the passage back to

Alexandria, while providing AA cover for ships loaded with troops, *Calcutta* was herself attacked by two Junkers 88s of the Luftwaffe. She received two bomb hits and sank in a couple of minutes, with HMS *Coventry* picking up 255 of her crew of more than 350.[8]

The final ship of the class to be converted was HMS *Colombo* and this took place in Devonport, completing in March 1943, after service in the Indian Ocean, the Red Sea and with the Eastern Fleet, including taking part in Operation *Ironclad*, the invasion of Madagascar. She deployed to the Mediterranean in her new role and participated in Operation *Husky*, the invasion of Sicily, and Operation *Dragoon*, the invasion of Southern France in August 1944. Placed in the reserve fleet prior to the ending of the war, *Colombo* survived and, like her sister ships, had a war record that demonstrated how badly needed these hard-worked AA cruisers were, and how the navy could have used double their number.[9]

Returning to the *Carlisle*, Nobby joined her in Devonport on 21 January 1940, when the ship was undergoing local sea trials to test her new equipment, prior to sailing to the Mediterranean for a short period to conduct further tests, concentrating on her new radar. As with her sisters, the *Carlisle's* conversion involved the removal of the single 6-inch mountings and the fitting of eight 4-inch Mark XIX guns in four twin mountings, accompanied by a quadruple 2-pdr mounting (known as a pom-pom) and two quadruple 0.5-inch

HMS *Carlisle*. (© Imperial War Museums (HU 471))

calibre machine guns. The twin 4-inch mountings had three covered sides and were open at the rear, turrets were not usually suitable for gun calibres of less than 5.25 inches. The four mountings consisted of, from fore to aft, No. 1 on the foredeck, No. 2 amidships and abaft the twin funnels, with No. 3 above the Captain's main cabin, superimposed upon No. 4 which was on the quarterdeck. The marine detachment, which totalled sixty, manned Nos 3 and 4 mountings with seamen gunners on Nos 1 and 2. An additional High Angle Control Station was fitted aft and *Carlisle* became the first Royal Navy warship to be fitted with Type 280 radar for the detection and tracking of aircraft. Once in the Mediterranean, *Carlisle* was based for a short period in Malta and ran a series of trials to test the new radar, which proved highly satisfactory, and she returned to the United Kingdom to join the 1st AA Squadron at Scapa Flow at the end of March. As part of this deployment *Carlisle* was sent to Humber Force to assist in the provision of AA cover in the North Sea but, on 9 April 1940, following the invasion of Norway by German forces, she rejoined the Home Fleet for participation in the ill-fated Norwegian campaign (see maps pp 138–9).

Churchill, as First Sea Lord, had been seeking since September 1939 to convince his Cabinet colleagues that it was in the Allies' best interests to take action against the German iron ore supplies from Sweden that were being transported from the northern Norwegian port of Narvik, then through the Norwegian coastal leads to Germany. This route, with the ore being taken by rail from Sweden to Narvik on the west coast of Norway, was used in the winter months as this coast was ice-free due to the effects of the warm Gulf Stream. In the summer months, the ore was shipped direct from the Swedish port of Lulea across the defended Baltic Sea to Germany, thus denying the Royal Navy and Royal Air Force, with the resources they had at their disposal, the opportunity to mount meaningful shipping strikes. Proposing firstly to mine the Norwegian leads, and secondly to send a force of destroyers to sink the merchant vessels carrying ore cargoes through them, Churchill ran into political problems caused by the neutral status of both Norway and Sweden. The question of breaching neutrality, which Prime Minister Chamberlain thought would harm the Allies' cause in the eyes of the wider world, set off a period of dithering and confusion over how this situation could be dealt with. The spell was broken by the Russian invasion of Finland at the end of November, which was met with a fierce and spirited Finnish defence that caught the imagination and sympathy of the public in Britain and France. In addition to supplying the Finns with arms, Churchill reasoned that supporting the Finns, with favourable public opinion, presented the Allies with an opportunity to get engaged in Scandinavia, thereby protecting Norway and Sweden against the Russian threat, while using their ports to attack Germany. At this stage of the war, popularly known as the Phoney War in the West, joint British and French strategy was in the hands of the Anglo-French Supreme War Council, which had first met, with both Prime Ministers attending, in Abbeville on 12 September 1939. More meetings followed and in Paris, on 5 February 1940, Churchill, First Lord of the Admiralty, was invited to attend for the first time by Prime Minister Chamberlain. Perhaps it was no coincidence, therefore, that the British delegation consisting, like their French counterparts, of their leaders, military advisers and foreign office ministers and officials, agreed with a French proposal to send a joint force to Narvik, provided that the consent of Norway and Sweden was obtained first. This was not forthcoming because the Scandinavians did not want to put their neutral status in jeopardy and, in any event, the scheme became redundant when Russia and Finland agreed an armistice on 13 March 1940. Churchill then pushed for the mining of the approaches to Narvik, in an operation given the code name 'Wilfred', which was, after much discussion about Germany's own Norwegian intentions, planned for execution on 9 April. Germany's plans and execution were, unfortunately, more focussed – and their invasion of Norway, involving six task groups and airborne forces, took place on the evening of the 8th and into the morning of 9 April. This operation, code named *Weserubung*, saw German forces swiftly take Oslo, Kristiansand, Egersund, Bergen, Trondheim and Narvik, thereby forming a chain of ports and airbases the length of Norway, threatening Britain, the North Sea and the North Atlantic with significant gains in terms of the shortening of range and protection. At the same time, German land forces marched into Jutland and then occupied Denmark. The stage was set for the invasion of France and the frightening prospect of Hitler controlling the European coastline from the top of Norway to the north of Spain. One glance at an atlas reveals just how threatening this was to British maritime operations, with the navy stretched beyond capacity to protect Atlantic- and Middle East-bound convoys. At one stroke the Kriegsmarine, especially the U-boat arm, had been freed from the shackles of operating from the Baltic and the southern North Sea, and the Luftwaffe was presented with bases from which more of the seas surrounding Britain, and Britain itself, could be attacked.

The reaction of the British government to this stunning turn of events led to a campaign in Norway whose failure ended with the replacement of Chamberlain by Churchill as Prime Minister. It can only be described as chaotic, in preparation and execution, as, for the first time, the navy and army were confronted with superior local air forces, which demonstrated the folly of trying to mount a hastily and ill-prepared amphibious operation without having obtained air superiority. These were lessons that were going to pay dividends later in the war but, in April 1940, HMS *Carlisle* and her crew underwent a professionally challenging and personally frightening baptism of fire. In the Allied counter-offensive to retake Trondheim, the ship was tasked with the landing of 'Sickleforce', consisting of an ill-prepared Territorial brigade at Andalnes, in Romsdalsfjord, south of Trondheim on 18 April. During this operation, the troops were carried from Britain in the merchant

Under the Royal Navy's protection. In spite of the menace of U-boats, aerial attack and bombardment by heavy guns from Channel ports under enemy occupation, Britain continued to carry on her trade by sea.

liner *Orion* and transferred at sea to the accompanying force of four cruisers, HMS's *Arethusa*, *Galatea*, *Carlisle* and her anti-aircraft consort *Curacoa*, for the approach to Andalnes. This was necessary as the Admiralty recognised the vulnerability of *Orion* to air attack, but the transfer only succeeded in exacerbating the problems caused by a failure to ensure that the troop's equipment had been properly loaded onto *Orion*. Such chaos arose from the many changes of plans that preceded this operation, due to earlier indecisiveness on intervention in Norway, and the German seizure of the initiative on the night of 8/9 April. After landing her soldiers, *Carlisle* assumed the role of AA Guard Ship covering, in succession, Romsdalsfjord, Molde, Andalnes and, north of Trondheim, the port of Namsos, before taking part in the evacuation of the latter on 3 May. For some fifteen days, this meant that *Carlisle* and the other vessels in the fleet were subjected to air attack by bombers of the Luftwaffe, flying from recently occupied airfields and reaping the benefit of a quick turnaround and internal lines of communication and supply. At this time of year, the nights were of a few hours duration, thereby limiting the time that port operations with resupply were possible. The corollary of this was that the extended daylight enabled the Luftwaffe to mount almost continuous daytime attacks on the supply vessels and the warships that were covering them. For the

AA ships, taking avoiding action by making successive turns at speed meant that achieving accuracy was as difficult for the ship's guns as it was for the attacking aircraft. Long hours at action stations and the firing of all guns to maintain an effective barrage made this an exhausting time for ship's crews, with rest only possible for some during the brief hours of darkness. Fighting for their lives, sailors and marines made an incredible physical effort to keep the guns firing and both *Carlisle* and *Curacoa* used prodigious amounts of ammunition in keeping the Luftwaffe at bay. To this was added the psychological effect of these ship's companies being well aware that as anti-aircraft cruisers, they were priority targets for the aircraft that sought so desperately to destroy them. Unsurprisingly, their luck, which depended so much on the ferocity of their own defence, did not hold out, for in the evening of 24 April *Curacoa* was severely damaged by a 500lb bomb that struck her foc'sle, killing eight of her crew and forcing her to return to the United Kingdom for repairs. *Curacoa* was later lost, on 2 October 1942, when she was rammed by the troop-carrying liner *Queen Mary*, whom she had been escorting. *Carlisle* remained as AA Guard Ship *Namsos* and sustained her first casualties when near-missed by a German bomber on 28 April; five ratings were wounded and Marine Stephenson was seriously wounded as a result of this attack.[10] After taking on board her allocation of evacuated troops, she sailed for Scapa Flow in the company of the County class heavy 8-inch cruiser HMS *Devonshire*, and the destroyers HMS *Afridi*, a French ship *Bison*, HMS *Grenade* and HMS *Imperial*. On leaving Namsos the Luftwaffe attacked and Ju 87 Stuka dive bombers succeeded in sinking *Bison* and then *Afridi*, after the latter had picked up survivors from the former. *Bison* lost 171 of its 236-strong crew, including 35 of the 61 survivors on board *Afridi*, which lost 53 of her complement and 13 of her embarked troops. The captain of *Afridi*, Captain Vian, was picked up and went on to make a significant contribution to the Allied naval effort, as an Admiral in the Mediterranean.[11]

The Norwegian campaign demonstrated the weakness caused by the failure to develop amphibious warfare between the wars, especially with regard to the proper planning of logistics and the specialised equipment required to deliver men and material onto a hostile shore. Although, as mentioned in Chapter 2, the Royal Marine Training Manual of 1932 had set out some instructions on the conduct of small-scale raids, the only peacetime larger scale amphibious exercise had been conducted by the army in July 1938. This was at the instigation of the then Brigadier Bernard Montgomery, commanding the 9th Infantry Brigade based in Portsmouth. Montgomery enlisted the help of the local Naval Commander-in-Chief, Admiral of the Fleet, Lord Cork and Kerry, who later commanded the Narvik forces, and was given the co-operation of the fleet and a dozen Fairey Swordfish aircraft with which to conduct his exercise. The brigade was loaded on ships in Portsmouth and taken to Slapton Sands, near Dartmouth in Devon, with the troops going ashore on the morning of 6 July and, according to the local press, 'taking the

The band greets a famous destroyer: HMS *Punjabi*, which participated in the morale-boosting second battle of Narvik, berths alongside a battleship after a period of patrol and is welcomed by a band of the Royal Marines.

Wessex defences totally by surprise.'[12] Montgomery's biographer, Nigel Hamilton, wrote this about the exercise:

> The *Times* recorded that 'the landing of an Infantry Brigade at Slapton Sands was carried out with great success this morning, under ideal weather conditions. The three regiments concerned, the KOSBs, the Lincolns and East Yorks were brought ashore in Naval cutters and whalers and in transport's lifeboats between one-thirty and four o'clock; and when dawn broke, the guns, tanks and lorries, accompanied by numerous stores were landed in flat-bottomed craft...'[13]

Montgomery's initiative and hard work was rewarded by the presence of Lord Gort, the Chief of the Imperial General Staff, and General Wavell, the recently appointed Commander-in-Chief of Southern Command. Wavell's professional opinion of the landing was in complete contrast to the report in the *Times*:

> It was a pitiful exposition of our complete neglect of landing operations. There was *one* so-called landing craft, an experimental one made many years before and dug out of some scrap heap for this exercise, in which I rather think it sank. For the rest the troops landed in open row-boats as they had done for the last 200 years and more. A storm came on, and the troops were unable to re-embark as had been intended...[14]

Indeed, the troops had to be put up overnight with the naval cadets at HMS *Britannia*, the Royal Naval College at Dartmouth, providing the exercise with an ignominious ending. The lessons of Norway had to be learned, and the fact that in the Western theatre of the war, a series of successful mass amphibious landings would be made between November 1942 and August 1944 is testament to the steep learning curve that was embarked upon after the Norwegian disaster.

Returning to the fleet and HMS *Carlisle*, the experience of Norway left Nobby and his shipmates in no doubt as to the supreme position of air power in modern naval warfare, and their first experience of prolonged, sustained air attack left them certain of what to expect in the future. Being a gun layer on an anti-aircraft cruiser now assumed, with the remainder of the gun crew, the transmitting station and gunnery control team, responsibility for maintaining self-discipline, exceptional gun drill and steady nerve to have any chance of successfully defending their ship and its charges. Courage, determination, and an ability to sustain a supreme physical effort had now become the new and almost constant reality, and a far cry from peacetime training. Following her return to Scapa Flow, *Carlisle* was reassigned for duty with the Mediterranean Fleet and sailed from Devonport on 18 May in company with two destroyers. Proceeding firstly to Malta, *Carlisle* then sailed to Alexandria, again accompanied by destroyers, to join the 4th Cruiser Squadron at the fleet's home base in Alexandria, Egypt, where she arrived on 26 May.

The strategic position in the Mediterranean had been altered by Italy's entry into the war on 10 May, Mussolini having finally committed his country following the success of Germany's forces in the West. Not wishing to miss out on the spoils of war, and with mainland France now out of the equation, Mussolini looked towards the southern Mediterranean and an offensive from Italian-controlled Libya towards Egypt, thus threatening the Suez Canal and its associated British imperial trade. This trade, however, must be put in perspective, because ships could be diverted around the Cape of Good Hope and, in any case, the survival of Britain was mainly dependent upon the Atlantic routes which, following the occupation of French west coast ports, required more protection than ever against the menace of the U-boat. Indeed, the four-year-long Battle of the Atlantic must be seen as the pivotal campaign of the war in the West. In this respect the First Sea Lord, Admiral Pound, invited Admiral Cunningham, Commander-in-Chief Mediterranean, to present his views about the withdrawal of the fleet to Gibraltar, with consideration of the need to keep the Red Sea open for the maintenance of British forces in Egypt. After a series of communications, Cunningham wrote the following to Pound on 27 June:

> I suppose the broad Naval Strategy will require some reconsidering. I hope it will not be necessary to abandon the Eastern Mediterranean: the landslide would be frightful. If the Spaniards leave us alone, I think quite a small force could hold that end, and if the efforts of the Eastern and Western Mediterranean are properly co-ordinated, I feel we can keep the Italians pretty well engaged... Malta is doing very well... If we had twenty or thirty fighters at Malta ready to operate over the fleet I think we could guarantee to make the Sicilians, anyway, very sorry that Italy had entered the war...[15]

By 3 July Churchill, the War Cabinet and the Chiefs of Staff had decided on the Mediterranean strategy, choosing to fight Italy in North Africa and Southern Europe, the only area at the time where British forces could engage the Axis powers on land. It would be nearly two years before Bomber Command could be made ready to attack Germany in a strategic air offensive. Seen in this light, the adoption of this blue water strategy appears almost inevitable, but it became a point of friction between the Combined Chiefs of Staff after America entered the war. Nevertheless, the die was cast and Britain was committed to the Mediterranean and the Suez Canal.[16]

To protect the canal, British forces were based in Egypt, under an Anglo-Egyptian treaty that had been agreed in 1936 and which itself had developed from Britain's virtual control of the country since the 1880s. South of the canal, the entrance to the Red Sea was covered by Sudan, which was effectively ruled by an Anglo-Egyptian arrangement. The other, eastern, side of the canal was covered by British forces in Palestine, which Britain held under a thirty-year mandate of the League of Nations, set up at the end of the war in 1918. On paper, therefore, it appeared that the legacy of long-standing treaties had secured Britain's defence of this important maritime artery, but there was not only a threat to Egypt from Libya, but also from the Italian colonies situated in what is known as the Horn of Africa, where the Indian Ocean meets with the Gulf of Aden into which the Red Sea flows. These colonies, which constituted Italian Somaliland and, following Italian invasion from there in 1935, Ethiopia and Eritrea, became Italian East Africa in 1936. Sandwiched between Eritrea and Italian Somaliland, on the southern coast of the Gulf of Aden, were the French colony of Djibouti to the north and British Somaliland to the south. Facing British Somaliland, on the north side of the Gulf, was the small British colony of Aden, strategically placed at the entrance to the Red Sea and having evolved, under British control, as a major bunkering port and international trading centre. Fearful of air attacks from Italian air forces based in Italian East Africa on merchant shipping convoys transiting the Red Sea en route to or outward bound from the canal, the Admiralty deployed additional vessels for escort. As part of this deployment, *Carlisle* sailed through the canal to Aden, where she took up her station as Flagship for the Red Sea Force, then under command of the British East Indies Fleet, in early June 1940.

Carlisle did not have to wait long for action as for three days, commencing 11 June, the Italian air force mounted a series of raids against the port and town of Aden. The anti-aircraft fire put up by the combined forces of shore batteries and the ships of the Red Sea Force resulted in the loss of approximately nine Italian aircraft. The effect of this was such that the Italian bombers only returned in early and mid-July, and the Red Sea Force was able to assume its primary task of protecting the Red Sea convoys. *Carlisle*'s duty in July consisted of escorting convoys for transit across the Red Sea from Aden to Port Sudan, a major port with good railway connections to Khartoum and the interior, and she also called in at the French port of Djibouti. The defeat of France had left Britain in a quandary with regard to the availability of the French fleet and, while this matter had been resolved in the western Mediterranean by the disagreeable action at Mers el Kabir, when British ships opened fire on their former comrades, Admiral Cunningham at Alexandria enjoyed a better outcome. On 7 July, after days of febrile negotiations, he reached a settlement with the French commander, Vice Admiral Godfroy, which allowed for the demobilisation of the large French squadron, including the battleship *Lorraine*. This prevented the ships from sailing under the Vichy flag or being acquired by Germany; neither of these possibilities were realistic, however, because Admiral Cunningham would have prevented this by force, however distasteful, but it remains the case that the Royal Navy was unable to add the French Mediterranean Fleet to its weakened ranks.

The Italian forces made their long-awaited move against British Somaliland on 3 August, employing vastly superior numbers against a local defence that, all in all, consisted of less than a full strength battalion. Although the arrival of Major-General Godwin-Austen with reinforcements, supported by air attacks from Aden, seemed to offer stiffer resistance, the advantage still lay with the Italians, and the decision to withdraw to the port of Berbera and carry out an evacuation was made on 15 August. In company with *Hobart, Ceres, Kimberley* and *Auckland*, HMS *Carlisle* arrived at Berbera the same day, and some 5,370 troops, 1,040 civilians and 175 wounded were landed at Aden seventy-two hours later.[17] After this action *Carlisle*, still part of the East Indies Fleet, was sent to Colombo in Ceylon (now Sri Lanka) for a much-needed refit, returning to Aden in October for duty as Guard Ship and Red Sea convoy escort. Between October and the end of the year, *Carlisle* was occupied with the escort of three convoys, WS3, WS4 and WS4B, which were part of the British effort to reinforce the army in Egypt ahead of the anticipated Italian attack from Libya. With the obvious government priority of defending Britain against a possible German invasion, it was not until the victory against the Luftwaffe in the Battle of Britain, in September, that convoys bound for the Middle East were authorised, planned and loaded. During this period about 50,000 troops – and as many aircraft, guns and tanks as could be spared – were safely shipped to Egypt via the Cape. *Carlisle* and her consorts were successful, in the face of repeated Italian aerial and submarine threats, in shepherding their charges to port, thus ensuring the safe arrival of the men and material that Wavell so desperately needed. On leaving WS4B and returning to Aden on 27 December, *Carlisle* developed a problem with one of her shafts, thus reducing her speed, and it was arranged that repairs would be carried out in Bombay (now Mumbai). Before this could be undertaken, however, she remained in the Red Sea and repairs were postponed when orders were received to join the Mediterranean Fleet in Alexandria. That *Carlisle*'s anti-aircraft capabilities were needed in the Mediterranean is undoubted, as earlier noted by Cunningham, when reflecting on the fleet action against the Italian navy at Calabria in July:

> We needed also an armoured aircraft carrier like the *Illustrious*, with fighters, an anti-aircraft cruiser like *Carlisle* and a couple of convoy sloops.[18]

With an enforced delay, due to the sweeping of aerial mines laid by Italian aircraft, *Carlisle* joined the fleet in Alexandria on 10 March 1941 and was immediately docked for repair, with her damaged shaft taken to Malta by submarine for specialist attention. She would emerge to begin a new phase of her very active wartime career, a phase that was, again, rightly acknowledged by Cunningham:

> There had been some changes and additions to the fleet which to some extent eased the strain on the overworked destroyers. We now had the three small anti-aircraft cruisers, *Coventry*, *Calcutta* and *Carlisle*, and no convoy was complete without one or the other of them.[19]

5

MEDITERRANEAN

At this point, as this narrative begins to focus more sharply on convoys, it is necessary to make some comments about merchant ships, so that their variety and different operational capabilities can be understood. This will put into context the challenges faced in mustering, escorting and protecting the various type of convoys that were deployed in the Atlantic, Arctic and Mediterranean. The term 'Merchant Navy' tended to give the impression of an homogenous fleet with, in today's parlance, an easily identifiable brand. At the outbreak of war in September 1939, the British-flagged merchant fleet, flying the Red Ensign, was the largest in the world, with in excess of 4,000 ships engaged in servicing more than 50 per cent of the world's trade. While the terrible wartime losses of over 2,000 merchant ships and more than 29,000 merchant seamen of many nationalities, gave credibility to any claim that the Merchant Navy was, in effect, the fourth armed service, the term is really a misnomer.[1] The merchant fleet was, in reality, a collection of dozens of different shipping companies, some of which, for legal reasons, owned a single vessel. The ships of these companies were sometimes collectively managed by a separate corporate entity, whereby a number of vessels were operated under a group umbrella. In broad terms the British merchant fleet was roughly

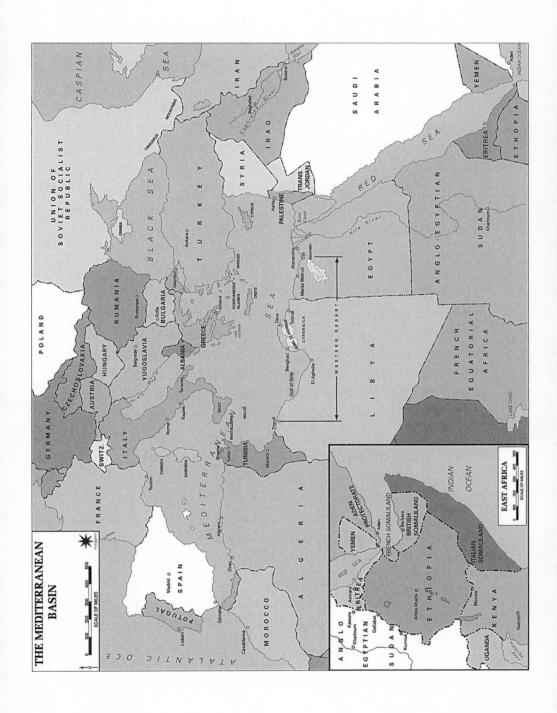

divided into two distinct parts: firstly, cargo and passenger liner companies – with household names such as P&O, Blue Funnel, Blue Star, Furness Withy, Shaw Savill & Albion, and Ellerman's – and secondly, tramp owners and operators, such as Runciman's and Ropner's. The first group owned ships designed to operate on liner routes conveying, for example, general cargo out to Australia, New Zealand, Africa, India and the Americas and returning with refrigerated and other produce and equipment required to be imported into the United Kingdom. The inability of the UK to feed itself was one of the reasons these lines were established, securing the regular supply of foodstuffs while adding passengers, mail and high-value commodities to generate further profit based on a regular, scheduled service.

The vessels were often of a high specification, increasingly powered by modern diesel engines and officered by 'company men' who enjoyed greater security of employment and conditions that were in excess of the legal minimums laid down in the Merchant Shipping Acts, overseen by the Board of Trade. Seamen from around the British Empire were frequently employed and Lascars, Indian and Chinese sailors were familiar sights in Britain's docks and port cities, where many settled. Cargo liners were able to operate at higher speeds than their tramp counterparts, so were ideally suited for convoys where a fast passage was required, with many such vessels being capable of more than 15 knots. This explains the make-up of MW6 (described below), with all four merchant ships being of the fast, cargo liner type. Tramp ships, on the other hand, made up the majority of the fleet and were operated to an entirely different business model, often carrying bulk exports such as coal from the UK to any willing market in the world, before commencing tramping through the shipbroking system. Ship brokers matched vessels with cargoes through institutions such as the Baltic Exchange in London, and ship owners had to bid for the business. Payment was arranged on a purely by-the-ton basis (freight) under a voyage charter, or by daily hire of the vessel under a time charter, and the market was driven by supply and demand, and logistical factors such as keeping non-earning ballast passages to a minimum. In order to maximise profits, tramp ships were fitted with the cheapest technology, utilising steam generated from coal-fired boilers to turn reciprocating engines. While their ability to handle a wide variety of bulk and break bulk cargoes was a definite asset, their speed was limited, with a rate of 8 knots or under being quite usual. This meant that when compared to cargo liners, tramp-based convoys, with speed set to that of the slowest ship, could take twice as long to cross the Atlantic, increasing the time exposed to submarine attack and making life difficult for the escorting warships. In the great majority of tramp ships the officers and crew were often paid, fed and accommodated to the minimum Merchant Shipping Act and Board of Trade requirements, with men selected from the industry pool of labour, on a voyage-by-voyage basis. Nor should it be forgotten that the clear majority of merchant vessels carried several boys or trainees, and these would have been as young as fourteen, the national school-leaving age. The Royal Navy had its fifteen- and sixteen-year-old boys as well, including marine buglers and boy seamen; it is a sobering thought to realise that when HMS *Hood* was sunk by the *Bismarck* in May 1941, about ninety boys perished with her.

Tramp ship crews were expected to sign Articles of Agreement that could mean up to two years away from their home port and, while monthly wages for an able seaman were roughly comparable to those of an equivalent naval rating, at around £6 per month, there was no paid leave. Furthermore, many tramp owners strictly followed the letter of the law by ending the voyage, and with it their obligation to pay further wages, at the time of sinking, so many a merchant sailor found himself suddenly becoming unemployed while struggling for survival in the water. Thankfully, this disgraceful and shocking practice was

HMS *Hood* was sunk by the *Bismarck* on 24 May 1941. The German battleship, in company with the heavy cruiser *Prinz Eugen*, was under orders to break for the North Atlantic, to destroy as many convoys as possible. The Admiralty confidently expected the battlecruiser *Hood* and the new, untried *Prince of Wales* to intercept and bring the *Bismarck* to battle. The possibility that the *Bismarck* might win the ensuing encounter did not enter anyone's head. *Hood* was struck by several German shells, exploded and sank. The loss affected British morale.

ended by the government in 1942, almost 100 years after a similar practice had been brought to a close in the Royal Navy, as a result of the after effects and mutiny that followed the wrecking of HMS *Wager* in 1841.

In a recently published (2011) memoir, Morris Beckman, who trained as a Radio Officer with Marconi before joining his first ship, an old tanker SS *Venitia*, described conditions on board as he sailed, aged 19, in his first Atlantic convoy in 1940. His first meal at sea, served in the saloon, set the scene:

The meal was terrible, consisting of carrot soup which was metallic to the taste, followed by what could have been grass cuttings and plasticine. This was eulogised as 'sea pie'. The dessert was a yellow mound of soggy dough covered with custard, which the cook said was Thames Duff. The same dessert was to become Texan delight in Galveston, Abadan Flan in the Persian Gulf, and ammunition to be aimed at bum boats in the Suez Canal.[2]

Morris became a little less light-hearted when recalling the terror of waiting to be torpedoed and witnessing the fate of survivors from a torpedoed merchantman:

(The Old Man said) The submarines will be hunting for victims, especially since we are homeward bound with full cargoes. So those off watch must stay mustered by their boats... 'Look, look!' It was Ginger. He was pointing frantically down at the sea at a small boat, probably a jolly boat, capsized and no more than twenty yards from us. Three men sprawled across its beam, hanging on, their faces white blobs. They were shouting at us but none could decipher what they were saying and in a flash we were past them. We felt very ashamed but there was nothing we could do. We knew that unless they were very lucky they would soon be dead.[3]

Efforts were made to offer merchant ships their own protection and many became Defensively Equipped Merchant Ships (DEMS), and were fitted with a gun, or guns, manned by service personnel. Some large, fast passenger liners had more extensive armament and a large naval complement that enabled them to act as auxiliary cruisers, but as in the case of the *Rawalpindi*, as soon as they encountered a modern warship they were virtually defenceless.[4] Merchant ships were, of course, primarily designed to carry cargo in large holds and were therefore very liable to swift flooding and loss when struck by a torpedo or bomb, a vulnerability that was compounded when the cargo consisted of oil, ammunition or explosives. While the escorting warships were better able to defend themselves, and had a higher level of compartmentalisation and manoeuvrability, the highly destructive capability of modern bombs and torpedoes rendered them almost as vulnerable as their charges, particularly when Axis tactics later concentrated on sinking the escorts before attacking the merchantmen.

Returning now to *Carlisle*, her first assignment in the Mediterranean was as part of the close escort to Malta convoy MW6, which departed Alexandria on 20 March for the three-day voyage to Valetta where, on arrival, the convoy was heavily attacked by Italian aircraft. The close escort comprised several destroyers and three anti-aircraft cruisers, the other two being HMS *Calcutta* and HMS *Coventry*, and they put up a fierce barrage in defence of the merchant ships, the harbour and the town. All four merchantmen, *Perthshire*, *Clan Ferguson*, *City of Manchester* and *City of Lincoln* were unharmed and were able to discharge the vital supplies they had carried to the island, while the cruisers returned to duty with the fleet, although the *Carlisle*, still awaiting its repaired shaft, was not available for major fleet operations due to her reduced speed. The close escort of MW6 was covered by the main force of Cunningham's Mediterranean Fleet, including the battleships *Barham*, *Valiant* and *Warspite*, the aircraft carrier HMS *Formidable*, and the cruisers HMS *Ajax*, HMS *Bonaventure*, HMS *Gloucester*, HMS *Orion*, HMS *Perth* and HMS *York*. This force dispersed to Alexandria and the British base in Crete on 26 March to prepare for a possible fleet action against the Italian navy. The Commander-in-Chief was not only keen to be in a position to counter any encroachment by the Italian fleet, but was running, at the same time, a series of troop convoys to Greece in Operation *Lustre*, at the behest of Churchill, following the death of the Greek Prime Minister Metaxas. It was expected that German forces would seize the opportunity to invade Yugoslavia and Greece, with Germany having already secured the allegiance of Bulgaria, Hungary and Rumania, thus strengthening its hand in Eastern Europe. Operation *Lustre* lasted until 24 April and involved the transfer of more than 60,000 troops and their equipment, but by the end of the operation the German conquest of Yugoslavia and her invasion of Greece had already come to pass. The decision, taken in London, to divert forces from Egypt and the Middle East to Greece and Crete had serious consequences for both military and naval operations. Wavell, for example, knew that the transfer of troops from Egypt would likely deny a complete victory in North Africa, at the very time when the desert army was threatening to expel the Italians from Libya. The situation was that after the Italian invasion of Egypt, from Libya in the autumn of 1940, their army had set up several strongholds as far east as Sidi Barrani in Egypt. Wavell counter-attacked and these fortifications were taken by the advance of the heavily outnumbered British and Indian XIII Corps, under the inspired leadership of Lieutenant-General O'Connor. With strong internal lines of communications, judicious use of all arms, and tactics that succeeded in cutting off each stronghold, the Italians were expelled from Egypt in one week. A further advance in January took O'Connor's Australian forces to Bardia, with XIII Corps poised to advance to Tobruk, thus explaining German intervention in North Africa and Rommel's arrival in the middle of February. If Wavell had been able to reinforce O'Connor earlier, it is very likely that the Italians would have been defeated before German intervention was practicable. The introduction of the Afrika Korps also added to Cunningham's burden, in that his command was now also expected to intercept and destroy the Axis supply convoys running between Italy and Libya, in addition to escorting his own convoys to Greece, Crete and Malta.

Admiral Cunningham fully understood that the desperate state of the battle of the Atlantic precluded any serious reinforcement of his fleet, regardless of the multiplicity of tasks that his fleet was faced with in the Mediterranean. This situation did not deter him, however, from taking the offensive against the Italian Fleet, as illustrated by the raid on Taranto on the night of 11/12 November

1940. This audacious raid demonstrated, yet again, the growing superiority of air forces deployed against ships, as a force of old, slow, Swordfish torpedo bombers took off from the carrier HMS *Illustrious* and sank half of the Italian battle fleet in a harbour thought too shallow for this type of attack. Cunningham did not rest on his laurels, for the force that had covered MW6 and returned to Alexandria on 26 March was then immediately deployed to attack an Italian battle fleet, consisting of one battleship, *Vittoria Veneto*, four heavy cruisers and several supporting destroyers who had set sail to interdict the convoys to Greece. Acting on intelligence from ULTRA (the code name for all intelligence coming from Enigma intercepters at Bletchley Park), Cunningham arranged for the Italians to be spotted from the air – protecting the real source of his intelligence – and set about attacking them with cruisers and aircraft from Crete, and with ships and carrier-borne aircraft from Alexandria. The ensuing battle took place south-west of Cape Matapan, after which the battle was named, which lay on the southern tip of Greece and was due west from Crete. It was a night action and, while some of Cunningham's ships had radar and the fleet was practised in fighting in the hours of darkness, the Italians were not. The combination of capability and determination ensured that the Royal Navy prevailed, sinking three of the four Italian heavy cruisers, two destroyers and torpedoing the *Vitorria Veneto*, forcing her withdrawal. British casualties were light, with the three crew members of a torpedo bomber being killed when their aircraft was shot down by the Italian battleship. Italian casualties were more than 2,000, in what was their greatest naval defeat.

The dynamics of the Mediterranean war at sea, clearly demonstrating the risks that were being run because of the many demands placed on limited resources, were highlighted by two events that occurred almost simultaneously to Matapan. Both were concerned with naval operations supplying and protecting the island of Crete, which had been garrisoned by British forces in October 1940 and was used as a naval base from which ships operated to protect convoys to Greece, as part of Operation *Lustre*. It was to Suda Bay, a natural harbour and main naval base on the north-west coast of Crete, that the *Carlisle* was sent after defending convoy MW6. On the day she arrived, 26 March, the heavy cruiser HMS *York*, also stationed in Suda Bay, was attacked by two small Italian motorboats packed with explosives. Severely damaged, and with the loss of two of her crew, *York* was beached and disabled, her war having come to a premature end. The loss of this heavy cruiser was a blow to Cunningham and his overworked fleet, but was soon followed by another. On 30 March, while engaged in convoy duty as part of Operation *Lustre*, HMS *Bonaventure*, a Dido class anti-aircraft cruiser that had been completed and commissioned in May 1940, was torpedoed by an Italian submarine south of Crete, losing 139 of its crew of approximately 480. One of the survivors was a young marine, John Marshall, who, in conversation with the author in 2005, mentioned that *Bonaventure* was his first ship, and that 'her maiden voyage was surrounded by secrecy as she shipped gold bullion from the Bank of England to Canada for safekeeping, after which we were sent to the Mediterranean.'[5] John also wrote to the author:

> I was serving on HMS *Carlisle* between April 1941 and August 1942... so was on her at the same time as Albert Elliott, although at the time he was a corporal... At the time I was a 15-year-old Royal Marine boy bugler who had joined 'Carlisle' after my previous ship [*Bonaventure*] had been torpedoed and sunk and we then experienced a dreadful year attempting to get convoys through to Malta and never succeeding as the merchant ships were always bombed and sunk. We were also a Suez Canal Guardship going up and down the canal continuously as well as escorting convoys up the Red Sea to the western desert.[6]

Marine Bugler John Marshall joined Corporal Nobby Elliott in *Carlisle* in early April 1941, following her return from Suda Bay to the main base at Alexandria. John recalled how cramped conditions aboard were, with the wartime complement being some 10–15 per cent higher than peacetime, and the extra weaponry installed after her conversion meant that *Carlisle* had more people to fit into less space. He also mentioned that the ship operated the canteen messing system so that the marines ate and slept in their barracks, taking it in turns to prepare food for cooking in the galley, and then collecting it for their mates. This was rudimentary enough in peacetime, but in wartime, with galley fires doused when the ship was at action stations, where most of the cooks and stewards were deployed in shell rooms and magazines, three hot meals a day were not frequent or even possible. When John joined, Nobby had one more year to serve on board and, as mentioned in John's letter, it was to be a truly eventful and frightening period as British fortunes waned in the struggle for supremacy and survival in the Mediterranean and North Africa.

On 24 April *Carlisle* sailed from Alexandria as part of an escort to convoy AG14, which was one of the last *Lustre* movements to Greece. On the following day, however, orders were received that required *Carlisle* to proceed directly to Greece for the evacuation of British and imperial troops to Crete, an operation appropriately code named Demon. The decision to evacuate had been made due to early Italo-German successes in pushing back Greek resistance, resulting in the taking of Salonica on 8 April and a continued advance thereafter. Despite the presence of over 55,000 British, Australian and New Zealand troops under the command of General Maitland Wilson, along with a substantial Polish element and all their equipment, there seemed to be little that could be done to stop the Axis advance. The Greek government surrendered on 23 April and, accompanied by the King of Greece, its members were flown to Crete in an RAF Sunderland aircraft, and Operation

Demon commenced. Commanded by Admiral Pridham-Wippell, who flew his flag on board the cruiser HMS *Orion*, the naval force designated for this operation included the *Carlisle*, *Coventry* and *Calcutta*, along with three other cruisers and twenty destroyers. Also available were the converted merchant ships HMS *Glenearn* and HMS *Glengyle* that had been fitted out as landing ships with specialised landing craft in place of ship's boats. Several smaller naval vessels and larger merchantmen acting as troop ships completed the resources at the Admiral's disposal. This was just as well, for the evacuation itself presented a very challenging proposition. On the military side, the army had been conducting a disciplined and tiring rearguard action from Salonica, and the lack of ports meant that evacuation was to be from a series of beaches between Raphtis in the east and Kalamata in the west, a distance of more than 150 miles. With the Axis air forces having air superiority, not only were the withdrawing troops subjected to frequent attack from the air, but the ships could only risk approaching the beaches in the hours of darkness, making sure that they were away by 0300. Sadly, the validity of this tactic was proved on 29 April when the Dutch merchant ship *Slamat*, unwilling to leave some soldiers behind, delayed its departure from Nauplia until 0415. Consequently, she was caught in open water a few hours later and was heavily attacked from the air, going down with the loss of approximately 500 men. Some survivors were picked up by escorting destroyers *Diamond* and *Wryneck*, while they too were being bombed. Overall, however, the decision to restrict the hours of operation was a success, as the Axis air forces did not appear at night, although its employment meant that the evacuation took six days rather than the originally envisaged three. The delay led to Cunningham's decision to send only the troop ships to Alexandria direct, in order to save on shipping, and to direct the warships and Glens to take their loads to Suda Bay, Crete, for a faster turnaround. As part of this task, on 26 April *Carlisle* carried more than 1,400 passengers, mainly consisting of New Zealand troops plus a small number of Greek nationals, from the port of Raphtis to Suda Bay. For this service, Captain Hampton, the *Carlisle's* Commanding Officer, received a letter thanking him and his crew for 'for their hospitality' on this passage, signed by five New Zealand army officers.[7] Operation *Demon* successfully evacuated in excess of 50,000 troops with the only major loss being that of the *Slamet* and, as at Dunkirk, the priority was troops not equipment, so much of the army's kit had to be left behind. The last troop convoy, GA15, left Greece on 29 April bound for Alexandria, with the cruisers *Carlisle* and *Perth*, sloop HMS *Auckland* and the destroyers HMS *Decoy*, HMS *Defender* and HMS *Kandahar* in attendance. GA15 docked at Alexandria on 1 May 1941. Cunningham later wrote of the pride he had in the men of the Royal and Merchant navies who had succeeded in getting the troops away:

> Of the men who were embarked only about 14,000 were brought away from recognised wharves or jetties. All the rest were taken off to the ships from open beaches in landing craft, ships' boats and any other craft that could be collected, a process which was depressingly slow at night. Yet one reads of the merchant ships each lifting up to 3,500 men a night, the cruisers up to 2,500, and the destroyers crammed with anything up to 800 and 850. The seamen did gallant work, and the cruisers and destroyers had been working at full pressure for weeks.[8]

There was also the wider situation to consider. With so many of his cruisers and destroyers deployed for the evacuation, Cunningham was unable to operate his main battle fleet out of Alexandria. Not for the first time was he grateful that the Italian navy seemed to prefer inaction and did not seek to take advantage of this situation.

With Greece lost, the situation in Crete now had to be reviewed and Churchill decided that the island had to be held. To firm up the defences, the finally assembled Royal Marine Mobile Naval Base Defence Organisation (MNBDO) had already been nominated for Suda Bay and sent round the Cape, arriving in Suez on 21 April. Unfortunately, and in a way reminiscent of the Norwegian campaign, its ships needed unloading and re-stowing, and were sent to the port of Haifa for this purpose. For the time being this meant that the MNBDO commander, the Marine Major-General Weston, was stranded in Crete, where he had arrived by air to take over command of the brigade-sized forces that made up the existing garrison. By the time the MNBDO arrived, in early May, General Wavell had decided that about 25,000 of the troops evacuated from Greece would remain in Crete, and sent General Freyberg, the New Zealand commander, to take overall control of the island, with Weston left in command of the defence of the naval base at Suda Bay. While the manpower situation on the island had improved, the original garrison having several anti-aircraft batteries and coastal artillery, supplemented by the MNBDO, the troops landed from Greece lacked equipment and the Axis control of the skies was making it increasingly difficult to supply the island.

Because of the considerable pressure being exerted by Axis forces in the Middle East, Churchill and his advisers decided that, in addition to holding Crete, further efforts had to made to supply and hold Malta, now more strategically important than ever, while sending much-needed armour and aircraft to Wavell in Egypt. With this in mind, Operation *Tiger* was put into action, involving the fast convoy MW7A and the slower MW7B proceeding from Alexandria to Valetta with, simultaneously, a military convoy, WS8, that was ordered to proceed to Egypt via the Strait of Gibraltar. An indication of the importance and risks attached to this operation is that the major covering forces for

WS8 were personally commanded by Admiral Somerville in the battlecruiser HMS *Renown* with Force H from Gibraltar, and Admiral Cunningham, who flew his flag in *Warspite*, covered MW7A and MW7B from Alexandria. Force H left Gibraltar on 5 May and Cunningham's fleet sailed from Alexandria shortly afterward. The five cargo liners in WS8 were carrying ammunition, artillery and aircraft and, when joined by Force H, were escorted by no less than one battleship, *Queen Elizabeth*, one battlecruiser, *Renown*, one aircraft carrier, HMS *Ark Royal*, three cruisers and several destroyers. This formidable force escaped the attention of the enemy until the afternoon of 8 May when, after being seen by a reconnaissance aircraft, the warships were attacked by German and Italian bombers, dive bombers, torpedo bombers and fighters. Somerville's ships and *Ark Royal's* aircraft put up a highly spirited defence, aided by the fact that, on this day, the cloud was at a reasonably low level and, despite many near misses and the frequent combing of torpedo tracks, the fleet remained intact. Now, as the convoy made its way through the heavily mined waters off the coast of Sicily, disaster struck when two of the merchantmen, *New Zealand Star* and *Empire Song*, struck mines. The former was able to continue her voyage but the *Empire Song* was lost, along with her cargo of tanks and aircraft and some eighteen members of her crew. Further east, Cunningham's fleet also experienced attack from the air on 8 May and his warships emerged unscathed from the Axis attacks. Meanwhile, en route to Valetta, *Carlisle* was part of the escort to MW7A, which consisted of four cargo liners that enabled the convoy to maintain a good speed of 15 knots. Accompanying *Carlisle* in the escort were four other anti-aircraft cruisers, *Calcutta*, *Coventry*, *Dido* and *Phoebe*, the total exceeding the number of merchant ships they were close protecting. Due to their staggered departure from Alexandria, MW7A combined forces with MW 7B and the convoys entered

Valetta harbour, after much minesweeping activity, on 9 May. Almost immediately, *Carlisle* and her fellow escorts regrouped and formed up to escort WS8 on the last leg of its voyage to Alexandria, where the remaining four merchant ships were safely delivered on 12 May. With the loss of a single cargo ship and no major naval casualty, the gamble taken in running Operation *Tiger* was fully justified. Or was it? The sheer size of the escorts and covering fleets demonstrated the importance of all the convoys involved in Operation *Tiger*, and clearly indicated the scale and strength of the aerial threat posed by the enemy air forces, but its success was due to a combination of good seamanship, fighting ability and poor flying conditions, circumstances which caused Cunningham to caution Churchill and the Admiralty against thinking that the run across the Mediterranean was easy:

> Unfortunately the apparent ease with which a convoy was brought through from end to end of the Mediterranean caused many false conclusions to be drawn at home, and I think made some people think that we were exaggerating the dangers ... Before long the dismal truth was painfully to be brought home to them.[9]

Cunningham also wrote to the Admiralty expressing his frustration that having run *Tiger* through to Alexandria at great risk, the saving in time made by the decision to enter the Mediterranean via Gibraltar instead of the Cape was rendered worthless by the fact that the tanks and hurricanes arrived unfit for action, having to go into storage to have sand filters fitted. When reading Cunningham's memoir, it is easy to agree with him when he writes:

> Why on earth these filters aren't fitted before they are shipped I can't think.[10]

This correspondence was followed on 13 May by another signal to the Admiralty regarding the Commander-in-Chief's concern about the shortage of anti-aircraft ammunition for his ships. Prolonged periods of air attack required the expenditure of copious amounts of this type of ammunition, to ensure that an effective deterrent by means of a sustained barrage could be maintained. In anticipation of a German attack or invasion against Crete, Wavell, Cunningham and their fellow Commander-in-Chief, Air Chief Marshal Longmore (who had started his flying career in the Royal Naval Air Service), knew there was insufficient aircraft to cover the fleet against the air superiority that the Germans would enjoy whenever they chose to make their move against the island.

After the arrival of the *Tiger* convoy in Alexandria, *Carlisle* was docked for much-needed heavy maintenance and repairs, and it was hoped that she would be able to fit her repaired shaft and be restored to her full operating speed. This was not to be, however, as she was hurriedly undocked when the Germans proceeded to invade Crete from the air just after sunrise on 20 May, an assault that took place following several days of heavy bombing of the island and its defences. While General Freyberg, commanding Crete, had disposed his 30,000 troops at key locations around the island in anticipation of an aerial assault, which he was confident of resisting, many of his troops were still short of equipment and ill recovered from their experiences in Greece. Defence was focussed on the three airfields at Maleme, Heraklion and Retimo, with the MNBDO and other forces defending Suda Bay. Such was the paucity of British aircraft on Crete that within a couple of days of the German bombing commencing on 14 May, the few fighters available, despite the gallant actions of their pilots, had been lost, leaving the island, its defenders and any ship operating in daylight hours fully exposed to the actions of the Luftwaffe. On the night of 14/15 May, however, Freyberg received welcome reinforcements at Heraklion in the shape of an infantry battalion from the Leicester Regiment, which also brought its full equipment. The battalion was carried from Egypt in the cruisers HMS *Gloucester* and HMS *Fiji*, and the landing ship *Glengyle* then delivered a battalion of the Argyll and Sutherland Highlanders to the south of the island on the night of 18 May. Cunningham responded to the airborne invasion by deploying his cruiser squadrons to intercept a possible German attempt to land ground forces from the sea. For this purpose, *Carlisle* joined the 15th Cruiser Squadron under the command of Rear Admiral King in HMS *Naiad*, with sister ship *Calcutta*, the Australian ship *Perth* and the destroyers HMS *Kandahar*, HMS *Kingston* and HMS *Nubian*, and proceeded towards Heraklion on the north side of Crete on the night of 21/22 May. At 2330 on 21 May, Rear Admiral Glennie in *Dido*, along with *Ajax*, *Orion* and the destroyers HMS *Hasty*, HMS *Hereward* and HMS *Kimberley*, located and attacked a German troop convoy about 20 miles off the north-west coast of the island. Glennie had the advantage of radar and experience of night fighting, and his ships were successful in sinking several of the troop-carrying fishing vessels and steamers in an attack that lasted more than two hours. It is estimated that 4,000 German soldiers were lost as a result of this night action. With daylight approaching, however, and having expended a great deal of anti-aircraft ammunition, Glennie withdrew to the south. This left King's squadron, including the *Carlisle,* to conform to Cunningham's orders for a sweep north-west of Heraklion, where they had arrived in the early hours of 22 May. The daylight hours exposed the squadron to heavy and sustained attack from the air, commencing at 0700. At 0830 a fishing vessel carrying soldiers was sighted and sunk by *Perth*, which was then heavily attacked by enemy aircraft. King ordered *Naiad* to go back and support Perth during this onslaught, and while *Perth* was able to return to the main body of the squadron, it was *Naiad*'s turn to face the bombers and she soon fell well astern of the squadron. With his ships restricted to 21 knots, due to the missing shaft in *Carlisle*, and with low stocks of anti-aircraft ammunition, King withdrew his ships to the west, after forcing another troop convoy to turn away from Crete. This withdrawal from the Aegean Sea did not lessen the ferocity of air attacks nor alleviate the great strain upon the ships' crews, who by now had spent many hours at action stations without a break. Instead the Luftwaffe mounted a strong attack that lasted over three and a half hours, with *Naiad* alone and still astern as a result of her earlier evasive action. During a two-hour period *Naiad* had 181 bombs aimed at her, while near misses put two of her gun turrets out of action and, with a number of her compartments flooded, her speed was reduced to less than 20 knots. At 1125, King ordered the remainder of the squadron to group itself around *Naiad* and then it was *Carlisle*'s turn to be hit.[11] The events of this day have been recorded in *Carlisle*'s log, which also noted that it was a clear day with a little cumulus cloud, light wind and a calm sea:

Thursday 22 May 1941

0500 Exercised action

0530 Commenced zigzag

0535 Opened fire on Dornier 17 knots

0545 Ceased ZZ

0550 Formed up on Naiad 15 knots

0600 Opened fire on Dornier 18 knots

0731 Opened fire on Ju88

0736 Opened fire on Dornier

0818 Opened fire on 3 Dornier

0820 2 Dornier

0826 6 bombs

0846 8 bombs stbd qtr

0900 sighted 12 troop carrying aircraft engaged 0902

Bombing of Naiad continued throughout

1030 6 bombs stbd qtr

1035 3 bombs port qtr

1042 2 bombs stbd beam

1130 20 knots all ships in company loose formation

1222 Engaged Ju88

1229 2 bombs near Calcutta

1235 Attacked by 3 Ju 87s [*Stukas*]

1236 Ship hit on No 2 Mounting, between funnels and near miss fwd. Fire in UD petrol stowage 9 killed

1242 Attacked by 2 Dornier Temp reduced speed

1245 Fire extinguished and RDF out of action

1256 16 knots.[12]

Damage reports filed after *Carlisle*'s return to Alexandria confirmed that she had been dive-bombed by three Stukas at 1236, the aircraft releasing nine bombs at an altitude of 800 feet. The bombs were identified as three of 500lbs and six of 100lbs, and the ship was hit by a single 500lb bomb and one 100lb bomb, the remaining seven missing and exploding down the port side of the ship. The heavier bomb struck the left gun of No.2 twin 4-inch mounting, situated between the funnels, killing eleven of its crew and wounding twenty-five, including Marine Babjohns. The mounting was completely destroyed, and the radius of the blast extended about 25 feet, wrecking the nearby direction finder hut, destroying the blacksmith's hut and severely damaging the after funnel. A petrol fire was started in the starboard waist and began to burn the ready use ammunition although, as noted in the log, this was extinguished by the ship's company in nine minutes.[13] It should be noted that where the log refers to 'RDF' it means the radar that tracked targets and assisted in the control of the guns. Strictly speaking, RDF means Radio Direction Finder, which was used to locate where enemy radio transmissions were coming from, but in this context the term RDF was used as a cover for radar, thereby disguising the fact that this new technology was now in use. Although the casualties and damage suffered this day were a serious blow to the ship, it could have been much worse, as explained in the after-action report from the Commander-in-Chief's office in Alexandria:

> But for the fortuitous circumstances in that the 500lb bomb scored a direct hit on no. 2 mounting thus allowing the main force of the explosion to vent freely, this vessel would have suffered much more severe damage.[14]

In other words, by striking the heavy duty mounting of the guns, the bomb was prevented from penetrating the deck of the *Carlisle* and exploding in a more vital area. Corporal Nobby Elliott was gun layer in No. 3 Mounting, aft of No. 2, when the ship was hit; the screams from the casualties stayed with him for the rest of his life. One of the effects of the explosion had been to create what seemed to Nobby to be a wall of fast moving and violent sea water flooding the upper deck. This forced everyone to hang on, with some unfortunates washed away and, despite their injuries, the rest clinging hard to any structure that would prevent them from being swept overboard. The memory was particularly potent and long-lasting; it physically moved Nobby when talking about it to the author thirty years after the event. Like his shipmates, Nobby had been at action stations, and in action, for seven-and-a-half hours by the time the Stukas attacked, and their ordeal was far from over. *Carlisle*'s log, again:

1257 3 torpedo planes 6 torpedoes fired
1312 Opened fire Ju88 & 2 fighters
1315 8 bombs stbd beam 1'
1350 Attacked by 9 Ju 87's Near miss stbd bow. Captain wounded by bullet. *Greyhound* hit twice

1630 Opened fire 9 Dornier

1625 16 bombs to stbd 5'

1637 6 bombs ahead

1642 6 bombs 4' to stbd 8 bombs stbd qtr 2'

1811 16 knots

1812 JU 88 dropped 4 bombs stbd qtr 5'

1920 Bodies of ratings buried at sea 35N 22 25E

2040 Captain Hampton and 2 ratings buried at sea 34 44N

2220 Joined up with battleships and others on 23 May proceeding Alexandria

1232 Sighted 8 aircraft

1234 Fleet opened fire

1237 Aircraft identified as friendly

Saturday 24 May in Alexandria 0215 No 2 mounting removed by crane and body of 1 rating removed.[15]

(Authors note: The symbol ' after a number indicates distance in cables from the ship. One cable equals one tenth of a nautical mile, or approximately 600 feet.)

The brief and matter-of-fact nature of the contents of the log, which were recorded on the bridge by a junior officer, barely reflect the terrifying nature of the prolonged onslaught from the air. The roar of aero-engines and the noise generated by the ship's own fans and machinery was accompanied by the shocking blast of the guns, reaching a roaring crescendo as each wave of aircraft approached the *Carlisle*. This was nothing, however, compared to the screaming dive of the Stukas and their terrifying vertical trajectory, followed by a horizontal levelling out that seemed to be almost at mast height. It was easy to be transfixed by this noise and sight but attention had to shift swiftly to the next target, a well-practised action that required the utmost in nerve and teamwork. Captain Hampton died five hours after being hit by two bullets from the single rear gun of a Stuka, as it flew over the ship after completing its dive-bombing run. The destroyer HMS *Greyhound* sank fifteen minutes after she was bombed and later in the afternoon the fleet lost the cruisers *Gloucester* and *Fiji* to further aerial bombardment, a fate suffered on the next day by the destroyers HMS *Kashmir* and HMS *Kelly*.

Analysis of *Carlisle*'s reports on the air attacks it received provides at least one explanation as to why she was hit so few times after so many attacks. For example, the Dornier attack at 0818 on 22 May resulted in fourteen bombs being dropped from a height of 11,000 feet, with the ship putting up no fewer than twenty-five salvoes of eight 4-inch shells. It was noted that nine salvoes were accurately predicted on the long-range RDF plot and that the enemy aircraft were effectively prevented from dropping their weapons at optimal range by the density of this barrage. It is also easy to see from these figures how AA ammunition stocks could be run down in a relatively short space of time; the *Carlisle* having expended 200 rounds of 4-inch anti-aircraft shells in less than ten minutes. This rate of fire also demonstrated that the hard, fast and accurate work demanded of gun's crews was absolutely critical to their survival.[16]

Other explanations for the effectiveness of ships' anti-aircraft defence were set out in a series of remarks by Captain William Powlett of *Fiji*. He identified four key elements. Firstly, there was the ability of cruisers to steam at high speed and take evasive action to dodge dive-bombers, secondly, the barrage was effective as a deterrent, until ammunition ran low. Powlett also observed that efforts to rescue the survivors of bombed ships, while air attacks were continuing, only served to endanger the rest of the fleet. Finally, he recorded that throughout 22 May every attack mounted against the *Fiji* was observed, thereby providing time for the ship's armament to respond, however:

It was an unobserved attack that finally immobilised the ship. RDF was out of action almost the whole day, but AA lookouts, after a taste of bombing, developed eyes which missed nothing.[17]

The *Fiji* was in fact hit by two single bombs dropped half an hour apart by two separate Bf/Me 109 fighters that came in low and fast and took her by surprise.

After No. 2 mounting had been removed in Alexandria, *Carlisle* proceeded to Port Said where she lay under repair for three and a half weeks. A new mounting, ex-HMS *Liverpool*, was installed and, at last, she was able to have her repaired shaft fitted. In addition to the repair of battle damage, *Carlisle* received some additional AA armament by way of several 20mm Oerlikon guns. One of the reports submitted to the Admiralty while *Carlisle* was undergoing repair dealt with the unusual fact that despite the 'shock' of her bombing, the electrical equipment on board, so vital to the control and firing of guns, continued to operate to a high degree of efficiency, as shown in the following extract:

3. There were NO important electrical failures, either with dynamos, and associated switchgear or Low Power and Fire Control equipment. The High Power switchboard maintained control of the three dynamos throughout the incident despite its proximity to the heavier impact...

5. Gun instruments and circuits on the damaged mounting were wrecked but, due presumably to the lack of short circuits and earths, the rest of the Fire Control system seemed to be unaffected and functioned normally during dive-bombing attacks which developed before these circuits could be isolated.[18]

This report is extremely important because it demonstrates the vulnerability of key electrical systems to damage from bombs, shells or torpedoes – ultimately resulting in a ship being rendered defenceless, as the control and firing systems depended on a constant and reliable source of power. Not only does this report explain how *Carlisle* was able to continue to fend off attacks after having been struck, but it also kept the Admiralty informed as to the efficacy of the system design and the robustness of its fitting.

As the cruisers were fighting for their lives, the German airborne invaders had, by 22 May, secured effective control of Maleme airfield, at the cost of great casualties resulting from desperate, ferocious fighting with the hard-pressed defenders. The effect of Axis air superiority against soldiers on land was as great, if not greater, than the damage inflicted against Cunningham's ships at sea and, while German reinforcements were flown into Maleme, the Luftwaffe continuously attacked the defenders – inflicting damage on both personnel and morale. The German success at Maleme virtually guaranteed her forces victory in Crete and, by 24 May, despite urgent messages from London insisting that the island must be held, the daylight denial to the navy of the Aegean and the waters surrounding Crete meant that Axis convoys could move with virtual impunity. By 27 May the number of German troops on Crete, about 35,000 men, exceeded defenders for the first time, and the latter were further denuded by the relentless bombing of the Luftwaffe. On the same day, Wavell ordered the evacuation of Crete and stated in his communication with London:

I fully regret failure to hold Crete... But it has become quite obvious that attempt to prolong defence will not only be useless but is likely to so exhaust navy, army and air resources as to compromise defence positions in Middle East... Result due to overwhelming enemy air superiority, He has been able to establish what practically amounts to box barrage of bombing aircraft around island.[19]

Ordering an evacuation was one thing, carrying it out presented Cunningham with an enormous challenge. Two ports were selected for this operation: Heraklion on the north coast and Sphakia on the south, although neither would be able to operate for more than a couple of hours at night. Nevertheless, the Royal Navy rose to the occasion, knowing it had a duty to rescue as much of the army as possible and accepting the very great risks involved in this operation. The evacuation was carried out over four nights, between 28 May and 1 June, commencing with the cruisers *Ajax*, *Dido* and *Orion*, accompanied by six destroyers, steaming to Heraklion, where they arrived offshore just before midnight, having been heavily attacked en route and using up half of their ammunition stock. After three hours and with about 4,000 men embarked, they set course for Egypt, but, as soon as the sun came up, they came under a nine-hour attack by Stuka dive-bombers. A destroyer was badly hit and beached – with her crew and soldiers taken prisoner – and both *Dido* and *Orion* were bombed, with heavy casualties among their crew and troops crowded into mess decks below. On arrival in Alexandria, it was reckoned that about 800 troops out of the approximately 4,000 that embarked had become casualties, and no further attempts were made to evacuate from Heraklion. By the ending of the evacuation on the night of 1 June, it is estimated that 18,000 troops got away, leaving about 14,000 dead, wounded or as prisoners of war. The cost to the navy was high with three cruisers and six destroyers sunk, and a further seventeen vessels damaged, including an aircraft carrier and three battleships. All the attacks upon the warships were carried out by German air forces, while the Italian Navy remained in harbour throughout. The human toll was just fewer than 2,000 sailors lost and about 200 wounded – a heavy sacrifice indeed.

In one of the war's great ironies, the Germans and Allies interpreted the success of the airborne invasion of Crete in two opposing ways. Firstly, Hitler and the German High Command were appalled at the extraordinarily heavy casualties, perhaps as high as 6,000, incurred by their airborne troops, which meant that the invasion was almost called off after the first night. This experience ensured that German airborne forces were never again used in this role. Secondly, the Allies interpreted the airborne invasion as highly successful – thus proving the concept of mass attack from the air – and set out to create what became, in 1944, an airborne army. Sadly, when used on large-scale operations rather than for raiding purposes, Allied airborne forces had a mixed record. In both Operation *Market Garden*, in September 1944, which failed in its object, and in Operation *Varsity*, the more successful crossing of the Rhine in March 1945, casualties were high. If there was any consolation arising from defeat in Crete, it was that the campaign in Greece and the Balkans delayed Operation *Barbarossa*, the German invasion of Russia (and the largest land invasion in history) by several weeks. Although this is still a matter of debate among historians, it remains the case that the invasion was launched too late to make the most of the summer weather in Russia west of the Urals.

Much has been made in this chapter of the insufficiency of Allied naval, military and air resources in the Mediterranean and Middle East for defence against the Axis and the execution of the wider strategy determined in London. This is highlighted by the fact that even while the situation in Crete was developing, Wavell was expected to achieve success in the Western Desert and Syria, the latter being controlled by the Vichy French with airfields out of which the Luftwaffe were able to operate against Allied interests. In addressing this matter, much of May was spent discussing action against Syria, with the involvement of the Free French and the diplomatic and strategic consequences of such a campaign. A plan was hatched, code-named Operation *Exporter*, to seize Lebanon and Syria, and a combined British and Free French force began their advance into both territories early on the morning of Sunday 8 June. It was anticipated that the advance would be relatively straightforward and with the presence of De Gaulle and the Free French, that the Vichy forces would, after satisfying honour, turn to the Allies. It was not to be, and a fierce campaign followed with the Vichy soldiers holding out and inflicting serious harm upon the Allied soldiers before an armistice was finally attained on 12 July 1941.

Having spent June in dock, during which time Corporal Elliott passed his second class school certificate, with an eye on promotion, *Carlisle* was deployed to Haifa as Guard Ship, and received orders to participate in *Exporter* by joining a naval bombardment in support of the army on 6 July. The seizing of Lebanon and Syria consolidated the Allies' position in the Middle East and Wavell, although irritated by the distraction, agreed that the campaign was both necessary and important. Shortly afterward, however, Wavell was replaced by General Auchinleck, at the express wish of Churchill, as they exchanged their commands in the Middle East and India. Air Chief Marshal Longmore had been sent home early, to be replaced by Air Marshal Tedder, thus leaving Admiral Cunningham as the sole 'surviving' Commander-in-Chief in the region. From the above account of the naval actions in the Mediterranean, which were far from over, it is not difficult to see why this aggressive, fighting Admiral remained in post.

With Churchill and his advisers pushing for a land advance across the North Africa desert, more aircraft, armour, men and supplies were now convoyed round the Cape so that Auchinleck could attack at the earliest opportunity. This route was chosen not only because of the vulnerability of large convoys transiting the western Mediterranean, but also because Alexandria was simply the only port available to Allied forces that could handle substantial quantities of men and materiel. It was not surprising, therefore, that *Carlisle* was sent to act as AA Guard Ship at Suez, with HMS *Coventry*, so that their armament and radar could afford protection to the convoys as they entered the final leg of their long voyage. This duty lasted until the end of October, interspersed with a voyage as escort to a convoy taking reinforcements and material from Alexandria to the army in Tobruk, Libya. After a further spell at Suez, *Carlisle* joined the fleet at Alexandria and, in company with three destroyers, provided the escort for *Glenroy*, leaving port on 22 November as part of the naval mission to resupply the surrounded garrison at Tobruk. The following day this small but vital convoy was subjected to heavy air attack, and the *Glenroy* was severely damaged and disabled by an aerial torpedo. *Carlisle* took the stricken ship in tow and *Glenroy* was eventually beached in Mersa Matruh, and later recovered to Alexandria. The next deployment for *Carlisle* centred on providing escort from Malta to Alexandria for the converted merchant ship, now naval auxiliary, HMS *Breconshire*, which had been sent to the Mediterranean to help with the resupply of Malta. Three cruisers, *Carlisle*, *Galatea* and the Australian *Hobart*, took over as escort on 7 December, the day of Pearl Harbor, relieving *Neptune* and *Ajax* before safely arriving in Alexandria the following day. On arrival in Egypt, Nobby Elliott was promoted to Temporary Sergeant and exactly one week later, on 15 December, *Carlisle*, *Naiad* and *Euryalus*, with seven destroyers, formed Force C under the command of Rear Admiral Vian. Force C sailed as escort to *Breconshire,* which had loaded much-needed supplies for Malta and, more importantly, carried 5,000 tons of oil in specially constructed deep tanks, all bound for the beleaguered island. Cunningham and Vian knew that an Italian convoy, escorted by heavy units of the Italian fleet, was in the offing and, late on 16 December, Vian sent *Carlisle* and a couple of destroyers towards the east, with the order to make a stream of radio transmissions in order to convince the Italian Admiral Iachino that heavier British units must be in the area. With the cruisers HMS *Aurora*, HMS *Penelope* and six destroyers racing from Malta to meet Vian, they joined forces on the 17th, being under the view of enemy reconnaissance aircraft who called in the bombers. Late in the afternoon Vian's force spotted some of the heavy units with the Italian convoy and, after sending *Breconshire* away to the south, he attacked in a highly aggressive manner, sending his destroyers and their torpedoes straight towards the enemy. This bold move, perhaps in addition to *Carlisle*'s deception, convinced Iachino that heavier British forces must be in the offing and he turned his two battleships, and the remainder of his convoy, away to the north. Known as the First Battle of Sirte, off the Libyan coast, this action lasted less than an hour, and *Breconshire* was safely escorted to Grand Harbour, Valetta, while Vian's force returned to Alexandria. Two days later, on 19 December, while moored at Alexandria, Cunningham's two battleships, *Queen Elizabeth* and *Valiant*, were disabled as a consequence of a brave and skilfully executed attack by Italian human torpedoes. Whereas *Queen Elizabeth*, although much lower in the water and with severe damage to her boiler spaces, maintained an appearance of normality, *Valiant*'s damage was such that she had to be quickly dry-docked.

At this point the fortunes of the British Mediterranean Fleet reached their nadir, as losses of cruisers and destroyers continued to be accrued in the interdiction of Axis convoys to Benghazi and Tripoli, with *Neptune* and *Kandahar* being lost to mines laid off the latter. Some relief was provided by the 8th Army's advance into the Cyrenaican bulge and the capture of Benghazi on Christmas Eve, although supplying this badly damaged port from Alexandria, some 500 miles to the east, presented another challenge. On this occasion, however, the opening up of airfields near the front in

Cyrenaica and an increase in Royal Air Force resources in Malta provided a measure of air cover for the convoys proceeding to Malta and Benghazi. Nevertheless, Cunningham realised, yet again, that there was little or no chance of receiving reinforcements because after the Japanese entry in the war and their attack on Malaya, threatening Singapore, the navy had lost the battleship *Prince of Wales* and battlecruiser *Repulse*, as mentioned in Chapter 3, to a devastating air attack on 10 December. With a fleet to be found in order to face this new enemy and threat, and with the battle for survival in the Atlantic continuing to dominate maritime proceedings, Cunningham had to use what he had in taking the fight to the Italian and German convoys to Africa and making sure Malta was protected and supplied.

It was to this task that *Carlisle*, now under the command of Captain Neame, was assigned from the middle of January until the end of April 1942. In what had become a familiar pattern, the convoy was in two parts, MW8A and MW8B, in the hope that this would help to disperse enemy forces. MW8A, escorted by *Carlisle* and her destroyers, sailed from Alexandria on 16 January, followed later the same day by MW8B, which was escorted by four destroyers – HMS *Gurkha*, HMS *Legion*, HMS *Maori* and the Dutch ship *Isaac Sweers*. Admiral Vian's Force K, *Dido*, *Naiad* and *Euryalus* with destroyers HMS *Foxhound*, HMS *Havock*, HMS *Hotspur*, HMS *Kelvin* and HMS *Kipling* – then sailed from Malta, but by the time the two convoys and Force K rendezvoused on 18 January the *Gurkha* had already been sunk by a torpedo from a U-boat although, thankfully, many of her crew were picked up by *Isaac Sweers*. It was now the duty of the escorts to get the four merchantmen, *Ajax* (not to be confused with the cruiser), *City of Calcutta*, *Clan Ferguson* and *Thermopylae*, through to Malta with nearly 40,000 tons of supplies. In the face of heavy air attack but this time with the aid of the RAF, three of the cargo ships got through and successfully docked on 19 January. The exception was *Thermopylae,* which had broken down in the early afternoon of the 18th and was ordered, under her reduced speed, to Benghazi with *Carlisle* and two destroyers as escort. For some reason, *Thermopylae* was diverted to Alexandria, the longer passage exposing her to air attack, and, despite the efforts of *Carlisle* and the other escorts, she was hit, badly damaged, and had to be sunk off Derna. *Carlisle* and her consorts returned to Alexandria, where they moored up on 21 January. Cunningham was relieved that so much of the precious cargo had safely arrived in Malta and was effusive in his praise of the RAF:

From the point of view of air reconnaissance and cover this operation was very well conducted. The work of the Royal Air Force 201 Naval Co-operation group was strikingly efficient and valuable. Very full reconnaissances were flown from Malta and Cyrenaica, while the fighter protection provided from the forward aerodromes in Cyrenaica worked well in difficult conditions. The Malta fighters also did an excellent job in protecting the convoy during its arrival. It showed what could be done with aircraft trained to work over the sea.[20]

Just as it appeared that lessons were being learned and applied with aplomb, Cunningham's plans to enrich and sustain Malta suffered a shocking blow. The Afrika Korps had again counter-attacked and, by 1 February, had driven the 8th Army out of the Cyrenaican bulge and back towards Tobruk, depriving the Allies of the forward airfields that had played such an important role in the passage of MW8A/B. When added to the Axis occupation of Crete, this meant that convoys to Malta were now faced with Luftwaffe airfields on either side – not for nothing was the sea between Crete and Cyrenaica known as 'bomb alley', so the future of the island was now bleaker than ever. Nevertheless, another attempt to reach Malta was made on 12 February, when convoys

MW9 A and B left Alexandria with *Carlisle* escorting the former. The operation was organised on the same basis as MW8 but that was where the similarity ended because, due to the strengthening of the Axis position, not a single merchantman was able to get through. This came about when the Luftwaffe attacked MW9 on Friday 13 February, so damaging *Clan Campbell* that she had to be detached and sent to Tobruk, where she was subsequently repaired, after a fashion, and was able to return to Alexandria. The next day, the German air force struck again, this time so disabling *Clan Chattan* that she had to be despatched by torpedoes fired from the destroyer *Decoy*. A third cargo liner, *Rowallan Castle*, also had to be sunk later that night, after being crippled from the air. These dreadful losses forced the cancellation of the convoy, and *Carlisle* was deployed with *Dido*, *Euryalus* and *Naiad* to escort return convoy ME10, which included the redoubtable *Breconshire*, from Malta to Alexandria. During this passage *Carlisle* suffered an engine room breakdown and had to stop to effect repairs. While in this vulnerable condition, she was screened by several Hunt class destroyers and saw off aerial attacks from the Luftwaffe, which scored several near misses without causing damage. With repairs complete, *Carlisle* and her escorts rejoined the convoy and entered Alexandria on 20 February. During the course of these events, Nobby heard that his promotion to Sergeant had become permanent, with effect from 16 February 1942, fifteen and a half years after his enlistment as a boy bugler.

The loss of the cargoes of MW9 accentuated the plight of Malta, which was itself coming under heavy, continuous bombardment from the air, perhaps becoming one of the most heavily bombed targets in the whole of the war. Furthermore, it had by now become impossible to supply the island from the western Mediterranean, and Cunningham received orders that a large convoy, MW10, to Malta from Egypt had to be attempted in March, with little regard to cost. For this purpose four ships, *Breconshire*, *Pampas*, the Norwegian *Talabot* and the hastily repaired *Clan Campbell*, were assembled and loaded in Alexandria, ready to depart at 0700 on 20 March. Their close escort was provided by *Carlisle*, and the destroyers *Hasty*, *Havock*, *Hero*, *Lively*, *Sikh* and *Zulu*, followed eleven hours later by the cruisers *Cleopatra*, flying the flag of Rear Admiral Vian, *Dido* and *Euryalus* with the destroyers *Jervis*, *Kelvin*, *Kingston* and *Kipling* as their accompanying destroyers. Cunningham had agreed with his fellow Commander-in-Chiefs, Auchinleck and Tedder, that the 8th Army carry out a feint attack towards the German front line and that the RAF would attack Axis airfields in Cyrenaica and Greece to divert the attention of the Luftwaffe. The RAF was also tasked to provide what fighter cover it could spare over the convoy and this operated until the morning of 22 March, after which the convoy was out of range. After the convoy and Vian's force closed up, in the early morning of the 22nd they were joined by the cruiser *Penelope* and destroyer *Legion* from Malta, and five Hunt class destroyers from Tobruk. These combined forces gave Vian an impressive anti-aircraft capability and, with 150 miles to go to Valetta, it seemed that the convoy had every chance of getting through. Regrettably, this proved to be wishful thinking because the convoy had been spotted by German aircraft, and both Cunningham and Vian received intelligence that heavy ships of the Italian fleet, with cruisers and destroyers, were departing from Taranto. Furthermore, almost immediately after the RAF fighter escort turned back at about 0900, the Italian air force attacked with bombers and torpedo bombers, and was beaten off by the fierce barrage put up by the escorts. The Luftwaffe turned up in the afternoon and attacked with great determination, but was greeted with an accurate, rapid and voluminous anti-aircraft barrage and achieved no substantial hits. Vian was, by early afternoon, well aware that the Italian fleet was fast approaching when *Euryalus* spotted smoke on the horizon at 1410 and twenty-four minutes later, the smoke of more Italian warships was observed. The practised plan for dealing with a surface threat to the convoy was now put into action, and the Second Battle of Sirte had begun. Essentially this involved the laying of a smokescreen, under cover of which his main force of cruisers and destroyers would attack with torpedoes, while *Carlisle* and her five Hunts took the convoy south, again under cover of smoke. The British ships were aided by the worsening of the weather, which meant that while the heightening seas were creating difficulties in gun control for the destroyers, the strengthening south-easterly wind was from an ideal direction for the laying of a thick smokescreen across the Italian interception course. This was just as well because the Italian ships bearing down on the convoy consisted of the battleship *Littorio*, with 15-inch guns, two heavy 8-inch gun cruisers, one 6-inch cruiser and a flotilla of destroyers; the heaviest armament at Vian's disposal was the 6-inch guns of the light cruiser *Penelope*. The Italian destroyers were also hampered by the rising sea and wind and were unable to put out the usual screen in front of their heavier units, and it soon became obvious that the Italian fleet did not want to enter the smoke, and turned to leeward to get around it. Between approximately 1440 and 1535, the British ships dodged in and out of the screen, firing at the enemy at long range, which was enough to make the Italian vessels turn away. An hour later, however, the Italians made contact with the destroyers *Sikh*, *Havock*, *Hero* and *Lively*, which held them at bay until Vian was able to come up with the remainder of his cruisers and destroyers. During the course of this gallant delaying action, *Havock* was damaged by a near miss from a 15-inch shell fired by *Littorio*, but she later made Malta under her own steam. Vian's destroyers, covered by *Cleopatra* and *Euryalus*, counter-attacked with torpedoes, perhaps scoring at least one hit on the Italian battleship. During the course of this attack, the destroyer *Lively* was straddled and hit by 15-inch shells and eventually made it back to Alexandria, but this was a small price to pay for driving the enemy off for a second time, at around 1900, never to return. After the battle, Vian's force made its way eastwards to Alexandria, the bad weather forcing it to make a daylight transit of bomb alley and endure further air attacks. For the final leg, however, the Royal Air Force put up fighter cover, and Vian arrived in Alexandria at 1230 on 24 March, the ships and their crews receiving a hero's welcome, and the Admiral an immediate knighthood.

While the British and Italian warships attacked and counter-attacked each other, the convoy had continued its westerly course, enduring a day of continuous attack from the air and emerging, thanks to some excellent ship handling and the efforts of *Carlisle* and the Hunts, unscathed. The official record shows that a total of twenty-eight attacks were made and four aircraft were shot down and many damaged by *Carlisle* and her destroyers, a truly magnificent effort.[21] Admiral Vian later noted that:

> Even at a distance of 8 miles the sound of the 4-inch fire from the *Carlisle* and the 'Hunts' was like continuous pom-pom fire ... The defeat of these terrific air attacks was one of the main features of the battle.[22]

However, expenditure of anti-aircraft ammunition was a concern, with the Hunts down to 40 per cent of their outfit, while the *Carlisle* had expended almost a third of hers. The Commodore of the convoy, Captain Hutchinson RN, in *Breconshire*, gave the order to disperse, not to be confused with the less orderly procedure of scatter, at 1900 on 22 March, with the idea being that the cargo vessels would attempt to make Malta overnight, while being covered by *Carlisle*, *Penelope*, *Havock*, *Legion* and *Kingston*. Daylight on 23 March, however, found the ships still short of their destination but with the assistance of Hurricanes and Spitfires from Malta, *Talabot* and *Pampas* entered harbour at 0915 and 0920 respectively. *Breconshire* was not so lucky for at 0920, just 8 miles short of port, she was bombed, with the result that she had to be later towed into Marsaxlokk, south of Valletta, where she was hit again and sank. After this attack, *Carlisle* unsuccessfully attempted to take *Breconshire* in tow, and was in collision with the destroyer *Avon Vale*, while taking evasive action against a combined bomber and torpedo bomber attack. *Carlisle* lost one sailor on entering Valletta when she was strafed by a lone Messerschmitt fighter. The fourth and final merchant ship, *Clan Campbell*, was slower than the other three and she was caught at daylight, 50 miles south of Malta, hit in the engine room and lost. During the course of the rescue of 112 of her crew, the destroyer *Legion* was bombed and had to be beached. For *Talbot* and *Pampas*, despite their arrival in Valletta, their ordeal was far from over because the condition of the harbour and the poor state of the cargo handling facilities, due to the ever-present air raids, meant that they were damaged and eventually sunk. The incessant bombing necessitated the swift extraction of the nine remaining British warships to safety at Alexandria, and they were withdrawn during the nights of 25 and 29 March, and 5 and 8 April. *Carlisle* sailed on 25 March and *Penelope* was the last to leave on 8 April, having had to re-ammunition after firing off her entire outfit in defence of the harbour and town. One destroyer, *Havock*, was lost on the way back, having run aground at high speed. So, for all the courageous and tireless efforts of its close escort, and the victory against all the odds of its brave covering force, MW10 managed to deliver only 5,000 tons of the badly needed 29,500 tons it had loaded. Malta's condition had gone from bad to worse, although it had, somehow, managed to hold on.[23]

The overall victory enjoyed by the Axis forces on this occasion should not be allowed to detract from the bravery and example of the officers and men of both Royal and Merchant Navies who took part in this operation. It was Cunningham's final operation before his departure to Washington, and he paid this tribute in a message to the Merchant Navy:

> There is probably no theatre of war in which more tenacity and courage has been required of the Merchant Navy than in the Mediterranean. During my tenure of command I have seen innumerable instances of the unobtrusive yet sterling work of the Masters, officers and crews under conditions often of great difficulty and danger... I thank you for your good work which we in the Royal Navy fully appreciate and which we greatly admire.[24]

In Admiral Harwood's Sirte despatch of 2 June 1942 (having replaced Cunningham as Commander-in-Chief Mediterranean) he wrote:

> The behaviour of all personnel throughout the many phases of this hazardous and testing operation was worthy of the highest traditions of the service.[25]

Sergeant Nobby Elliott left the *Carlisle* for the last time on 2 April for transport home, via the Cape. In the two years and just over two months that Nobby had served in *Carlisle*, the ship's company, radar and anti-aircraft capability had made her an invaluable asset to the fleet and the merchant ships she defended. From a brutal baptism of fire in the confined waters of the Norwegian fjords, to the daylight cauldron of the frequently clear skies above the Aegean and Mediterranean, the officers and crew mastered their craft and fought ferociously and tirelessly. After Nobby's departure, *Carlisle* went on to take part in Operation *Husky* – the invasion of Sicily – on 10 July 1943, and her luck ran out three months later when she was bombed when transiting the Scarpanto Channel, east of Crete, between the islands of the Dodecanese. She was towed to Alexandria and was not repaired, remaining as a base ship until the end of the war, before being broken up in 1948. It is believed that *Carlisle* held the record for most enemy aircraft shot down by a single Royal Navy ship – eleven. Considering *Carlisle*'s extraordinary performance with MW10 it comes as no surprise to record that Sergeant Albert Thomas Elliott RM, Ply X100, was duly Mentioned in Despatches for his actions in the Second Battle of Sirte.[26]

6

HMS *JAMAICA*

Nobby arrived home in Plymouth in early May 1942 and enjoyed some well-earned leave with Rose and young Syd, spending the next five months training in Plymouth Division, becoming familiar with the latest equipment and gunnery techniques before his next posting. In the two very active years he had experienced in the Mediterranean, the Battle of the Atlantic – the longest and most pivotal campaign of the war – had stretched the resources of the Royal Navy and the merchant navies of the free world to their utmost. It has already been acknowledged that the Mediterranean theatre had been deprived of the necessary naval and shipping capacity required to guarantee victory, in every one of the multiplicity of tasks that were placed in the hands of the local Commanders-in-Chief. The very survival of Britain, and with it the future of the free world, was at stake, particularly after the fall of France in May 1940, which gave Hitler's U-boats direct access to the Atlantic. While President Roosevelt ensured that armaments, food and supplies were able to be shipped under the Lend-Lease Act, which hardly seemed compatible with the neutral status of the United States, Britain and her Empire stood alone until 7 December 1941 when, following the Japanese attack on Pearl Harbor, Roosevelt and his administration were at last able to enter the war as fully fledged combatants. Even more important to Britain was the German declaration of war against the USA, issued only four days later, which enabled the President to publicly announce the policy of Germany first. This policy had already been agreed by Roosevelt's cabinet and advisers, with the exception of some elements of the US Navy, who wanted absolute priority to be given to the Pacific. In some respects, however, the policy of Germany first was a continuation of the actions already taken by the United States in defence of Atlantic convoys, while still technically in a state of neutrality. Put another way, if the United States was to defeat Germany, then the United Kingdom had to be the forward operating base for the Allies, and, if the UK was to survive and fight, then the convoys had to get through.

The experience of the First World War and the devastating attacks on transatlantic shipping by unrestricted U-boat warfare in 1917 had resulted in the slightly belated – due to disagreement in the Admiralty – introduction of the convoy system. This had the almost immediate effect of halving shipping losses and, just as vital, permitted the safe transfer of more than a million US soldiers to the Western Front. Learning from this experience, the British government and Admiralty prepared, from 1937 onwards, for the immediate introduction of convoys and the machinery by which they could be organised and controlled. This involved a high level of co-operation between the Admiralty and the Board of Trade, which oversaw British flagged shipping companies and certified ships – in conjunction with classification societies such as Lloyd's Register – as well as examining and licensing officers and crew. Out of this co-operation grew the Ministry of Shipping, later the Ministry of War Transport, which co-opted experienced managers from the shipping industry to supplement its own expertise. During the same pre-war period, several thousand officers attended Merchant Navy Defence Courses, which instructed them on the legalities and practicalities of operating in convoys under Royal

Naval command, and what to do if they were in foreign ports or on the high seas when war was declared. For the ships that were to be engaged in the North Atlantic, Mediterranean and Arctic convoys, as well as in the troop and supply movements convoyed to the Middle and Far East, convoy command and control was soon highly developed. Unfortunately, despite the timely preparations and the willing co-operation of both service and civilian personnel, the fact remained that the Royal Navy entered the war without anywhere near a sufficient number of vessels to fulfil the tasks assigned to it. This was particularly the case as far as escort vessels were concerned and, before the necessary corvettes, sloops and frigates could be built, many convoys in the period 1939–1942 were escorted by a small number of various warships, including converted trawlers and old destroyers with limited range. In fact, up to the point when the United States fully entered the war and the Canadian Navy achieved a fiftyfold expansion of its fleet, Atlantic convoys were routinely escorted for only 300 miles out from the westernmost shores of Britain and the eastward shores of Canada. With speeds of convoys adjusted to that of the slowest ship, a long, slow passage across the Atlantic exposed all ships and their crews to extended periods of danger. Seamen found themselves in the position of wishing for bad weather and rough seas, increasing the maritime danger they faced in a North Atlantic winter but knowing that such weather acted as a welcome deterrent to enemy reconnaissance and U-boat attack. Conditions in the small escorts were particularly bad, with overcrowded messes, long periods at defence, cruising and action stations all resulting in the most prolonged bouts of weariness. In these conditions, personal and ship hygiene was almost impossible to maintain and sickness caused by poor diet, stress and damp concerned both the medical officers and the Admiralty. The combination of a wild ocean and a ruthless underwater enemy served to weld escort and convoy, the former with an increasingly large proportion of hostilities-only seamen on board, and the latter with civilian crews from Britain and overseas that continued to sign on, voyage after voyage, despite the desperate situation they faced. There were different dangers for the ships that could not be convoyed until the last leg home. For example, the fast cargo liners that plied their trade from Australia and New Zealand had to undertake long voyages alone until they could meet up with a homeward-bound convoy. This meant three to four weeks' crossing the Pacific or two to three weeks' croissing the Indian Ocean, dependent upon their speed and ability to keep out of trouble. If they did meet trouble, via

HMS *Ajax*: A stern view of Commodore Harwood's flagship at the Battle of the River Plate.

discovery by a U-boat or surface raider, their chances of avoiding disaster were virtually nil.

In the early days of the war, as with the British escorts, the German navy itself was not ready to mount a full-scale unrestricted submarine campaign, with the shipbuilding priority being given to surface warships in anticipation of a war commencing around 1944. Hitler's exploitation of Allied weakness over Czechoslovakia, the signing of the Nazi-Soviet pact and the six-week destruction of Poland rendered the German timetable redundant, and so the German navy could only employ a handful of submarines (fewer than ten at any one time) to attack the vital transatlantic trade. The tragic sinking by U-30 of the liner SS *Athenia*, off the Atlantic coast of Ireland, just a few hours after the declaration of war on 3 September 1939, and the early successes of the raider, or pocket battleship, *Graf Spee*, later scuttled in December in Montevideo after a brief fight off the River Plate with three British cruisers, *Achilles*, *Ajax* and *Exeter*, gave little indication of the onslaught to come. That is not to say that the relatively few U-boats operating in 1939–40 were ineffective; the loss of the *Royal Oak* in Scapa Flow and the sinking of more than 100 merchantmen by the end of December 1939 served to confirm the potency of the small U-boat fleet.[1] The sight of merchant seamen survivors, often distinguishable by their obvious wounds or dressings, brought home to the general public that while there was a 'phoney' war over the Channel, there was nothing false or quiet about the war at sea. Many shipping companies did not wear uniform and for those that did, their officers and crew would normally be seen ashore in civilian clothing. In an attempt to boost morale and public recognition the authorities introduced a badge, consisting of a crown above a circle of rope with the initials MN in the centre, for seamen to wear on their lapel. Another reason for its issue was to prevent seaman of military service age being stopped in the street and questioned as to why they were not in uniform.

As explained earlier, however, trying to give a collective identity to the disparate community of merchant seamen belied the actuality of their existence, and did not always improve the reputation and standing of seamen in society. The author sailed with a senior officer in the early 1970s who recalled that when the badge was issued, some of the lads turned it around so that it read NW, or 'Not Wanted', instead of Merchant Navy.

By the summer of 1940, however, German access to the French Atlantic ports provided a new set of U-boat bases which, by avoiding the 450-mile-long voyage around the top of Scotland, greatly increased the frequency and range of U-boat patrols in the Atlantic. Coupled with an increase in U-boat construction and the determined leadership of Admiral Doenitz, a decorated U-boat commander of the First World War, the U-boats began to inflict serious losses among Allied ships in what was to become the Battle of the Atlantic. In September 1940, Doenitz introduced the wolf pack system, and almost immediately the number of sinkings rose dramatically: in excess of sixty vessels were lost during that month alone. As the threat of invasion was reduced, Churchill and the Admiralty diverted more ships from anti-invasion duties to escort duties, but the navy remained woefully short of the number required. This prompted Churchill to pursue an earlier approach to the United States for the loan of some fifty destroyers, and this was agreed in September 1940 in the 'ships for bases' deal. Even so, the new class of escort destroyer – the Hunts – would not be available until 1941 and, in the meanwhile, construction of corvettes, based on a deep sea trawler design, continued apace, as did the expansion of the Royal Canadian Navy to provide eastward cover from the large and vital convoy assembly port of Halifax, Nova Scotia. Throughout this period, however, losses as a result of U-boat action continued to be severe, with variations due to bad weather and the behind-the-scenes activities involving codebreakers on both sides. In many ways, 1941 was the most pivotal year of the war, with the United States moving towards the end of neutrality with the signing of the Lend-Lease Act in March, and the first attack by a US warship, USS *Niblack*, on a U-boat while defending the recently declared security zone in the Atlantic. As the US Navy became more active in the Atlantic, the sinking of the destroyer USS *Reuben James* pushed the United States to the brink, although it was Pearl Harbor and the subsequent declaration of war by Germany that finally sealed the full participation of the USA. Churchill was much relieved, but the preceding months of 1941 had been an extreme trial for Britain and her empire. The events in the Balkans and Middle East in the late spring were followed by the German invasion of Russia in June, to which Churchill responded quickly and with resolve. Despite some doubts about the ability of the Red Army to resist the Wehrmacht, and understanding that British production and Lend-Lease were still far from providing all the equipment needed for a more aggressive prosecution of the war, Britain sent eight small convoys to North Russia with tanks, aircraft and other military essentials as an immediate contribution towards the Soviet effort. All eight, despatched between August and December, arrived safely in port, while the German navy was focussed on the Atlantic convoy routes and the supplies to Erwin Rommel in the Mediterranean. Churchill may have been confident that the entry of the USA, with its overwhelming productive capacity, manpower and political will, would mean victory, but the questions of how and when remained in the balance.

The year 1942 began with the expansion of the Japanese empire, and Britain, after the loss of the *Prince of Wales* and *Repulse* and the subsequent fall of Singapore, was struggling to meet the need for more naval resources in the Far East, while fighting bitterly in the Atlantic and Mediterranean and somehow finding the shipping for North Russia. There was, however, much comfort to be had in the fact that if the Soviet Union could be sustained, then the brunt of the land war would fall upon the Red Army, thus sparing the Western Allies and the soldiers of the British Empire a repeat of the dreadful casualties of the Western Front some twenty-five years before.

Against this backdrop, one of the Royal Navy's latest light cruisers, HMS *Jamaica*, entered the fray, straight from her working up after being commissioned in June 1942. *Jamaica* was one of eight Fiji, or Colony, class cruisers whose design conformed with the Second Naval Treaty of London, 1937. With a full load displacement of about 10,500 tons, she was 555 foot long with a beam of 62 feet and a draught of just under 20 feet. Driven by four shafts, and powered by geared turbines delivering 80,000 shaft horsepower, *Jamaica* had a top speed in excess of 32 knots, and carried a wartime complement of 920 officers and ratings, including a marine detachment of 122. Armament consisted of twelve 6-inch guns, mounted in four triple turrets, eight 4-inch high angle guns, two quadruple pom-poms, six 21-inch torpedo tubes and two aircraft housed in a hangar immediately aft of the forward funnel.[2] To achieve the reduction in weight required by the 1937 treaty, the *Jamaica*'s hull length had to be shortened, and this was achieved by situating her after boilers alongside each other, rather than in the conventional one-behind-the-other configuration.[3]

After joining the 10th Cruiser Squadron, Home Fleet, *Jamaica*'s first mission was to take part in a minelaying expedition around the Faroe Islands on 1 September, after which she proceeded to North Russia with convoy PQ18 and then back with QP14. By this time, the German commanders had fully woken up to the threat posed to their army by the supplies being conveyed to Archangel and Murmansk. In the summer of 1942, the U-boat bases, airfields and surface ship anchorages along the Norwegian coast enabled the Germans to take full advantage of the protracted hours of daylight in locating and attacking from above, on and below the sea, with shocking effect. The near-total destruction of PQ17, following an order to scatter sent from the Admiralty late on 4 July, demonstrated weaknesses in the Royal Navy's centralised command system which, unlike the other two fighting services, did not have a fully developed staff to which responsibilities could be delegated. This meant that the First Sea Lord had an operational role in addition to the day-to-day responsibility for managing fleets and resources. Given the extent and sheer size of the Royal Navy's commitments, this appears, in hindsight, to have placed an unacceptable burden on the office holder, thereby increasing the likelihood of poor decision-making on occasion. The German occupation of Norway also demonstrated the almost paralysing effect of a naval doctrine that has become known as a 'fleet in being', in this case heavy German units like *Tirpitz*, whose mere presence in the fjords demanded constant monitoring and cover. Thousands, if not millions of words have been expended on the tragedy of PQ17 and the resentment felt by the crews of the destroyers that were ordered to leave their charges to their own fate, and the bitter recriminations of the merchant seamen, many of them American, who felt abandoned to the enemy. The Admiralty's overwhelming concern was to protect the merchant ships from annihilation by *Tirpitz* and the pocket battleship *Admiral Scheer*, and the First Sea Lord believed that this threat was imminent when he issued the fateful order. This caused consternation among the close escort and the larger covering force from the Home Fleet that was shadowing the convoy at a distance. With the First Sea Lord having access to signals intelligence from ULTRA, which was denied to the Commander-in-Chief Home Fleet, the basis for controversy, mistrust and misunderstanding was well and truly laid. Churchill and the Admiralty had to take action to restore Russian faith in the restoration of this vital supply line, rebuild the navy's reputation and improve morale in both the Royal Navy and its multi-national merchant counterpart.[4] That this was achieved, to a large extent, by the running of the next convoy, PQ18, is testament to the courage, determination and skill of all those involved. The scale of protection provided for PQ18 was exceptional and demonstrated that the Admiralty and the Commander-in-Chief Home Fleet (Admiral Tovey) had learned painful lessons from the experiences of July. Convoy PQ18 comprised forty merchantmen, twenty of which flew the flag of the United States, and was covered by a total of more than fifty warships. Admiral Tovey decided that the best location from which he could exercise command and maintain communication with his fleet and the Admiralty was Scapa Flow – so he sent his deputy, Vice Admiral Fraser, to sea in the battleship HMS *Anson*, accompanied by sister ship *Duke of York*, *Jamaica* and four destroyers. This was the distant covering force that would attack any large German surface units that threatened the convoy, while acting as a barrier to any enemy ships seeking to break into the North Atlantic. The efficacy of this deployment was questioned after the event, as the Admirals continued to use their experience to master the strategy and tactics demanded by the modern, three-dimensional war at sea. Tovey also initiated a Fighting destroyer Escort, or FDE, which consisted of a flagship, the light cruiser HMS *Scylla*, under the overall command of Rear Admiral Burnett, and sixteen destroyers in two flotillas. Although the primary task of Burnett's ships was to act as close protection of the convoy, it could also be used for other tasks in an independent capacity, thereby providing a useful degree of flexibility when responding to unforeseen developments. PQ18 also had its own light aircraft carrier, HMS *Avenger*, accompanied by two destroyer escorts, and further warships accompanied tankers to Spitsbergen, where they would be available to refuel the ships of the FDE, thus enabling this force to provide cover for both outward (PQ) and homeward (QP) convoys through the area of greatest threat. Finally, some sixteen warships, destroyers, trawlers, corvettes and submarines made up the close escort to PQ18, which finally departed its anchorage at Loch Ewe on 2 September.

Bad weather imposed itself on the convoy early on, and the Commodore had great trouble in keeping station discipline among his mainly inexperienced charges. Unfortunately for the convoy, the Germans had anticipated its departure and had reinforced their bomber and torpedo bomber squadrons based in Norway, and had long-range reconnaissance aircraft, Focke Wulf Condors, as well as a line of U-boats patrolling across the convoy's predicted course. German preparations were assisted by the delay between PQ17 and PQ18, caused by the planning considerations described previously and the fact that so much of the Royal Navy was occupied, in August, on Operation *Pedestal*, a vitally important Malta convoy. First contact with PQ18 was made on 8 September and this was followed by a series of heavy aerial attacks throughout the 13th and 14th, with the convoy losing ten ships. However, the formidable anti-aircraft fire put up by the escorts and merchantmen, and the bravery of the fighter pilots from *Avenger*, caused heavy casualties among the Luftwaffe aircraft, perhaps as many as forty in total. In the cold and unforgiving Arctic sea, few air crew survived and the Luftwaffe lost many highly trained pilots that they could ill afford to replace. Further attacks on the convoy were made on 15 and 18 September before it entered the safety of the White Sea and its Russian escort. In all, thirteen merchant ships had been lost but the failure of the German surface ships to emerge, the ineffectiveness of the U-boat screen, which lost two of its number to escorts, and the heavy losses of the Luftwaffe all combined to restore the situation in this most harsh of maritime campaigns. Meanwhile, on 17 September, Admiral Burnett had led his ships away from PQ18 to join the nearby homeward-bound QP14, which contained the survivors from the ill-fated PQ17. While

Jamaica remained at sea patrolling with Admiral Fraser's distant covering force, it was Burnett's ships and the close escort that now had to endure, day after day, U-boat attack and aerial bombardment. Of the seventeen ships in the convoy, six were sunk on the voyage back to Loch Ewe, and the Royal Navy lost HMS *Leda*, minesweeper, and the Tribal class destroyer HMS *Somali* to U-boats. The surviving merchant ships and escorts finally arrived in Loch Ewe on 26 September, thereby bringing the tragic saga of PQ17 to its bitter end.

Meanwhile, *Jamaica* and the other vessels of Fraser's force had returned to the Home Fleet's base anchorage at Scapa Flow, where they anchored on 24 September. Arrangements were made for crew transfers and leave, and Sergeant Nobby Elliott joined *Jamaica* on

HMS *Jamaica*. (© Imperial War Museums (FL 22384))

2 October, at the beginning of what was to be, for him, another commission of just over two years' duration. Having completed his leave from *Carlisle* and the training and barrack routine that followed in Plymouth, Nobby took up his berth as gun layer in the marines' turret, X, situated aft and superimposed on the aftermost Y turret. Despite Nobby's long service and years of turret drill and practice, the operating environment in the *Jamaica*, inside the armoured triple turret, was quite distinct from the open mountings on the *Carlisle*. *Jamaica*'s turrets weighed 175 tons and each one mounted three Breech Loading Mark XXIII 6-inch guns, with a maximum rate of fire of eight rounds per minute, meaning that X turret alone could deliver twenty-four rounds every 60 seconds with a well-drilled crew. Each shell weighed one hundredweight and the maximum range of the guns was 14 miles. Inside the gun house, at the top of the turret, a crew of seven marines were required to operate each gun, with the gun layer being responsible for elevating the barrel until the settings received from the gunnery director aloft via the transmitting station below were matched. Beneath the gun house, marines were stationed in the shell rooms and magazines, placing shells and cordite charges into their respective hoists for delivery to the loaders and rammers above via a system of flash protected shutters.[5] On joining *Jamaica*, Nobby had prepared himself for what looked likely to be prolonged service in the dangerous waters of the Arctic.

Before this could happen, however, wider developments had overtaken planning priorities, and Nobby was soon scheduled for a return to the Mediterranean. With the United States now fully engaged in the war, the American administration and public were looking to see where their country's forces could get to grips with Germany, which had, after all, been made the priority in Washington. At the same time, Stalin had urged Britain and the US to open a second front as early as possible to relieve the USSR's plight, because the Germans had mounted another strong summer offensive in the east. The US Chiefs of Staff, accompanied by the

President's Special Envoy, Harry Hopkins, had flown across the Atlantic to meet their British counterparts in a visit that lasted a week, from 18 July, during which the British government and Chiefs of Staff argued that no second front in Europe was possible in 1942 because there simply was not the air, land and sea resources to carry out such a risky attack across the English Channel. The Americans eventually accepted the British argument, after Roosevelt had cabled his agreement, and, according to the diary of General Brooke, the Chief of the Imperial General Staff (CIGS), Roosevelt also wrote that he was:

> ...in favour of attack in North Africa and was influencing his Chiefs in that direction.[6]

From this agreement came the decision to undertake Operation *Torch*, the full-scale invasion of the western part of North Africa, where the Vichy French were in control of Morocco and Algeria. The overall strategy behind the concept of *Torch* was to drive all Axis forces out of North Africa, as a precursor to an invasion of Sicily and then Italy. This would open up what has been termed 'the soft underbelly of Europe', and thereby avoid, or at least delay, the cross-Channel invasion so dreaded by Churchill and his military advisers. The day before the President had cabled London, General Auchinleck had launched an attack against Rommel's forces in the First Battle of El Alamein, and Churchill was keen for Auchinleck to drive the Afrika Korps westwards, to later fall into the arms of the Anglo-American forces that were to be landed in *Torch*. As it turned out, Auchinleck's action managed to halt Rommel's advance into Egypt, aided by the fact that the German troops were at the end of a very long line of supply. The halting of the German advance permitted the 8th Army to prepare for a more decisive attack, using the additional troops and equipment that were continuing to arrive in theatre. Churchill, however, construed this as a delay, and when he visited Egypt with Brooke in early August, Auchinleck was removed and Generals Alexander and Montgomery took over the theatre command and the 8th Army respectively. Montgomery then took his own time in preparing and training for the decisive Second Battle of El Alamein, which was finally launched on 23 October. By 4 November, after several days of heavy fighting, Rommel was forced into a long retreat to the west. The *Torch* landings commenced four days later, on 8 November, and so the first steps of the Western Allies' land strategy for the defeat of the Axis in the Mediterranean were taken. The opening of the second front in North Africa did nothing to reassure Stalin because not only did it take place outside Europe, but also the shipping requirements for *Torch* meant there were to be no more Russian convoys until late December and early January 1943. This was unavoidable as the Home Fleet could not cover Arctic operations and *Torch* at the same time, even though the period between October and the New Year provided the best weather conditions – darkness, low cloud, storms, rain and snow – for running convoys to North Russia. The decision not to run a convoy was not taken lightly and Churchill, as ever, was keen to do so until he was dissuaded by the Chiefs of Staff. In fact, the possibility of running such a convoy had been considered as early as 10 September, as Brooke recalled in his diary of that day:

> We discussed the likelihood of being able to carry out the North Africa attack before November 15th, and in that case the desirability of trying to put in an extra convoy to Russia before it. Many various facts to consider, danger to naval forces employed, thus rendering them possibly non-available to support North African venture. Secondly, result of locking up some 80 ships in Archangel during whole winter etc. etc. PM as usual trying to get the last ounce out of the Naval forces and consequently wanting to run the convoy if possible.[7]

Churchill's aggressive attitude is well illustrated here as he sought to commit the Navy to tasks for which it did not have enough resources; however, he did eventually accept the advice of the Chiefs of Staff.

Operation *Torch* saw the emergence of General Eisenhower as Supreme Commander, and the establishment of an Anglo-American command system that lasted through to victory in Europe. The overall naval commander was Admiral Cunningham, late of the Mediterranean, whose deputy was Admiral Ramsay, the commander of Operation *Dynamo*, during which he oversaw the evacuation of the army from Dunkirk in May 1940. From a naval point of view, *Torch* required the deployment of what was then the largest invasion fleet in history, with some 600 vessels sailing from ports in Britain and the United States. They were tasked with landing 65,000 soldiers at three points – Casablanca, on the Atlantic coast of Morocco, and Oran and Algiers, on the Mediterranean coast of Algeria. These landing points were chosen after prolonged deliberation in London, Washington, and at Eisenhower's headquarters in Gibraltar. Ideally, the main objective would have been Tunis, thus placing the western arm of the Allied pincer very much closer to Rommel's supply base at Tripoli, but air cover from nearby Luftwaffe airfields in Sardinia and Sicily ruled this out. Complications in the availability of shipping, as already mentioned, were another integral part of the Allied calculations, as was the attitude of the Vichy French in Morocco and Algeria. Vichy forces consisted of more than 110,000 French and colonial troops in Morocco and Algiers, and, given the conflict between the British and the Vichy Navy at Mers-El Kebir, and the resistance of Vichy forces to British imperial arms in Syria and Dakar, it was decided that American troops, who made up the majority of the Allied forces, were to make the landings at Morocco and Oran. In addition, the American General Mark Clark was sent in secret, by submarine, to talk to Vichy military representatives and secure their co-operation or at least to gauge how they might react to the invasion. At the tactical level, Allied commanders had learned amphibious warfare lessons from raiding, and the disastrous assault on Dieppe, which had taken place as late as 13 August 1942, marked a key turning point in appreciation of what was needed to get substantial amounts of troops and their supporting arms ashore. Dieppe's heavy casualties, particularly among the Canadian troops deployed in the frontal assault, was the price paid for the acquisition of this knowledge, which included the avoidance of an attack against a fortified point, the use of heavy naval bombardment and the necessity of having co-ordinated command and control on the spot, in a suitably equipped headquarters' ship. In some ways, therefore, it is quite remarkable that within two months of Dieppe, the plan for *Torch* was distributed, taking these lessons into account. There were three task forces, the first being the Western Task Force, commanded by General Patton with 35,000 US troops to take Casablanca. Patton's force was transported directly across the Atlantic from the United States, in a shipping movement of nearly 100 vessels, including Admiral Hewitt's Task Force 34, that had three battleships, four escort carriers, a fleet carrier, seven cruisers and more than forty destroyers and minesweepers at his disposal. The second task force, Central, and the third, Eastern, operating in the Mediterranean for the landings at Oran and Algiers, had their naval cover entirely provided by the Royal Navy. To do this, Cunningham had taken over command of the portion of the Mediterranean that was west of a line between Tunis and Sicily, also drawing on units from the Home Fleet and Force H from Gibraltar. On the military side, the landing forces at Oran were commanded by the American General Fredendall, with 18,500 soldiers, and the Eastern Forces, attacking Algiers, consisted of 20,000 mainly American troops accompanied by a British infantry brigade and commando units. United States

General Ryder led the landing force, although overall military command in this sector belonged to the British General Anderson.

As noted, it was considered that American prominence in *Torch* would lessen the chances of resistance from the Vichy forces and, as far as the western landings in Morocco were concerned, this was mainly true. In fact, the surf conditions on some of the beaches proved to be far more hazardous than any enemy action and provided another lesson for future amphibious operations. At Mehdya, north of Casablanca, the Vichy French opposed the landing with some vigour and it took two days' fighting for the Americans to secure the town and airfield on 10 November, following the agreement of an armistice on that day. To the east, in Algiers, however, resistance was potentially of a much tougher nature because in addition to substantial ground forces, the Vichy French had several fighter and bomber squadrons based nearby, as well as heavy coastal artillery. As it turned out, a combination of successful ground advances and the use of air power from the fleet and direct from Gibraltar captured the airfields and secured an early ceasefire. Within the port itself, an attempt by two Royal Navy destroyers, HMS *Broke* and HMS *Malcolm*, to land troops to secure the port's facilities was met with heavy fire from both coastal and inshore artillery. Both ships were hit and damaged, resulting in the loss of the *Broke* on the following day, and the temporary abandonment of in excess of 200 troops ashore. For the Central Task Force in Oran, they had initial technical, navigational and weather difficulties in landings to the west of Oran, although the largest ship and troop movements in this sector took place to the east of the city. This part of the landing was covered by the headquarters ship *Largs*, indicating the importance of this section of the attack, accompanied by the cruisers *Aurora*, *Jamaica* and *Delhi*, with several corvettes and destroyers in attendance. The troops here were landed with minimal opposition, but this was far from the case for the groups of soldiers that had been sent in destroyers to attack and seize the port in the hours of darkness that preceded dawn on 8 November. The two ships carrying the US Rangers on their port seizure mission, *Hartland* and *Walney*, came under attack from the Vichy French warships *Epervier*, *Typhon*, *Tornade*, *Tramontane* and *La Surprise*. Both of the British ships were lost, with heavy casualties, and the Vichy destroyers then took the bold decision to leave harbour and attack the Royal Navy task force outside. In a one-sided action that lasted into 9 November, all the destroyers were lost, succumbing to the superior gunfire of *Aurora* and *Jamaica*.

Sergeant Nobby Elliott's first action in *Jamaica*'s X turret had seen him engage ships of a former ally, marking his return to the Mediterranean where, in this instance, he experienced for the first time a fight where local air superiority belonged to the Allied not Axis forces. This action, however, was not quite the end for *Jamaica* in this campaign, because the following day, 10 November, she joined in a final bombardment with the battleship *Rodney* (one of Nobby's previous ships) and *Aurora*, to end resistance and seal the fate of the Vichy authorities in North Africa. A ceasefire and then surrender was agreed between Eisenhower and Admiral Darlan, the deputy leader of the Vichy government in France, who was visiting Algiers to see his son. This convenient happenstance meant that the necessary authority was in the right place at the right time to give the Allies and Eisenhower what they wanted. For his pains, the Nazi collaborator Darlan was made High Commissioner, a practical solution to a local problem but not one that was popular with many politicians or the press in Britain and America. Cunningham commented on this when he wrote a few days after the agreement with Darlan:

I found the General – Eisenhower – rather in despair over our politicians not much liking his dealings with Darlan. They are curious people, always wanting to have it both ways.

Of course our obligations to de Gaulle make it difficult for them to justify our dealings with D.[8]

Cunningham was later destined to deal with politicians day in and day out when he was appointed First Sea Lord in October 1943, after the death of Admiral of the Fleet Dudley Pound. Cunningham's deputy, Ramsay, played the major role in completing the plans for the Central and Eastern sector landings, and went on, after further experience in the planning of the invasions of Sicily and Italy, to become the Naval Commander for Normandy in 1944.

The Darlan deal delivered to the Allies the security of this part of North Africa as a firm base for advancing towards Tunis, and of knowing that the French fleet in North and West Africa was now firmly in the Allied camp. This left the Allies considering the position of the final piece of the French naval jigsaw in the Mediterranean, the fleet at Toulon, in unoccupied Vichy France, and how to deal with it.

Darlan's acceptance of the High Commissionership provided the solution to this problem, because his action prompted Hitler to immediately order the occupation of Vichy France, which resulted in Darlan ensuring that the French fleet in Toulon was scuttled. Hitler also moved to strengthen his army and air force in Tunisia, in preparation for the next phase of the battle in the Mediterranean. Darlan's treachery was rewarded by his assassination on Christmas Eve 1942.

On 14 November, four days after the bombardment of Oran, *Jamaica* was released back to the Home Fleet. The return of *Jamaica* highlighted the way in which the Admiralty was forced to shuffle ships around in order to continue to attempt to meet its many commitments. Victory in *Torch* had, as far as shipping was concerned, added another supply burden that became complicated when U-boats started to sink ships in the sea corridor between Algiers and Gibraltar. Nevertheless, *Jamaica* was now required to assist in the resumption of convoys to North Russia and, to this end, she reached Scapa Flow on 20 November. Three weeks later she joined forces with another cruiser, HMS *Sheffield,* and several destroyers to form Force R, which was established to provide cover and escort for the convoys to what was now the freezing north. The time had arrived for the Admiralty to take advantage of what remained of the harsh winter weather and a large convoy was put together, eventually sailing from Loch Ewe in two parts, JW51A on 15 December and JW51B one week later, on the 22nd. The Admiralty, notwithstanding the poor weather forecast, remained concerned at the number of German heavy surface units that they knew or suspected to be in Norway, including *Tirpitz, Scharnhorst, Gneisenau, Lutzow* and heavy cruisers *Hipper* and *Prinz Eugen.* For this reason, their Lordships arranged for the usual deep cover to be provided by a force led by Admiral Tovey in *King George V,* in addition to the close escort and the cruiser cover of Force R. Assembled to cover both parts of the JW51 convoy, Force R, under the command of Admiral Burnett, who flew his flag in *Sheffield* in company with *Jamaica* and the destroyers HMS *Beagle,* HMS *Matchless* and HMS *Opportune,* went to sea on 17 December. In the context of probable enemy action, 'poor weather' may seem to offer a crumb of comfort, but the harshness of the marine environment in these high latitudes offered little solace. Frequent gales, blinding snowstorms and a freezing sea made life on board ship extremely unpleasant and often downright dangerous. There is no doubt that a well-built ship, properly loaded and with a professional and experienced crew, was (and is) expected to be able to cope with extreme weather and sea conditions, but even without the presence of an enemy the Arctic presented two distinct challenges to survival. Firstly, there was the accumulation of ice on deck and around the gun barrels, derricks, cranes and every other surface on a vessel's superstructure, threatening a ship's stability. Crews had to work hard to remove the ice, while the ship pitched, rolled and corkscrewed around the ocean. The sheer physical effort of handling heavy steam hoses and chipping away at the ice on an exposed and slippery deck added to the weariness of watch-keeping and, for the warships, to the tension of frequent periods at action stations. For the individual sailor, contact with metal by any uncovered part of the body resulted in nasty burns, and spray froze as it came over the bows. For those serving on ships with open bridges and lookout positions, the frozen spray turned into sharp needles that penetrated any exposed skin. Internally, the sleeping and working environment was no better. Frozen water systems combined with a lack of heating, failure of galley equipment and the ever-present condensation to produce unhealthy and unhygienic living conditions, exposing the crew to sickness and disease. Secondly, atmospheric conditions in this region often caused navigation and communication equipment to fail or otherwise to malfunction. In bad visibility this had a disastrous effect on station keeping, as ships took what action they could to avoid collision. When ships found themselves isolated and having to rely on dead-reckoning, because no celestial observations were possible, calculating a true position was nothing more than an educated guess at best. Worse still, if a ship's gyro compass failed and magnetic compasses had to be used for steering a course, the dramatic magnetic variations in the high latitudes of the Arctic made it almost impossible to steer accurately without some point of celestial or land observation. It is worth noting that many of the older merchant ships, or those that were run on a shoestring, only had magnetic compasses to begin with; gyro compasses were not made compulsory on merchant ships by international regulation until 1974.

Returning to Admiral Burnett's deployment, Force R sailed out to the west of the convoy then closed on JW51A after it had passed Bear Island, and the two cruisers then proceeded ahead, arriving in the Kola Inlet on Christmas Eve, where they observed the safe arrival of the convoy on Christmas Day. JW51A had been attacked from the air, without loss, on Christmas Eve, as it entered the last leg of its voyage, and had made no contact with any German surface vessel. On 27 December, Force R left Murmansk to screen the inbound second part of the convoy, JW51B, and to be available to reinforce the escort for its final leg through the Barents Sea.

The Russian navy, as a matter of routine, was also due to send out a number of destroyers to help bring the convoy in. These extra warships were needed because, despite any deviation from a direct route that a convoy had made to a point north or south of Bear Island to avoid or shake off any enemy observers, there was little opportunity to do so as the ships traversed the Barents Sea towards the entrance to the Kola Inlet. If a convoy could be observed and tracked by a U-boat or reconnaissance aircraft in the Barents Sea then it became extremely vulnerable to attack from the air, where the proximity of the German airfields in northern Norway posed a particular threat, from patrolling U-boats, and, if alerted in time, surface units of the Kriegsmarine. The threat from the latter awaiting JW51B was slightly muted because Hitler, alarmed by a number of raids on the Norwegian coast, was more concerned with a possible invasion of Norway. Consequently he ordered that the heaviest units were not to be risked in convoy action. This priority was set even though the destruction or disruption of supplies to the Red Army would have helped the German armies fighting on the Eastern Front, where the Battle of Stalingrad had been raging for four months, with the surrounded German 6th Army facing disintegration. Nor was this restriction on deployment known by the Admiralty, whose intelligence, however, had been able to warn JW51B about the presence of U-boats. One of these, U-354, alerted by air reconnaissance, had indeed located the convoy, steaming in a single column because of ice floes, and had begun reporting its course and speed to German headquarters in France and Norway.

These reports caused a stir of activity when it was realised that JW51B had been blown to the south by a force ten storm, and was therefore closer to the main German anchorage at Altenfjord (now known as Altafjord), about 100 miles south of the North Cape, than was usual. Admiral Raeder, head of the German navy, then seized his chance to prove the worth of his surface fleet to Hitler by pointing out that this was an outstanding opportunity to destroy a valuable convoy and he ordered that a pre-planned operation, *Regenbogen* (Rainbow), be immediately put into action. On 30 December, under the command of Admiral Kummetz, two small groups of German warships consisting of the flagship, the heavy cruiser *Hipper*, armed with eight 8-inch guns, and accompanied by three destroyers, together with the pocket battleship *Lutzow*, a sister to the lost *Graf Spee* with six 11-inch guns, in company with another three destroyers, sailed north from Altenfjord. Plotting a north-easterly course to intercept the convoy JW51B, Kummetz prepared to execute *Regenbogen* by placing the *Hipper* group in a position to attack the convoy from the north, thereby drawing the escorts towards her while the merchant ships turned away to the south. This would enable the *Hipper* to engage the destroyers of the escort with all the advantages of her superior armament, while the *Lutzow* group approached JW51B from the south. This deployment was designed to permit the *Lutzow*'s 11-inch guns to pick off and destroy the fourteen merchant ships of the convoy, laden with tanks, aircraft, fuel, ammunition, trucks and thousands of tons of general supplies.

Providing that the tracking of the convoy continued to be relayed to Kummetz, the simplicity of the *Regenbogen* concept gave Kummetz every chance of successfully completing his mission. The simplicity, however, was now corrupted by further messages and orders from high command that again cautioned Kummetz that he was not to risk his two heavy warships, causing a conflict between the need to attack the convoy and the avoidance of an encounter with an enemy force of equal or greater strength. Kummetz had no choice, therefore, but to act cautiously, adopting an attitude that tempered any determination to attack, and it must have had a less than positive effect on the morale of the German crews. Kummetz had therefore been placed in a position where he had to take very careful stock of any opposing force that he encountered, and he was fully aware of the convoy's destroyer escort, which consisted of HMS *Onslow*, HMS *Obdurate*, HMS *Obedient*, HMS *Orwell* and HMS *Achates*, under the command of Captain R. St V. Sherbrooke in *Onslow*. The four 'O' class destroyers were modern vessels, having been launched between March 1941 and April 1942. They displaced 1,540 tons, with the leader *Onslow* being slightly larger at 1,610 tons, and were armed with four single 4.7-inch guns, eight torpedo tubes and were capable of a speed in excess of 36 knots. The *Achates*, which had the same armament as her 'O' class consorts, was slightly smaller at 1,350 tons, at least a knot slower, and had been in service for more than ten years.[9]

These ships were several times smaller than the *Hipper* and *Lutzow*, and heavily outgunned, but the bravery and determination with which they were handled, the threat of their torpedoes, and the constraints under which the German ships were handled all tested Admiral Kummetz's command to breaking point.

Furthermore, Kummetz had no idea of the presence or whereabouts of Admiral Burnett's Force R, the cruisers *Sheffield* and *Jamaica*, sailing on a course between the Kola Inlet and North Cape on its way to find JW51B. Burnett was a seasoned Arctic commander and kept his ships as far north off the coast as he dare, so as to be out of the range of any unwelcome reconnaissance until he was in a position to decide, based upon intelligence and an instinctive appreciation of the enemy's intentions, when to commit his ships in support of the convoy. The stage was now set for the German ships to execute Operation *Regenbogen*, and for the escorts and Force R to defend the convoy.

By the morning of 31 December, on which the crews had woken up to a heavy frost, icing and a large swell, JW51B was approximately 230 miles north-west of the entrance to the Kola Inlet when at 0820 the Flower class corvette, HMS *Hyderabad*, part of the convoy's close escort, observed two destroyers astern from its position on the starboard quarter of the merchant ships. The captain, thinking that these vessels were the expected Russian destroyers coming out to meet the convoy, made no report to Captain Sherbrooke on the *Onslow*, and maintained his course and speed. Ten minutes later, however, lookouts on the *Obdurate* also sighted the two destroyers, accompanied by a third, and immediately signalled Sherbrooke with the news. Sherbrooke replied with an immediate order to *Obdurate* to investigate and, as she turned towards the destroyers, they retreated to the north-west, in the direction of *Hipper*. Still unsure of the exact identity of these ships, *Obdurate* signalled a challenge, which was, somewhat suspiciously, unanswered. All doubt was removed when, at 0930, the German destroyers opened fire on the pursuing *Obdurate* at a range of less than 5 miles. Seeing the flash of gunfire, Sherbrooke ordered his ships to take up pre-planned positions that would allow the four 'O' class ships to attack the enemy, while the *Achates* and the smaller close escort vessels began laying a thick smokescreen to cover the convoy. During this manoeuvre, *Hipper* was identified by Sherbrooke and he immediately radioed the Admiralty and Burnett. In similar fashion, at 0940, Kummetz radioed headquarters ashore to confirm he was engaging JW51B and ordered *Hipper* to fire at the smoke-laying *Achates* which, for the time being, remained unharmed.

The convoy under the command of Commodore Melhuish, in *Empire Archer*, moved away from *Hipper* and her destroyers at 1000, taking a course to the south-east, under cover of the thick smokescreen that was now between the convoy, close escort and the enemy. This was, to an extent, playing into the hands of

Regenbogen, as the *Lutzow* and her destroyers were positioned in this approximate direction, less than 10 miles from the convoy, forming the southern arm of the pincer that was the very essence of the German plan. Captain Sherbrooke, in the meantime, after noticing that the *Hipper* moved northwards after his destroyers engaged the German ships with radar-controlled fire, was convinced that the German fleet was more than just wary of the torpedo threat posed by his destroyers. He decided to split his forces and ordered *Orwell* to join *Onslow* in his pursuit of the enemy, and sent *Obedient* and *Obdurate* to reinforce the convoy and add their smoke to the heavy screen that had already been created. As the convoy moved towards the *Lutzow*, the *Hipper* and her consorts' northerly track took them towards Force R, Burnett having made his decision to steam south, towards the action, just before 1000.

Fifteen minutes later action came thick and fast as Kummetz turned *Hipper* towards *Onslow* and *Orwell* and several 8-inch rounds hit *Onslow*, severely damaging the ship, putting the forward guns out of action, destroying communications and wrecking the bridge. Splinters severely wounded Captain Sherbrooke, who continued to command despite having had an eyeball dislodged and lying against his cheek, only going below after he had made arrangements to transfer command of the flotilla to *Obedient*. More than forty of her crew were killed or wounded and *Orwell* made smoke and shielded the *Onslow*'s forced retirement to the south, which enabled them to rejoin the convoy; a convoy now in sight of the *Lutzow* and her destroyers. The destroyer escorts, now under the command of Commander Kinloch in *Obedient*, closed on the convoy and positioned themselves off the port quarter, where *Achates* continued to lay down the thick smokescreen that had distracted the German ships. Indeed, it was the combination of heavy, intermittent snow showers and the smokescreen laid down by the escorts that prevented *Lutzow* from springing a shocking surprise attack on JW51B. In trying to gain a fighting advantage by placing itself across the head of the convoy, *Lutzow* lost contact in the poor visibility and her commander, Stange, decided to remain on his present course to await the merchantmen and their escorts. In doing so, not only did *Lutzow* lose the element of surprise, but also destroyed the planned pincer movement because she, like *Hipper*, was now placed to the east of JW51B. Unknowingly, the German ships had in fact put themselves between the convoy and the fast approaching Force R, with Burnett's cruisers heading south towards the action at more than 30 knots.

Before Force R could engage Kummetz's ships, at around 1115 *Hipper* opened fire on the *Achates*, which was steering out of the smokescreen to close the convoy. *Achates* received several hits from the heavy guns of *Hipper*, losing her forward armament and, with her bridge destroyed and captain killed, the remaining crew began a desperate fight to save her from the many fires and leaks that permeated their ship. Responding swiftly to this action, Commander Kinloch took *Obedient*, *Orwell* and *Obdurate* on a course towards *Hipper*, placing his destroyers between the convoy and the German cruiser. Once again, the German response was tempered by the fear of torpedo attack and, after discharging a salvo targeted on *Obedient*, *Hipper* turned away to the north-west, initially followed by Kinloch who then ordered his ships back to a position astern of the convoy. It was at this point, between fifteen and twenty minutes after *Hipper* had fired upon *Achates*, that Force R, led in by the radar on *Sheffield*, sighted *Hipper* making her turn at a distance of about 7 miles. Both *Sheffield* and *Jamaica*, the latter with her forward turrets only due to the angle of approach, now engaged the *Hipper*, firing several salvoes that inflicted enough damage to make Kummetz turn away to the south west at reduced speed. *Hipper* had returned fire, after a delay caused by the surprise achieved by Force R, but achieved no hits on the British cruisers, which continued their pursuit. It was now just after 1135 and Kummetz, for the first-time sighting and realising that *Lutzow* was on the same side of the convoy as he was, ordered a general retirement of all his ships to the west. Burnett continued the chase and *Sheffield* and *Jamaica* sank two destroyers, *Friedrich Eckholdt* and *Richard Beitzen* respectively, as they pursued the enemy. Despite having been ordered to withdraw, the *Lutzow*, positioned to the south-east of *Hipper*, now chose this moment to fire upon the convoy, and was attacked by the three 'O' class destroyers from their covering positon astern. *Lutzow* exchanged fire with the destroyers before finally obeying Kummetz's order to withdraw, just after noon.

No vessel in the convoy had been damaged. In what was to be the denouement of the Battle of the Barents Sea, Burnett's cruisers exchanged fire with Kummetz's ships as they moved to the west, and the action was broken off just after 1230. Just to be sure, *Sheffield*'s radar monitored the German ships progress for another hour and a half and, with Burnett still to locate the convoy and aware of the possibility that other enemy units could be out from their Norwegian bases, Force R turned south. The aggressive and decisive actions taken by the British commanders, and their hard-fighting crews, enabled convoy JW15B to reach its destination without any further difficulty. *Achates*, in which at least forty sailors had been killed, capsized while preparing to be towed by the commissioned trawler *Northern Gem*, whose crew then risked immersion in the freezing ocean to recover the survivors from Carley floats and the water itself. Their swift action, and the seamanship of Skipper Aisthorpe, prevented many further losses and demonstrated a courageous determination to overcome the worst excess of the freezing and unfriendly Arctic environment. In summing up his report on the battle, Admiral Tovey, Commander-in-Chief Home Fleet wrote:

... that an enemy force of at least one pocket battleship, one heavy cruiser and six destroyers, with all the advantages of surprise and concentration, should be held off for four hours by five destroyers and two six-inch cruisers without any loss to the convoy is most creditable and satisfactory.[10]

The success of the action in the Barents Sea had two major and significant effects upon the prosecution of the war at sea. Firstly, as far as the Allies were concerned, the reputation of the Royal Navy was somewhat restored, following the debacle of PQ17, and JW51B exemplified the high level of ability and discipline that the American, British and neutral merchant ships achieved, while operating in some of the worst conditions of the war. The combination of learning from experience, which was not without its cost in lives and trauma, and sailing with a competent commodore and escort commander paid hard-earned dividends. Secondly, the aggressive tactics employed by the escorts and Force R, underwritten by experience in anticipating an enemy's intentions, both deterred the German ships and protected the convoy. These bold, brave, but not reckless actions pushed Kummetz into a conflict between using his heavier armament to destroy the convoy or applying the caution urged upon him by the constraints in his orders about preserving his ships. Notwithstanding the torpedo threat of the destroyers, the poor visibility due to snowstorms and smoke, or even the unexpected arrival of Force R upon the scene, Kummetz's fleet had enough firepower to carry out his mission.

It seems that once he discovered that the Lutzow had rendered the original pincer plan inoperable, he deduced that, not being able to divide opposing forces in the way originally envisaged, the preservation of his fleet now overrode the destruction of the convoy. Kummetz's order to withdraw can certainly be supported by this line of reasoning, when taking into account the directives he had received before embarking on this mission, but the effect on German naval operations and policy was profound; the German surface fleet had now reached the end of the road.

Once Hitler had heard the news, on this occasion through the BBC before his own naval channels had reported that the convoy was unscathed, he immediately called for the scrapping of every ship larger than a destroyer. Ironically, it could be argued that it was Hitler's own misunderstanding of naval warfare, and the consequent issuance of the contradictory orders to Kummetz, that created the situation in which the German surface fleet was rendered virtually redundant. Within a month of the ending of the battle, Grand Admiral Raeder resigned and, at the end of January 1943, Admiral Doenitz, commander of the U-boat fleet, was promoted over the head of many senior officers to become Commander-in-Chief of the German Navy. This was rational as the main German naval effort was now concentrated in the U-boat arm, and many of the released ship's crews were transferred to the expanding submarine service.

As it happened, the threat to scrap the major ships was not carried out and while the majority were declared obsolete or redundant, two ships, *Tirpitz* and *Scharnhorst*, were allowed to resume their 'fleet in being' status in the northern fjords of Norway. Interestingly, this adjustment to Hitler's policy was made after some keen lobbying by Doenitz himself. As a result of these decisions, the Royal Navy found itself contemplating a worsening situation in the North Atlantic as U-boat attacks and resources increased, while the retention of a 'fleet in being' in Norway, albeit smaller than before, still required the deployment of close and distant covering forces from the Home Fleet for the protection of the Arctic convoys.

7

BLOCKADE, ICE AND BATTLE

Jamaica and her crew remained at sea to provide cover for the homeward-bound convoy RA51, which had departed from the Kola Inlet on 30 December. Further cover, in the form of a large force led by Tovey himself in *King George V*, had sallied forth in the hope of catching the *Hipper* and *Lutzow* on their way back to Altenfjord, but no sighting or contact was made. In any event, *Jamaica* was so far north of the convoy (about 150 miles), that, like the other covering ships, it seemed to the merchant seamen that RA51 was just bait, and 'the feeling of being decoys was inescapable.'[1] The success of JW51B was followed by the sailing of two further outbound convoys, JW52, which left Loch Ewe on 17 January 1943, and JW53 one month later. Despite air and U-boat attack, JW52 – consisting of thirteen 'experienced' merchant ships with a large close escort supported by cruiser and distant, heavy cover – arrived in the Kola Inlet, unharmed, on 27 January. The way in which this convoy was fought though, with concentrated anti-aircraft fire and the use of HF/DF technology to locate U-boats, demonstrated what an experienced, well-equipped and highly trained escort force could do, while the merchant ships were able to execute well co-ordinated manoeuvres, keeping the enemy at bay. A similarly large escort was provided for the next return convoy, RA52, which, having been delayed by the slow rate of discharge in Russia, not helped by frequent visits from the Luftwaffe, finally arrived in Loch Ewe on 8 February. Despite a waiting line of U-boats, only one cargo ship was lost, to U255, and all its American crew were rescued by the corvettes and trawlers in close company.

In what proved to be the final outward-bound convoy of this period, JW53, which sailed on 15 February with another large escort, it was the weather that threatened. Big seas and storm-force winds made station-keeping a nightmare, and forced the merchant ships and smaller warships to heave to, in order to respectively keep their deck cargoes on board and to literally ensure their preservation. Cruiser cover was again provided by Admiral Burnett, this time flying his flag in HMS *Belfast*, accompanied by *Sheffield* and HMS *Cumberland*. As the cruisers ploughed through the heavy, icy sea, the *Sheffield* suffered an astonishing blow when the armoured roof of A turret was ripped off and blown over the side by a crashing sea. In accordance with normal Arctic practice, the turret, when not in action, was trained abeam, avoiding an ingress of spray that, on freezing, would damage the rifling in the barrels when the guns were fired. It therefore seems more than likely that the angle of the turret, combined with the direction and force of the sea, contributed to the extraordinary result of this massive impact.

Sheffield was replaced by the Arctic veteran HMS *Norfolk* and, when the weather began to settle, the convoy, forced south by the extent of the pack ice, found itself in good order when approaching Bear Island. Observed from above and below on 23 February, JW53 came under attack from U-boats and bombers; like JW52, the weight and skill of the escort, which by now included no less than thirteen destroyers, led by Captain MacIntyre in *Scylla*, saw the convoy through to Kola.

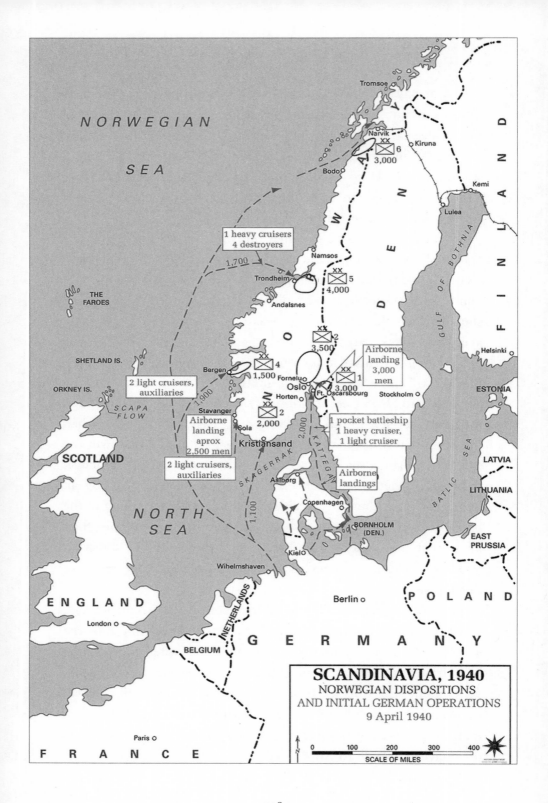

NORWEGIAN

SEA

Tromsoe

Narvik
XX
6
3,000

Kiruna

Bodo

Kemi

Lulea

GULF OF BOTHNIA

Namsos

1 heavy cruisers
4 destroyers

1,700

Trondheim

XX
5
4,000

S W E D E N

F I N L A N D

THE
FAROES

Andalsnes

Helsinki

XX
3
3,500

SHETLAND IS.

Bergen

XX
4
1,500

Airborne
landing
3,000
men

ESTONIA

ORKNEY IS.

2 light cruisers,
auxiliaries

1,900

Fornelu

XX
1
3,000

Oslo

Ft. Oscarsbourg

Horten

Stockholm

SCAPA
FLOW

Stavanger

Sola

XX
2
2,000

N O R W A Y

1 pocket battleship
1 heavy cruiser,
1 light cruiser

LATVIA

SCOTLAND

Airborne
landing
aprox
2,500 men

Kristiansand

2 light cruisers,
auxiliaries

1,100

SKAGERRAK

2,000

KATTEGAT

Airborne
landings

BALTIC SEA

LITHUANIA

NORTH
SEA

Aalborg

Copenhagen

BORNHOLM
(DEN.)

EAST
PRUSSIA

Kiel

Wihelmshaven

NETHERLANDS

ENGLAND

London

BELGIUM

Berlin

G E R M A N Y

P O L A N D

Paris

F R A N C E

N

SCANDINAVIA, 1940
NORWEGIAN DISPOSITIONS
AND INITIAL GERMAN OPERATIONS
9 April 1940

0   100   200   300   400
SCALE OF MILES

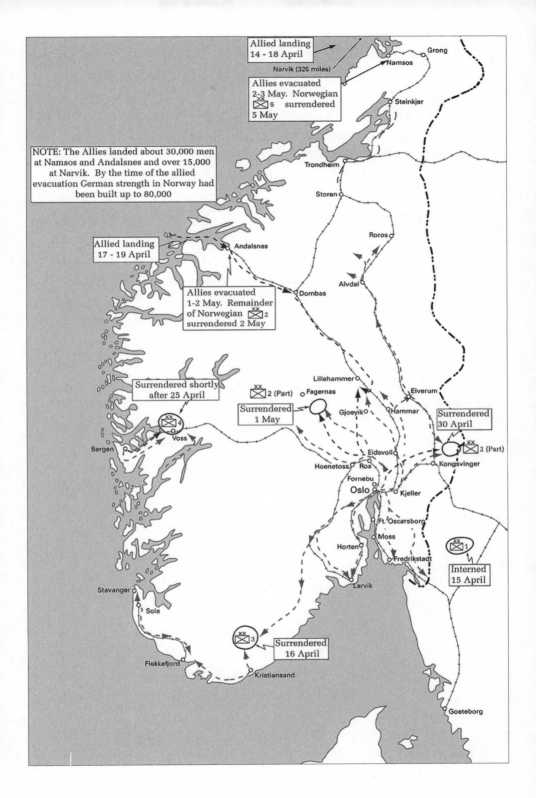

Allied landing
14 - 18 April

Narvik (325 miles)

Allies evacuated
2-3 May. Norwegian
⊠5 surrendered
5 May

Grong

Namsos

Steinkjer

NOTE: The Allies landed about 30,000 men
at Namsos and Andalsnes and over 15,000
at Narvik. By the time of the allied
evacuation German strength in Norway had
been built up to 80,000

Trondheim

Storen

Roros

Allied landing
17 - 19 April

Andalsnes

Alvdal

Dombas

Allies evacuated
1-2 May. Remainder
of Norwegian ⊠2
surrendered 2 May

Lillehammer

Elverum

Surrendered shortly
after 25 April

2 (Part) Fagernas

Surrendered
1 May

Gjoevik

Hammar

Surrendered
30 April

⊠4

Voss

Eidsvoll

2 (Part)

Kongsvinger

Bergen

Hoenetoss Roa

Fornebu

Oslo

Kjeller

Ft. Oscarsborg

Moss

⊠1

Horten

Fredrikstadt

Interned
15 April

Larvik

Stavanger

Sola

⊠3

Surrendered
16 April

Flekkefjord

Kristiansand

Goeteborg

139

Both sides made operational decisions in March that were to affect the war at sea. In Britain, the decision was taken to halt the next two Arctic convoys on the grounds that wolf pack activity in the Atlantic now required the deployment of more escorts, while the approach of lighter, longer days added to the risks of running ships to Murmansk. In Germany, Doenitz put his 'fleet in being' into operation, sending *Scharnhorst* to join *Tirpitz* and *Lutzow* in Altenfjord by 20 March, thereby compelling the Admiralty to reinstate the cruiser patrols that had previously been established in the three gaps comprising the Denmark Strait and the passages between Iceland, the Faeroes and Shetland that offered access to the Atlantic. The intensification of the war at sea in the western hemisphere yet again highlighted the shortage of escorts, but the halting of the Russian convoys allowed the Admiralty to divert corvettes, destroyers and frigates from the Home Fleet in numbers sufficient to create hunting groups of escorts. This ensured that using the tactics developed by Commander, later Captain, Walker in HMS *Starling*, the Royal Navy went on the offensive against Doenitz's wolf packs, beginning in the late spring of 1943. In the Home Fleet itself, the opportunity was taken to reorganise the heavier ships, releasing, for example, the latest King George V class battleship, HMS *Howe*, for service in the Mediterranean where she performed heavy shore bombardments in support of the landings in Sicily. To help with the containment of the Norway-based 'fleet in being', the United States Navy sent over two battleships, USS *Alabama* and USS *South Dakota* to work with the Home Fleet. The resumption of cruiser patrols, in the face of the same threat, was also a clear example of how Britain's deficiency in cruisers, in terms of number and firepower, had resulted in this 'jack of all trades' being extremely overstretched, with more commitment to come.

After covering, albeit distantly, the return convoy RA52, *Jamaica* and Nobby Elliott, now an experienced Arctic veteran, rejoined the Home Fleet in Scapa Flow. At the end of January *Jamaica*, with several other cruisers, including *Sheffield* and HMS *Sussex*, was selected to join an operation designed to intercept the cargo carrying blockade runners that were attempting to cross the Atlantic with strategic supplies destined for German occupied ports. These cruisers were given independent patrol lines spread along various courses, ranging from the western approaches to the Azores, with occasional periods spent as cover for convoys in anticipation of surface raiders. *Jamaica* carried out two fruitless patrols in February, but at least Nobby and his shipmates were spared the crushing routine of freeing the gun barrels of ice at least eight times every watch, then attempting to, while snatching sleep in the confines of X turret in the short intervals between chipping and action stations. Gone, too, was the exhaustion fed by tiredness, poor diet and the constant tension that so typified

Ice was a perpetual problem for ships on the Russian convoys.

the voyages through the icy northern wastes; wastes to which the *Jamaica* would return later in the year.

As *Jamaica* returned from her second patrol at the end of February, having seen nothing of the enemy, two Royal Marines were preparing to cross the Pyrenees on their way back to the United Kingdom, via the Resistance and the British Consulate in Barcelona. Major Hasler and Marine Sparks were the sole survivors of Operation *Frankton*, which was a daring and extremely hazardous canoe-based assault on several German blockade runners, who thought they were safely berthed in the French port of Bordeaux, some 70 miles upriver from the estuary of the Gironde. *Frankton* was the brainchild of Hasler, a temporary officer with a penchant for sailing and canoeing, who proposed to Combined Operations a novel solution to the blockade running problem. This problem, and the Admiralty's apparent inability to deal with it, unsurprisingly, due to the lack of sufficient cruisers to provide an effective screen, had become a major source of irritation to the War Cabinet. Churchill and his colleagues were well aware, through intelligence reports from the French Resistance and agents of the Special Operations Executive, that several fast cargo liners were bringing valuable war materials from the Far East to support armaments manufacture in the Third Reich. The mission to destroy the blockade runners in situ was passed to Combined Operations, and Admiral Mountbatten swiftly approved Hasler's proposal. In order to carry out the mission, Hasler formed a special unit of selected volunteers, the Royal Marines Boom Patrol Detachment (RMBPD), which commenced training in the summer of 1942 at Eastney Barracks, Portsmouth. As a cover name the RMBPD was ideal, because the formation of this unit was no less than the forerunner of what would become known later as the Special Boat Service, the Royal Navy's equivalent to the Army's Special Air Service. In addition to training the men, Hasler himself initiated and co-designed the two-man canoes, which he named Cockles, and armed them with magnetic limpet mines that were to be attached underwater to the side of the target ship, preferably adjacent to a large cargo hold, engine room or other vulnerable compartment. Hasler placed the highest priority on the fitness and determination that would be needed to tackle this astounding operation, which, in its execution, required six Cockles and twelve marines to be loaded on board a submarine for passage to the Gironde estuary. On 30 November 1942, the submarine HMS *Tuna* stealthily departed the Clyde, with Hasler, the Cockles and their crews safely stowed below for the week-long passage to the mouth of the Gironde. Lieutenant Raikes, Captain of *Tuna*, had to take every precaution in avoiding detection, a task that became increasingly difficult as the boat approached the coast of France. Submerged during the day, Raikes had to take particular care on the surface at night, when recharging the *Tuna*'s batteries, so as to avoid the inshore patrol vessels and reconnaissance aircraft deployed by the local German forces. As *Tuna* edged its way towards the drop-off point, Hasler, who was accompanied by Marine Sparks in the Cockle *Catfish*, took the opportunity to deliver a final briefing on the attack. Hasler's raiding party consisted, in addition to Sparks and himself, Sergeant Wallace and Marine Ewart in *Coalfish*, Corporal Sheard and Marine Moffat in *Conger*, Corporal Laver and Marine Mills in *Crayfish*, Lieutenant Mackinnon and Marine Conway in *Cuttlefish*, with Marine Ellery and Marine Fisher in *Cachalot*. The briefing summarised the details of the plan, with the Cockles being paddled during the hours of darkness only, and then camouflaged among the marshland and reed beds during the day. Knowing the importance of avoiding detection and dealing with river traffic, fishing boats and tidal conditions, Hasler had planned for a long, careful and slow approach to the target, the cargo ships in the tidal basin of Bordeaux port. As soon as the limpet mines had been placed and their time fuses set, the marines were then to attempt to escape overland, using Resistance contacts. When the time came to disembark *Tuna*, the *Cachalot* was damaged and Hasler had to leave her and her crew behind, finally leading the five remaining Cockles towards their objective at around 2215 on 7 December 1942. Almost immediately the Cockles ran into trouble, with *Coalfish* and *Conger* both succumbing to the fast, turbulent waters of the rip tide found at the entrance to the Gironde. The three remaining Cockles, *Catfish* and *Crayfish* in company, and *Cuttlefish* out on its own, continued their dangerous passage up the river for the next three days and nights. Hasler commenced the final attack at 2110 on 11 December, separating *Catfish* and *Crayfish* so as to improve their chances of avoiding detection and getting through to their targets. *Catfish* successfully attached its limpet mines to a German naval vessel, a tanker and two cargo vessels, while the *Crayfish* placed its limpets on two large cargo vessels. Meeting briefly after the attack, the four marines congratulated one another and then, in accordance with the plan, split up to make good their evasion and escape.

Hasler had had no further contact with *Cuttlefish*, but the six marines from the three surviving Cockles did make it ashore to begin the long walk to safety. For the attack, the marines wore military insignia and uniform, in addition to the kit they had adapted for use in the Cockles; once ashore, however, they resorted to civilian clothing to aid their escape, everyone knowingly taking the risk of being caught and shot as a spy. Unfortunately, only Hasler and Sparks were to make it back to the United Kingdom, Major Hasler via an RAF Dakota from Gibraltar and, after a lengthy stay in Spain, Marine Sparks was transported home at a more leisurely pace in one of His Majesty's troopships. Sadly, the other eight members of this operation were either lost at sea or executed after capture by a highly embarrassed local German command, although it is fair to say that evidence has yet to be found confirming exactly what happened to Marine Sheard. There is no doubt that Operation *Frankton* demonstrated the extra capability that a small, highly trained unit could bring to the prosecution of a modern war. However regrettable, a relatively small number of losses could be incurred for more valuable gains and, in the case of *Frankton*, the slim chance of escape, evidenced by the lack of detail in this part of the plan, seems to indicate an attitude of expendability and, in extremis, 'suicide mission'. But what of the gains? It can be argued that *Frankton* was not as successful as envisaged because the ships were empty and settled on the mud in the basin, allowing them to return to use soon afterwards. The German reaction, however, belied this partial failure as they came to terms with the threat that such small raiding parties or commandos presented to their harbours and naval bases. As a consequence of this realisation, thousands of military personnel were deployed to act as guards of these important installations, removing men and equipment, for example, from the Eastern Front.

In addition, the raid did have positive consequences for the future of the Royal Marines, at a point when those with foresight could see that their traditional role at sea was threatened by changes in ships, technology and weapons.

Finally, there is a postscript to the *Frankton* story. Recent research has shown that, at the same time that *Frankton* was being planned and executed, the Special Operations Executive had a team of agents and Resistance fighters close to the docks in Bordeaux. Their plan was pre-empted by the smallest of margins, when the limpet mines from Hasler's two Cockles exploded. Apparently neither the Chiefs of Staff, Combined Operations or the Special Operations Executive were aware of the co-existence of the two plans.

It can only be a matter of speculation as to which of the two or a combination of both could have been more successful. In the summer of 1943, for the purposes of a study in preparation for another similar operation, Hasler's own remarks concerning *Frankton* were recorded in the subsequent report:

The previous operation [*Frankton*] was carried out in a condition of almost flat calm which is most exceptional and the odds are against it ever occurring again. In spite of the calm weather two of the five canoes capsized at the mouth of the river and Major Hasler is of the opinion that, under any other sea conditions, it is unlikely that any of the canoes would get through the race.[2]

Nevertheless, in Britain, although the raid and its aftermath were kept secret for operational reasons, *Frankton* did represent a breakthrough for Combined Operations and its charismatic leader, Admiral Mountbatten. His organisation had taken on a mission that had proved impracticable for conventional forces and had, almost as a by-product, provided a pathway for the Royal Marines to finally assume the amphibious raiding role identified within the Madden Report some twenty years beforehand. As we have seen, there were no resources available between the wars to implement this role, especially as the Royal Navy needed to retain the gunnery skills of its 'blue water' marines. The year 1942, therefore, with the formation of the first Royal Marine Commando (40 Commando RM) and Operation *Frankton*, can be judged a pivotal year in the development of the future employment of the Corps. In the same year, Royal Marine Commandos took part in the raid on Dieppe and, despite the controversial failure of this mission, Mountbatten had sufficient faith in their capability to promote the breaking up of the Royal Marine Division in order to expand commando forces, thereby clearly placing them in the Corps domain.[3]

For the 'blue water' marines in *Jamaica*, March 1943 was a quiet and welcome period of service, as she was released from the Home Fleet in Scapa Flow for a long docking in the shipyard of Vickers Armstrong, Barrow-in-Furness. The shipyard carried out repair work to the damage inflicted by exposure to the Arctic weather and attended to the *Jamaica*'s radar sets, which had shown a tendency to shatter, or be otherwise incapacitated, when her main armament was fired. This was one of the reasons why *Sheffield* had taken the lead in the pursuit of *Hipper* during the Barents Sea action, when visibility had been foreshortened by the presence of smoke and snow. These repairs were undertaken while Vickers Armstrong undertook the main purpose of the docking, which was the replacement of *Jamaica*'s 6-inch gun barrels. All gun barrels have a limited life, due to wear and tear, which is mainly caused by the frequency of firing and the weather. In the tropics, for example, gun barrels were frequently hosed down between salvoes while, in the freezing air and seas of the Arctic, the ice and extreme temperature took their toll. As the wear in a barrel had a marked influence on the performance of a gun, due allowance had to be made in the calculations processed by the transmitting station, to keep the weapon on target. In extreme cases when, for instance, a barrel was nearly worn out, the chances of a dangerous, even catastrophic, misfire and explosion were increased well beyond any recognised margin of safety. For *Jamaica*'s crew, the work at Barrow provided a more than welcome opportunity to take some home leave, and Nobby Elliot took full advantage of this to visit his wife and son back home in Plymouth. It must have been very hard, therefore, to have to leave his young family and rejoin the ship, but Nobby was now an experienced and seasoned serviceman. With three years' war service behind him, including sustained periods of action, Nobby, as one of two sergeants in *Jamaica*'s marine detachment, knew where his duty lay and what was expected of him. *Jamaica* rejoined the Home Fleet and was used during April to cover convoys passing through the North-Western Approaches on their way to discharge their vital cargoes in the ports of the United Kingdom.

The Battle of the Atlantic was at its height and, due to the tactical and technical developments mentioned in the previous chapter, the Royal Navy was beginning, at long last and after desperate losses of men and ships, to wrestle the initiative from Admiral Doenitz and his fleet of U-boats. Perhaps the critical juncture came at the end of March 1943, when the first of the American-built escort carriers, USS *Bogue*, came into service, flying the flag of the United States. Convoys were now offered air cover for the duration of their transit across the ocean, and three of *Bogue*'s sister ships came into service with the Royal Navy shortly thereafter. Events in April further improved the prospects of successfully defending the convoys, and increasing the detection and destruction of the U-boats, at the very time that Doenitz had more than 200 at his disposal. This month also witnessed the belated introduction of a greatly increased number of Very Long Range aircraft, equipped with radar and depth charges, that virtually closed the air gap that had for so long provided U-boat packs with a certain freedom of manoeuvre and undetected attack. On the surface of the sea, the Royal Navy was now able to deploy its escort groups as vessels released from Arctic Ocean and Mediterranean operations joined the escorts. These closer escorts, which had benefitted from the rapid expansion of the Royal Canadian Navy and its volunteer crews, had by now developed an operating capability that reflected the hard lessons learned since the autumn of 1939. Supported by Enigma-sourced intelligence from Bletchley Park, the escort groups, the escort carriers and the closing of the air gap, ship losses in April were reduced to half that of March, and it is significant to note that the biggest single deterrent to the wolf packs proved to be the increase in long-range and local air cover. The transformative effect of this much-needed improvement was very marked; it effectively turned the hunters into the hunted, exposing the U-boats to attack from both above and on the ocean. Events in the Atlantic in May, when the Western Allies decided to fight convoys through large wolf pack concentrations, ended in success for their navies, eventually forcing Admiral

Doenitz to withdraw his cherished submarines from the field of battle. All of the convoys that had braved the dangers of crossing the Atlantic in all weathers rightly deserve mention but, in the context of this momentous change in Allied naval strategy and tactics, three deserve particular description: ONS5, HX237 and SC129. ONS5 was a convoy outbound from Britain to Halifax, Nova Scotia, and both HX237 and SC129 were fully loaded eastbound convoys, sailing from Halifax to the United Kingdom. The latter's initials stood for slow convoy, for vessels with a typical speed of less than 10 knots, whereas the faster HX convoys grouped vessels that could sustain a speed of between 10 and 14 knots. The availability of escort groups and carrier groups now allowed the Royal Navy, where Western Approaches were now commanded by Admiral Sir Max Horton, a submarine veteran of the First World War – as was his adversary Doenitz – to deploy these groups in positions where they could defend a number of convoys sailing in opposite directions.

ONS5 was a large convoy of forty-two merchant ships, the majority in ballast, and was escorted by eight destroyers, frigates and corvettes, under the command of Commander Peter Gretton. Doenitz had placed between thirty and forty U-boats in a line to intercept the convoy, which was first sighted by U-258, whose transmissions were decoded in Bletchley Park. Sea conditions were appalling, with the empty merchantmen and the small escort ships pitching and rolling through heavy seas, with the result that long-range aircraft were unable to fly, and the U-boats lost contact on 1 May. It took another three days for the U-boats to re-locate the convoy and, meanwhile, the Royal Navy had sent the five destroyers of the 3rd Escort Group (Captain J. McCoy), to reinforce Gretton. These reinforcements were both timely and welcome, but the appalling weather conditions, to which had been added the perils of ice drifting down from the north, prevented refuelling at sea. Consequently, Gretton had to take his own ship, HMS *Duncan*, to St Johns on 3 May for fuelling and this was repeated by two ships of the 3rd Escort Group on the following day. The convoy escort was now commanded by Lieutenant Commander Sherwood, an experienced Royal Naval Reserve officer, and this reduced force now faced an onslaught from the waiting U-boats on the night of 4/5 May. Five of the merchant ships were sunk as the depleted escort struggled with the darkness, weather and the sheer weight of the attack. As the weather eased back during the day, refuelling at sea became possible once more, and the convoy welcomed the arrival of a lone long-range aircraft. It was to no avail, however, as the concentrated U-boats mounted a further series of attacks during the day and then the night of 5/6 May, ahead of the arrival of the Canadian local escorts later in the morning. Seven cargo ships were sent to the bottom during this period, with the result that ONS5 had lost twelve of its forty-two charges, but the aggression, persistence and fighting capability of the escorts had sunk five U-boats, with another two succumbing to attacks from the air. Other U-boats were damaged and Doenitz was beginning to realise that the rate of attrition to his boats and, more decisively, his valuable crews, was approaching unsustainable levels. This was brought home personally to him by the loss of his youngest son, when the U-954 was sunk with all hands in the North Atlantic, just two weeks after the battle with ONS5. Following the battle, ONS5 received further reinforcement from the 1st Escort Group, and the remaining ships made it safely to port. This deployment alone clearly illustrates the transformation in the balance of resources between the belligerents; Horton was able to commit not one, but two escort groups to a single convoy, allowing several escorts to track, attack and destroy the enemy, displaying a great deal of courage, skill and determination.[4]

During the week after the transit of ONS5, the fully laden eastward-bound convoys HX237 and SC129 took on the thirty or more U-boats that had been directed to intercept them. The former, in addition to the close escort, was provided with the services of the 5th Escort Group and was covered by long-range aircraft. The 5th Escort Group included one of the new escort carriers, HMS *Biter*, giving the convoy increased aerial capability, and this combination of surface and air defence succeeded in sinking three U-boats for the loss of three of the merchant vessels, thereby maintaining extreme pressure upon Doenitz's resources. The *Biter* and its Escort Group were then ordered to reinforce SC129 and between 12 and 14 May, aircraft and warships struck back at their underwater foes – with two merchantmen and two U-boats being lost as a result. With the initiative now firmly in the hands of the Allies, the next three convoys enjoyed heavy support on and above the waves, and proceeded to their destinations without losing a single cargo ship. The threat to Britain's Atlantic lifeline had, after three and a half years of brutal conflict, been dealt a mortal blow, but caution needs to be exercised when looking at this change in fortune from a longer perspective. The thousands of ships, and the many thousands of seamen and women that were lost to the U-boats, paid a dreadful and heavy price for their vital part in what had become, to all intents and purposes, an economic and technical race for supremacy in the Atlantic. Economically, the shipbuilding capacity and power of the United States enabled the Allies to stay, albeit precariously, in the race. The technical innovation and operational experience of the United Kingdom and the Royal Navy came to maturity just in time, because Doenitz, in the spring of 1943, finally had the numbers of U-boats he needed to win the battle. The Battle of the Atlantic was decided by the smallest of margins, with the outcome uncertain until May 1943. Without victory in this ocean, there was no way the Allies could contemplate large amphibious operations in the Mediterranean, and there would have been insufficient shipping resources available for an eventual invasion of France. It was that important.

8

RETURN TO THE FROZEN NORTH

After her covering duties in the Atlantic were completed, *Jamaica* returned to Scapa Flow and the Home Fleet. Within a relatively short time of her arrival, no doubt all on board were very pleased to receive the news that *Jamaica* had been scheduled for a twelve-week refit, to take place in the naval dockyard at Portsmouth. Sergeant Nobby Elliott looked forward, with his shipmates, to some time at home and, if only temporarily, a respite from the daily grind of gun maintenance and the ever-present underlying tension experienced at sea in wartime. What made this respite more than just welcome, however, was the fact that *Jamaica* was being thoroughly overhauled and prepared for another long winter's deployment in the Arctic. Nobby and his mates would not, of course, have been aware of this at the time, but mess deck rumours and a shrewd observation of dockyard additions and supplies would have given the game away to many of the crew when they went back to her in early September. *Jamaica* underwent a series of machinery tests and trials before rejoining her squadron and the Home Fleet in Scapa Flow on 18 September 1943. Eight days earlier, while working with Churchill in Washington, the First Sea Lord, Admiral of the Fleet Sir Dudley Pound, suffered a stroke and tendered his resignation.

Pound had been suffering from ill health for some time, with a painful hip joint that disturbed his sleep. This was complicated by the discovery of a brain tumour, and it is easy to appreciate the stress caused by having the double responsibility for policy and operations, and the relentless hours of work that running the navy entailed. In addition, Pound had to keep up with the pace of the Prime Minister, and Brooke noted how this affected his ability to concentrate at Chiefs of Staff committee meetings.[1] The fate of the ill-starred Russian convoy, PQ17, and in particular, the obstinacy that Pound displayed after issuing the order to scatter, when intelligence indicated that the *Tirpitz* remained at anchor, was the most profound example of the effect of his tiredness and micro-management mentality.

To his credit, Pound been relatively successful in diverting Churchill from pursuing some of his wilder strategic ideas, without losing favour with the Prime Minister, an achievement he shared with Brooke. This can be contrasted with Winston's handling of Auchinleck and Wavell in the Middle East, and bore fruit as Pound successfully made the case for the highest priority to be given to the life-and-death struggle in the Atlantic. In a later note in his diary, Brooke paid this tribute to his colleague:

> A very gallant man who literally went on working till he dropped. I am certain that he had been suffering from his complaint for some time... He was a grand colleague to work with, and now that I realise how sick a man he was lately I withdraw any unkind remarks I may have made in my diary concerning his slowness and lack of drive.[2]

Pound was replaced by Admiral Cunningham, who travelled to London from the Mediterranean where he had resumed command after the departure of Harwood in the spring of 1943. Churchill wanted Admiral Sir Bruce Fraser, who had relieved Tovey as

Commander-in-Chief Home Fleet in May, having been the latter's deputy, to be appointed First Sea Lord, perhaps because he wanted to avoid having the considerable presence of Cunningham on the Chiefs of Staff Committee. Fraser demurred in favour of Cunningham, who was the Royal Navy's most experienced and battle-hardened fighting commander, with an appreciation of the wider picture and possessed of sound judgement.

When *Jamaica* rejoined the Home Fleet, Fraser's appreciation of the situation facing his command included a firm belief that the convoys to Russia should not be resumed until at least October. To some extent his appreciation and understanding were underwritten by wider events in Russia and North Africa, where the Germans had suffered two extremely heavy defeats. In the first, the surrender at Stalingrad in February put the German invaders on the retreat, with casualties in excess of 700,000. This was followed by the surrender of German forces in Tunisia in May, when nearly 250,000 prisoners were taken by the British and American armies under the overall command of General Alexander. This victory, the first major land success of the Western Allies, completed the clearance of North Africa, and was the culmination of Operation *Torch* and the Battle of El Alamein. Success in North Africa removed any threat to Suez and the Middle East oil fields, and provided a platform for the Allies to invade Sicily and then, in September, Italy. These advances forced Hitler and his commanders to withdraw resources from the East to reinforce their newly threatened southern flank. It is, therefore, fair to say that with the taking of the initiative in the Atlantic, Russia and the Mediterranean, the early autumn of 1943 was when it was realised that the Allies were going to win the war. Economically, production in all three of the major allies had increased, and the trained manpower becoming available to the United States and, on an even greater scale, to the USSR pointed in one direction. Strategically, and tactically for the Royal

Navy, this turnaround in fortune had reduced the pressure on the Western Allies to send cargoes via the hazardous northern sea route, even though there had been no convoys to Kola since March. Supplies continued to go to Stalin via an overland route through Persia, and the United States ran a few convoys across the Pacific to the Russian port of Vladivostok. Stalin, however, was anxious that the Arctic convoys be resumed, due to the higher volume of cargoes that could be carried over this shorter sea route, and he maintained the pressure on Roosevelt and Churchill to open a second front in North West Europe. As the government and the Admiralty prepared for the resumption of convoys in November, Fraser's second concern remained the German 'fleet in being' in Norway. He was conscious of the need to maintain vigilance off the Norwegian coast, and to keep enough heavy units to hand in Scapa Flow to deal with any possible breakout, although the pressure had been reduced by a midget submarine attack in September. To deliver Operation *Source*, as this mission was named, the Royal Navy had six purpose-built X Craft, each of which was just over 50 foot long, armed with two 1-ton charges, known as side cargoes, which were packed with high explosives. Attached to the sides of the craft, the side cargoes could be dropped under the hull of a target vessel or attached by limpet with the help of an on-board diver. X Craft were crewed by four highly trained volunteers, and all six were towed by conventional submarines to a point close to the entrance to the Norwegian fjords that harboured *Tirpitz*, *Lutzow* and *Scharnhorst*. Two of the X Craft, X8 and X9, were lost at sea during the difficult transit from north-west Scotland to the northern part of Norway. This left four boats for the final approach: X5, commanded by Lieutenant Henty-Creer; X6, Lieutenant Cameron; X7, Lieutenant Place, and X10, commanded by Lieutenant Hudspeth. Lieutenant Place was the only regular officer in the group as Cameron was RNR and Henty-Creer and Hudspeth were from the RNVR, the latter being in the Australian equivalent of that service. X5, X6 and X7 all had *Tirpitz* as their target and, as they approached the anchorage in Altenfjord where she was positioned behind an array of anti-submarine and anti-torpedo nets, X5 was lost, in circumstances that remain unknown. X6 and X7 pressed home their attack, avoiding patrol boats and cutting their way through the defensive nets, and succeeded in planting their side cargoes under the hull of the enemy. With much of his equipment rendered unserviceable, Lieutenant Cameron brought X6 to the surface and ordered his crew to bail out, after which their X Craft was scuttled and the survivors awaited rescue by the Germans. They were taken on board a motorboat and sent to the *Tirpitz* for questioning. Lieutenant Place's X7, meanwhile, had managed to get away, but it proved impossible to control the depth of the craft and its intermittent periods on the surface were greeted by automatic fire. Coming alongside a target raft in the fjord, Place and one other managed to escape and they too were taken aboard the *Tirpitz*. All six survivors were present in the *Tirpitz* when the four side cargoes exploded, so damaging the hull and engines that the German battleship was put out of action for six months, until mid-March 1944. While X6 and X7 completed their mission, X10 had steered towards its target, *Scharnhorst*, which was believed to be in Kaa Fjord, a branch of the Altenfjord. Regrettably, X10 suffered compass and machinery problems, which left Hudspeth no alternative but to take her down to the bed of the fjord to make repairs. After several hours, Hudspeth brought X10 up to observe the target, but the *Scharnhorst* had sailed out to the Norwegian sea for training drills. With no target Hudspeth set X10 on a course for one of the waiting submarines that could tow the craft home. Astonishingly, it took six days for X10 to find the submarine and rig a tow, with the craft and its crew experiencing difficult sea conditions en route and running low on fuel. Despite this excellent display of seamanship, worsening weather conditions meant that X10 was scuttled before base could be reached in Scotland. Operation *Source* was a success because, although it did not manage to sink the *Tirpitz*, she was removed from the Arctic convoy situation for the remaining winter months, and added to the paranoia of the German High Command and their obsession with keeping the 'fleet in being' intact. Lieutenants Cameron and Place were both awarded the Victoria Cross for their bravery, determination and leadership in this operation. Further relief for Fraser followed soon after Source's ending, when the German High Command ordered the *Lutzow* back to Germany. Embarrassingly, the pocket battleship completed her voyage without being seen or touched by the search that was mounted to intercept her – now only *Scharnhorst* remained as the 'fleet in being'.

With the new situation in the Atlantic, Fraser assigned *Jamaica* to Norwegian interception and patrol duties, which were duly carried out throughout the month of October. These patrols were uneventful, although useful in completing the working up of *Jamaica* following her refit, changes in personnel and the need to become ever more familiar with new equipment. The interruption to the Arctic convoys had left several merchantmen and their crews stranded in Russia, where treatment by their hosts left a lot to be desired and added to the misery of German air raids and generally poor living and welfare conditions. To recover these ships, the Admiralty assembled them in Archangel as convoy RA54A, and they sailed for Loch Ewe during the early morning of 2 November. In accordance with the established operational routine, the twelve empty cargo vessels were given a large close escort, which included no fewer than nine destroyers. This force was supplemented by three cruisers, once more under Admiral Burnett's command – *Belfast, Kent* and *Norfolk* – which provided cover across the Barents Sea and then west of North Cape. A third, heavier and more distant layer of protection was commanded by Fraser's deputy, Vice Admiral Sir Henry Moore, in the King George V class battleship *Anson*, with the fleet aircraft carrier HMS *Formidable*, *Jamaica* and five destroyers drawn from the Royal Navy, the United States Navy and the Royal Norwegian Navy. Weather conditions for the voyage to the north-west coast of Scotland were favourable, as the persistent fog and mist prevented the Germans from sighting the ships as they made their wary way home, in conditions that favoured collision above enemy action. RA54A anchored safely on 14 November, thankfully unscathed, and with the merchant seamen no doubt relieved to be back in the United Kingdom. In the meantime, ships of the distant covering force, including *Jamaica*, arrived back at Scapa Flow on 8 November after completing their shadowing task. Almost immediately after refuelling, *Jamaica* was ordered back to sea as part of the cruiser cover for the first outbound convoy of the season, JW54A. This heavily laden convoy of nineteen ships left Loch Ewe on 15 November, the day after the arrival of RA54A, and *Jamaica* again joined the *Anson*, in the hope that the *Scharnhorst* would be tempted out by the close passage of the merchant ships. Yet again the weather came to the aid of the merchantmen and their close escort, and they escaped the attention of their enemy, who was certainly aware, through radio intelligence, that the convoys had resumed. The pattern was repeated with JW54B and the return convoy RA54B, and, while their safe passage must have given some encouragement to their crews, there was no respite from the continuing dreadful weather. On board *Jamaica*, Nobby and his fellow gunners had a new gunnery officer, Lieutenant Commander Rupert Wainwright, who brought his experience and know-how to bear on the difficulties of gunnery in the Arctic. Confronted by the problems caused by frozen spray in the gun barrels, Wainwright came up with a novel solution that prevented this from happening. He ordered discs to be made from millboard, and then had them heavily greased and place in the mouth of each 6-inch barrel. Once fitted, the discs froze and sealed the barrel in place until the guns were fired, with the first blast blowing away the disc, without any damage or significant effect upon the performance of the weapon.[3] Wainwright also grappled with another problem, that of condensation within the gun houses that froze on the deck, making movement inside the turret dangerous. If untreated, this ice played havoc with gun drills, limiting the effectiveness of the many hours that the gun crews exercised their routines to maintain a very high rate of fire. In action, one slip could slow the whole process as well as lead to the loss of an injured crew member, with consequences for the uninterrupted teamwork that characterised the way the guns were serviced.

Although relieved at the successful transit of the latest convoys, neither the Admiralty nor Fraser were under any illusions as to the serious threat that continued to be posed by the Norwegian-based U-boat packs, reconnaissance aircraft and, above all, the *Scharnhorst*. They considered it would only be a matter of time before the convoys were attacked and Fraser, in particular, was of the opinion that *Scharnhorst* would venture out soon. In recognition of this, he set sail in his flagship, *Duke of York*, with *Jamaica* and four destroyers, HMS *Savage*, HMS *Saumarez*, HMS *Scorpion* and the Norwegian *Stord*. This force, now designated Force 2, set out to cover convoy JW55A, but *Scharnhorst* did not show. Taking advantage of this situation and, with a view to fostering better relations with his Russian counterparts, Fraser took his ships through the Kola Inlet and on to Murmansk. Here the Force stayed for two days, while Fraser met with the local naval liaison staff and visited Admiral Golokov, the local Commander in Chief. The visit, which lasted two days, demonstrated two truths. First, there was the need to add the personal touch to encourage a good working relationship between the Russian and British forces in the Arctic war, and to improve the welfare of the British seamen during their time in Murmansk or Archangel. Second, Fraser's willingness to take his battleship, a cruiser and their destroyers through the Kola Inlet indicated that the threat from the air was much diminished, as the Germans were having to send air forces to aid the weakening Eastern Front. It is also entirely possible that in Fraser's judgement, because of the new air situation, he was becoming even more convinced that the German's would attack, to disrupt what had now become a highly successful series of heavily laden cargoes destined to add to the woes of the German Army in Russia. With this in mind he sailed from Murmansk on 18 December, taking his force to Akureyri, Iceland, for refuelling and to prepare to cover the next outbound and homebound convoys, JW55B and RA55A. It was no coincidence that both these convoys had ten destroyers in their close escort and, in addition to Fraser's own covering ships, Burnett had three cruisers, *Belfast, Sheffield* and *Norfolk* designated Force 1, deployed together to intercept the *Scharnhorst* should she leave the protection of the fjords. Fraser put to sea on 23 December, with ULTRA intelligence reinforcing his calculation that *Scharnhorst* was about to come out and, due to the limited range of his destroyers, he realised that Force 2 could not cover JW55B all the way to Kola. He therefore planned to reach a position to cover the convoy when it was closing Bear Island from the east, steaming at 15 knots to conserve fuel. Before departing Iceland, Admiral Fraser assembled the commanding officers of his warships and urged them to make doubly sure that their crews were fully prepared for a night action. He was conscious of the fact that the Home Fleet had a relatively high turnover of men, with transfers between various types of escort vessels, promotions, training and sickness all to be taken into account. Fraser therefore appreciated the fact that Force 2 had been working closely together for a couple of weeks, and the prudent and thorough Admiral had already taken several opportunities to conduct night exercises. Nevertheless, at sea on Christmas Eve, he put Force 2 through a series of manoeuvres with the *Jamaica* acting as the target, rehearsing the tactics he intended to employ when encountering the enemy battlecruiser. According to Admiral Fraser's own report, he had decided on three actions to take in the event that his ships came across the *Scharnhorst*:

(a) To close the enemy, opening fire with starshell at a range of about 12,000 yards.

(b) To form the four destroyers of my screen into sub-divisions and release them in time to take up positions for a torpedo attack.

(c) To keep the JAMAICA in close support of DUKE OF YORK but with freedom of action to take drastic avoiding action and open the distance if engaged.[4]

An examination of these tactics reveal how successful Royal Navy Admirals such as Cunningham, Fraser and Vian concentrated on the offensive, while appreciating the armament and speed of each type of ship available to opposing fleets. If Fraser had to engage *Scharnhorst* with Force 2 alone, then he knew that the superior 14-inch guns (there were ten) of the *Duke of York* could exchange fire with *Scharnhorst*, which had nine 11-inch guns as her main armament. Unlike the *Duke of York*, the *Scharnhorst* was a battlecruiser and had lighter armour, and would need to avoid plunging fire from her main adversary by closing the range, not only to flatten the directory of *Duke of York's* shells but to ensure that her own smaller calibre guns remained in effective range. However, by doing so, *Scharnhorst*, if sailing alone, then exposed herself to torpedo attack by the destroyers, operating in pairs (sub-divisions) and approaching from different directions. This still left the 6-inch cruiser *Jamaica*, operating with a measure of freedom of action and which, in addition to her relatively light main armament, carried a full complement of torpedoes, along with the necessary speed to attack and despatch them. If *Scharnhorst* attacked on her own, or in company with several destroyers as would normally be the case, her prospects of getting through to the merchant ships were far from bright; and that is without taking account of the twenty destroyers escorting JW55B and RA55A, let alone Burnett's cruisers, which included the eight 8-inch guns of the *Norfolk*. The Royal Navy's chance had come.

During the course of Christmas Eve, Fraser had been made aware that JW55B was being shadowed by German reconnaissance aircraft, and this made him conscious of the fact that the convoy only had its close escort to hand at this point and was vulnerable to a surface attack. Fraser took swift and decisive action, and at 1400 he broke radio silence to order the convoy to reverse course for three hours, while Force 2 increased speed to 19 knots. This, he hoped, would prevent the convoy from being attacked in what little daylight remained; however, he received further information advising that JW55B was not steaming as fast as planned, and that RA55A had safely passed Bear Island, coming, of course, in the opposite direction towards the covering forces. Admiral Fraser deduced that the lack of German attention toward RA55A indicated that U-boats were being concentrated on JW55B, in response to it being shadowed from the air. In a message to the Rear Admiral commanding the Home Fleet's destroyers, Fraser issued orders that required RA55A to steer north in order to 'clear the area', and for four fleet destroyers to be transferred from this convoy to reinforce JW55B. When these instructions had been carried out, Fraser felt confident that, in the event of an attack by *Scharnhorst* and/or U-boats, the convoy's increased escort and the nearby presence of Burnett's Force 1 could either repel or delay her, giving Force 2 the opportunity to destroy the enemy. But what of the *Scharnhorst*? After much debate within the German High Command and the Kriegsmarine, Doenitz had finally instructed the *Scharnhorst* and a force of five destroyers, under the command of Admiral Bey, to execute Operation *Ostfront* and attack JW55B. The name of the operation provides a clear clue as to Doenitz's intent, which was to relieve the pressure on the German Army on the eastern front. The prize for the *Scharnhorst* was that, if she could evade the covering forces and deal with the close escort with her vastly superior weapons, then she could set about the merchant ships. *Scharnhorst* had the capability and wherewithal to destroy all of the merchant ships, inflicting greater losses than the U-boats had achieved in the final quarter of 1943. The order was issued while Doenitz was visiting Berlin, and so it is more than probable that it was a gesture of support for the army, and a justification of the 'fleet in being'. Ironically, by sending out *Scharnhorst* the whole concept of the 'fleet in being' was put at risk, but these were turning into desperate times as the fortunes of war swung against Germany. Doenitz's naval staff and commanders in France (he was now based in Paris after taking command of the Kriegsmarine) and Norway were aghast at the notion of this sortie. The minimal, almost non-existent daylight over this period made it clearly more sensible to deploy destroyers rather than the battlecruiser. The orders given to Admiral Bey were clear:

(a) Action of the First Battle Group, consisting of the Scharnhorst and five destroyers, against the convoy on December 26 at dawn, i.e. at about 1000 hours.

(b) Battle line in close order only if battle conditions were favourable, i.e. tolerable weather conditions with good visibility, permitting a full appreciation of the enemy's dispositions.

(c) If the tactical situation was not favourable for the Scharnhorst, the destroyers were to attack alone, the battleship standing by to pick up the destroyers while remaining herself at a distance from the target area. If necessary she was to withdraw to the outer fjord.[5]

It can be seen in part 'c' of these orders that the High Command did, in fact, appreciate that under certain conditions the destroyers could be sent in alone. Admiral Bey, however, had no intention of obeying this part of his instructions; 'if the tactical situation was not favourable' he would withdraw all of his ships until dawn on the following day. This argument became academic, however, as the weather was to have the last word.

Scharnhorst and her destroyers left Altenfjord at 1900 on Christmas Day, and her departure was confirmed by the Admiralty at 0339 in a signal to all ships, meaning that every escort and covering group commander, and the commanding officers of all of the warships involved, now knew the enemy was out and that the chase was on. Armed with this information, Fraser was worried that Force 2 was still too far away from the convoy should *Scharnhorst* attack at first light, which was about 0830 on Boxing Day. The dawn consisted of a glimmer or a pale twilight as the sun struggled to get above the horizon, creating a bleakness that made life extremely difficult for lookouts. Breaking radio silence for a second time, he ordered the convoy to steer north, while he established the position of Force 2. Once this was known, Fraser altered the course of the convoy, just before 0630, to the north-east and ordered Force 1 to close on JW55B. The combination of the convoy's destroyer escorts, Burnett's cruisers and destroyers, would then be able to execute Fraser's plan to deter or attack *Scharnhorst* if she appeared on the scene before the arrival of Force 2. With these dispositions in hand, and with full knowledge of the position of all the ships under his command, Fraser altered course towards the convoy and increased speed to 24 knots. This was not without difficulty as the weather, which had been poor since before Christmas Eve, now intervened as a factor in the movement of both British and German ships. A full-blown gale from the south-west was accompanied by rain that further restricted visibility, which was already limited. A deep swell and very rough seas forced the *Scharnhorst*'s destroyers back to Altenfjord, thereby abandoning their search for the convoy which, thanks to Fraser's prompt orders, had evaded their clutches. They also abandoned the *Scharnhorst* and Bey, completely unaware of the presence of British covering forces, continued his hunt for the merchant ships. The sea conditions also affected Fraser's vessels, including his own flagship, *Duke of York*:

> During the night of 25/26 December, the battlefleet steamed to the eastward at 17 knots. There was an unpleasant sea and conditions in DUKE OF YORK were most uncomfortable, few people obtaining any sleep.[6]

If such were the conditions on board a 35,000-ton battleship, for the four destroyers attempting to keep pace with *Duke of York* it was a night of seas smashing over decks and chaos below as both men and unsecured gear in cabins and working compartments were thrown around without respite. Fraser's increase of speed to 24 knots presented a tremendous challenge to the seaworthiness of his destroyers and the seamanship of their crews who, by now, expected to go into action at any time. That the Allied destroyers stayed in the hunt was testimony to their design, being smaller and sleeker than their German counterparts; they pitched, rolled and carved their way through the sea. Uncomfortable as it was, and provided power and steering were available to avoid broaching to, these ships were capable of handling the conditions, in stark contrast to the *Scharnhorst*'s escorts. Burnett's Force 1, in obeying the order to close the convoy, also found the weather difficult, and his response to the wild conditions was to alter course so as to approach the convoy from the south. This reduced the exposure of his ships to heavy seas crashing directly over the bows, thereby maintaining the effectiveness of their forward armament, particularly with regard to the guns of 'A' turret. Once in action, Burnett knew that he would need every one of the cruisers' main weapons if he was to deter or drive off their more powerful adversary. Fraser and Burnett needed to find the enemy first and, as Forces 1 and 2 converged on the convoy, *Scharnhorst* did the same. In the pale twilight, lookouts strained their eyes, while radar sets were monitored continuously as the ships prepared for action in the morning.

The first sighting of *Scharnhorst* was made at 0840 on Boxing Day, 26 December, when *Belfast*'s radar identified her at a range of nearly 20 miles, less than half the distance that Burnett had estimated in his own calculations. Altering course to south, Burnett led his cruisers towards the enemy and a further sighting of the *Scharnhorst* was made at 0921 from the bridge of the *Sheffield*, with the range now down to just less than 7 miles, well within the capability of Force 1's main armament. Three minutes later, *Belfast* opened fire with starshell, to illuminate the enemy, and *Norfolk*, with her more powerful 8-inch guns, opened up with a full salvo at 0930, maintaining her fire for the next ten minutes. *Norfolk*'s first salvo had been delivered at a range of 5½ miles, but the *Scharnhorst* lost no time in escaping in a southerly direction and increasing speed to 30 knots, giving her an advantage of 6 knots over the British cruisers. In a demonstration of how quickly this turn of speed could alter the situation, *Norfolk*'s final salvo, at 0940, had to travel a distance of more than 13½ miles to reach the target. *Norfolk* achieved a hit with one of her early salvoes, inflicting damage to the bridge upperworks, causing casualties but not eliciting any retaliation from the German battlecruiser. In his later analysis, Admiral Fraser thought that Bey was under the impression that *Norfolk* was on her own, because the *Belfast* and *Sheffield* did not fire on this occasion, and this consequently led to the German Admiral's fateful decision to make another attack on the convoy. Bey certainly intended another attack but, after withdrawing from his encounter with *Norfolk*, he remained out of contact with the merchant ships and the shadowing warships. As far as the latter were concerned, Fraser, with Force 2, continued to make progress towards the convoy, while Force 1 successfully located JW55B by radar at 1050. Burnett then took his cruisers to a point 10 miles ahead of the convoy, placing his vessels in a protective screen ahead of the merchant ships. Half an hour earlier, Force 1 had been joined by the four fleet destroyers, HMS *Musketeer*, HMS *Matchless*, HMS *Opportune* and HMS *Virago*, that Fraser had earlier ordered detached from RA55A for this purpose. These valuable destroyers were deployed ahead of Burnett's cruisers, and all seven of the warships now in Force 1 commenced zig-zagging as a precaution against U-boat attack. For the next ninety minutes the loss of contact with *Scharnhorst* created some worrying moments for Admiral Fraser, as he contemplated the fuel situation of his destroyers and the lack of knowledge of the *Scharnhorst*'s actual position. If the pursuit continued for much longer, the Admiral would have to take his force back for refuelling or commit to a passage all the way to the Kola Inlet. In an attempt to locate *Scharnhorst* at the earliest possible opportunity, Fraser considered detaching ships from Force 1, but Burnett advised that he was confident that the German battlecruiser would approach the convoy from the north or north-east, and was unwilling to divide his forces. Burnett was well aware that the *Scharnhorst* held a 4–5 knot advantage in speed, and his reluctance to detach ships to go searching for the enemy was accepted by Fraser, for whom the clock was still ticking with only a few hours of feeble daylight remaining. Relief, however, was soon at hand because *Norfolk* made radar contact with what was believed to be *Scharnhorst* at 1137, but this signal was lost a few minutes later, and nerves were jarred yet again. Then, at 1205, *Belfast*, some 9 miles ahead of the convoy, which was on its port quarter, picked up a firm echo at a range of just over 17 miles on a bearing of 75 degrees. It was not only in the bridges, wardrooms and messes that the tension was deeply felt. The First Sea Lord, Admiral Cunningham, wrote:

> At the Admiralty we listened, watched and waited with what patience we could muster. There was nothing we could do to help. There were dismal faces. But Burnett's appreciation had been perfectly correct... Our suspense at the Admiralty lifted.[7]

Sixteen minutes later, *Sheffield* sighted the enemy ship and as the opposing forces converged, Burnett ordered his cruisers to open fire when the range was closed to 6¼ miles and sent the destroyers to mount an attack with torpedoes. Hearing this encouraging news back in the *Duke of York*, Fraser knew that his worries were much reduced, and that there was now a very good chance that Force 2 would finally catch up with the enemy. In the meanwhile, Force 1's destroyers had difficulty with the weather and the size of the seas that were sweeping along their path, and it was not long before it was realised that a torpedo attack was impossible. The accuracy of the salvoes from the cruisers and the onrush of the destroyers had forced *Scharnhorst* to withdraw once again, this time to the south-east, peppered by splinters and sustaining a possible hit. The destroyer *Musketeer* approached closest, engaging the enemy with shell fire at ranges down to 2¼ miles, before *Scharnhorst* quickened to 28 knots. Unlike the previous encounter, however, this time the *Scharnhorst* retaliated with accurate fire from her 11-inch guns, damaging both *Norfolk* and *Sheffield*. There were two hits on *Norfolk* the first incapacitated the marines' X turret and caused the magazine to be flooded, while the second exploded amidships killing an officer and six sailors. Damage to *Norfolk*'s radar was also attributed to this second hit, although she retained the use of her Type 284 set, which was used to control the main armament. Damage to *Sheffield* was slight, consisting of a number of large shell fragments from an 11-inch salvo that exploded close alongside. In spite of this show of defiance, Force 1 had again driven off the enemy, in an action that lasted about twenty minutes, Burnett's crews displaying an aggressive determination that protected the convoy and, on this occasion, allowing the cruisers and destroyers to continue to shadow the *Scharnhorst*. There would be no escape this time.

What Bey had not predicted, as he took the battlecruiser towards the south and south-west for the three hours following his exchange with Force 1, was that he was heading for Force 2. Although it now seemed likely that Bey had given up on the convoy, Fraser appreciated that *Scharnhorst* still had an opportunity to either turn back towards the convoy or break off from her pursuers and return to Altenfjord before *Duke of York* could reach her. To remove the latter possibility Fraser, at 1539, ordered the destroyers of Force 1 to attack *Scharnhorst* with torpedoes but, as before, the condition of the sea prevented such an attempt, and so they were ordered to place themselves in a position between *Scharnhorst*, the convoy and Altenfjord. All this time Fraser had the comfort provided by the knowledge that the cruisers were maintaining a radar watch on the enemy, out of visible range, and able to report regularly on her course and speed. Suddenly, between 1603 and 1610, this continuity was threatened when *Norfolk* and *Sheffield* had to reduce speed to deal with, respectively, a fire and mechanical breakdown. Although *Norfolk* was soon able to regain her position in Force 1, *Sheffield*'s repairs took longer and she was to remain some 10 miles astern of her consorts, throughout the action that was soon to follow.

Meanwhile, *Belfast* continued to shadow and keep *Duke of York* informed. It was this information that provided Captain E. H. Thomas, Master of the Fleet and the officer with overall responsibility for the navigation of the Home Fleet, with a meticulous estimate of the enemy's position, course and speed. This meant that when, to everyone's relief, excitement and, no doubt, trepidation, *Duke of York* made contact with *Scharnhorst* on her radar at 1617, within just a few minutes of Thomas' estimate, that contact had been lost, Fraser would still have had every chance of finding the enemy.[8] The radar contact was made at the very long range of nearly 26 miles, and gave time for Fraser to issue the orders for the execution of the tactics he had practised on Christmas Eve. *Jamaica* was ordered to steer parallel with the flagship towards the enemy, and at 1637 the destroyers were deployed in two screens, one on either bow, in readiness for a torpedo attack. Three minutes later Fraser received the news he had been waiting for. *Belfast*, which was 11 miles north west of *Scharnhorst*, made radar contact with *Duke of York* at 1640 at a range in excess of 20 miles. With the battlecruiser heading southwards, the *Duke of York* steamed towards her on her starboard side, as Force 1 closed from the rear. *Scharnhorst*, meanwhile, had commenced a zig-zag pattern on a base course of 160 degrees. Plotting her movements in the flagship, Fraser brought his ships round to bear and opened up the A arcs of his main armament, ready to unleash all ten 14-inch guns upon his beleaguered opponent.[9] *Belfast* fired starshell over *Scharnhorst* at 1647, quickly followed by more of the same from *Duke of York*, and the sight of the illuminated enemy allowed Fraser to make an enemy report to the Admiralty at 1650, before opening fire. Astonishingly, the *Scharnhorst* appeared to her enemies with her main armament, the three large 11-inch turrets, aligned fore and aft, indicating that the starshells had caught her completely by surprise; she must have had little idea that her enemies were so close. Fraser believed that *Duke of York* hit the *Scharnhorst* at least three times with her main guns, inflicting some serious damage both above and below the waterline. On board the battlecruiser a report was made to the Gunnery Commander:

A turret is no longer reporting. Fire and smoke around the
turret prevent entry.[10]

The first shell from *Duke of York* had hit the turret and jammed
the training gear. With its three guns pointing skyward, the turret
could not be moved; A turret would never fire again.

Scharnhorst had lost a third of her main armament, and Bey
turned to the north, away from the unwelcome attentions of
the *Duke of York*. The battlecruiser managed to fire a couple
of salvoes as the British battleship manoeuvred in response, but
the inaccuracy of her shooting evidenced a lack of preparation,
no doubt due to the sudden shock of encountering Force 2, but
this would improve as the action developed. Her turn to the
north gave no relief, however, as *Belfast* prepared to attack with
her torpedoes and then *Norfolk* let fly with her 8-inch main
armament. At 1708 *Scharnhorst* altered course, this time towards
the east, a turn that opened up her A arcs, thereby permitting
Bey to shoot at *Duke of York* and *Jamaica*. No hits were scored
and a pattern now began to emerge as the *Scharnhorst's* crew of
nearly 2,000 men fought for their lives. Bey had the ship turn to
the south before discharging a broadside, then turned to the east
while preparing the next salvo. In so doing, he hoped to throw the
gunnery of the British ships, but their gunnery control radar, and
the experience of their director and transmitting station crews,
kept up the pressure. As *Duke of York* and *Jamaica* continued
to follow from the south, Force 2's destroyers, *Savage* and
Saumarez, crept closer to the enemy on her port quarter, while
Scorpion and *Stord* approached on the opposite flank, dodging
the occasional fire from *Scharnhorst's* secondary armament. To
the north, *Belfast* and *Norfolk* exchanged fire with the enemy
until 1712, then followed her to the east – making sure that they
maintained position to the north of her track. In the dark, freezing
and heavy waves off the North Cape, near the junction of the

Barents and Norwegian Seas, the men of the *Scharnhorst* must have realised that they were now trapped between Fraser's forces. The prospect of being killed or wounded by explosion and fire or succumbing to a freezing death in the icy waters of a dark, hostile sea must have been terrifying, but they fought on. Their tenacity was rewarded with a series of salvoes that straddled the *Duke of York*, inflicting no damage, although it was later discovered that both masts had been shot through by 11-inch shells that failed to explode. It soon became apparent that *Scharnhorst*'s improving accuracy, at this stage, was not rewarded, probably due to the failure of a significant proportion of her shells. The earlier damage to *Sheffield*, when a straddle riddled her with large splinters, piercing her hull and superstructure, showed what happened when a near miss from a heavy shell exploded, and the fact that *Duke of York* remained unscathed is testimony to the unreliability of the German ammunition.

In company with *Duke of York*, and in accordance with Fraser's planned tactics, *Jamaica* steamed six cables astern of the flagship, moving between her port and starboard quarters as changes of course demanded. Opening up at 1652, just two minutes after the battleship, *Jamaica* fired at the enemy whenever opportunity presented itself for some fifty minutes, when she ceased fire to avoid interfering with the operation of the *Duke of York*'s gunnery radar. During this period, *Jamaica* managed to hit the target on at least one occasion, but when *Scharnhorst* fired back, the gunnery officer, Lieutenant Commander Wainwright, recalled seeing the approaching echo of the 11-inch shells on his radar, 'with every appearance of accuracy', and was no doubt much relieved when they missed.[11] After *Jamaica* ceased fire, *Duke of York* and *Scharnhorst* continued to shoot at each other until 1820, when the latter stopped firing as a result of more hits by the British battleship, which was making, in the dark and wet weather, the most of its superior gunnery radar and weight of shell. Fraser kept firing for another twenty-four minutes when he observed that the *Scharnhorst* had slowed down, a clear indication of the damage inflicted by the flagship's 14-inch salvoes. As a result of this reduction, Fraser's destroyers were at last able to close the range on the enemy with the *Savage* and *Saumarez* coming up from astern, while *Scorpion* and *Stord* were on the starboard beam of the looming battlecruiser. When the range dropped to less than 6 miles, the *Scharnhorst* fired furiously at the fast-moving destroyers, but her aim appeared to be out. Fraser later wrote that intelligence gathered from the survivors included a story of chaos and disagreement within the gunnery department of the *Scharnhorst*, exacerbated by an earlier order sending the secondary gun crews below, when *Duke of York* first opened fire. Apparently, some of the crews did not receive orders sending them back to their action stations, and the response of the remainder was slow and confused.[12] Their fire was mainly but poorly directed at *Savage* and *Saumarez*, who were bravely drawing the German fire, while *Scorpion* and *Stord* stealthily moved in as they prepared to release their torpedoes. As the damaged battlecruiser continued to lose speed, at 1849 *Scorpion* fired starshell over the target and both destroyers, at a range of about a mile, sent eight torpedoes each on their way to the illuminated enemy ship. Turning towards, so as to comb the tracks of the torpedoes, *Scharnhorst* was struck by only one of the sixteen, believed fired by *Scorpion*. Having avoided more serious damage, the *Scharnhorst*'s turn placed her in the perfect position for a torpedo attack from *Savage* and *Saumarez*, who moved in under their own starshell and exchanged fire with their target, as their torpedo tubes were being set. The first to fire, at 1855, was *Savage*, who launched eight torpedoes from about 2 miles off the starboard bow of the *Scharnhorst*, followed by a spread of four torpedoes from *Saumarez*, fired from half the range. Both during the attack and their subsequent withdrawal away to the north, the two destroyers exchanged fire with the enemy, *Saumarez* receiving a number of hits from smaller calibre shells and splinters from near misses. Unfortunately, ten of her crew were killed and a similar number wounded, and the damage reduced her to a single engine, limiting her speed to 10 knots. The cost had not been in vain, however, because the *Scharnhorst* was hit by three torpedoes from this joint attack, the explosions being clearly heard by both *Duke of York* and *Belfast* on their respective sides of the action. The side armour and heavily compartmentalised structure of the battlecruiser saved her from fatal damage, but a boiler room and shaft were disabled, reducing her speed to around 22 knots, and some of her after compartments had to be sealed off to halt flooding. *Scharnhorst* now continued south and at 1901, just six minutes after the destroyers had launched their torpedoes, *Duke of York* and *Jamaica* came steaming in from the west and opened fire at a distance of 6 miles. *Norfolk* joined in from Force 1 to the north, but after a few minutes she became wary of hitting the wrong target, and ceased fire. Force 2's heavy fire now pummelled *Scharnhorst* and multiple hits were obtained, resulting in fires and explosions that were visible to her attackers. The *Scharnhorst* was being slowly destroyed and when *Belfast* got into the act, at 1915, she responded by steering to the north, but to no avail as by 1928 her speed had been reduced to a mere 5 knots. In addition to this drastic loss of speed, the stricken battlecruiser, which had earlier lost the use of A turret, had difficulty in maintaining fire from B turret. This left only the after turret, C, capable of firing continuously throughout the battle, while much of the exposed secondary armament had been destroyed by the barrage from the *Duke of York* and *Jamaica*. Fraser ceased fire at 1928, having ordered, nine minutes before, *Belfast* and *Jamaica* to administer the *coup de grace* with their torpedoes. *Jamaica* fired first, at 1925, sending three torpedoes at the target, but two missed and the third was a misfire. *Belfast* then fired her first three torpedoes, two minutes after *Jamaica*, and these also appeared to miss, requiring both vessels to turn and prepare their remaining three tubes for another attack. As they approached the target, *Jamaica* continued to fire her 6-inch guns and scored several hits on *Scharnhorst,* which retaliated with uncoordinated fire from the few remaining light weapons. Taking her chance, *Jamaica* sent her three torpedoes towards the target at 1937 and, while no explosions were seen, because of the shroud of smoke that was wrapped around the battlecruiser's hull, two underwater tremors were felt, indicating that *Jamaica* had struck home with two of her salvo. The number of ships now around the enemy coupled with the difficulty of obtaining a clear sight prevented *Belfast* from following suit, and she steamed around to a better firing position at 1948. After putting starshells over the target, *Belfast* observed nothing but wreckage, the *Scharnhorst* had been sunk and the Battle of the North Cape had reached its deadly end. Lieutenant Commander Paul Chavasse, *Jamaica*'s First Lieutenant and Torpedo Officer, later recalled this final episode in the battle when he gave an interview to the *Daily Telegraph* on returning to Scapa Flow:

By starshell we saw the black mass of the *Scharnhorst* and as we closed with her we let fly with our torpedoes. At the *moment critique* [sic] the target was blacked out with smoke. We then did another 'swing' and fired three more from our starboard tubes. The enemy seemed to resent this, and blazed away with secondary armaments and close range weapons, but most of his stuff went over our heads. There were two heavy explosions… When the smoke cleared we saw the *Scharnhorst* lying on her side. She looked like a whale that had come up for air, except that she was ablaze from stem to stern.[13]

The senior surviving member of the *Scharnhorst*'s company, Acting Chief Petty Officer Godde, described what happened just before Captain Hintze, commanding officer, issued the order to abandon ship:

> [We] heard reports coming in from all parts of the dying ship; in accordance with the Captain's orders to prepare for scuttling, the damage control parties had fitted the explosive charges and one by one the various installations were being destroyed or rendered useless.[14]

As the ship continued to heel over to starboard, 'Abandon Ship' was broadcast and Captain Hintze ordered everyone on the bridge, including Godde, to slide into the water down the port side, as the starboard side was now almost under, the waves continuing to break over the hull. Surrounding the stricken German ship at the time of her demise were *Duke of York*, *Jamaica*, *Belfast* and *Norfolk*, and the eight destroyers that had accompanied Forces 1 and 2. No actual sighting of the sinking was made, or indeed possible, although Fraser reported that the fleet 'heard and felt' a tremendous underwater explosion at 1945, three minutes before *Belfast* spotted the wreckage.[15] The British crews (and Norwegians in *Stord*) were aware of survivors in the water, whose chance of life dwindled with every second of their immersion in the freezing sea. Added to this, the hundreds of tons of oil that came to the surface from the wreck of the *Scharnhorst* brought further discomfort, as the oil choked many of the weakening survivors, making it difficult to breathe and burning the lungs. The destroyers were sent in to look for survivors and *Scorpion* picked up thirty and *Matchless* six. Only thirty-six German seamen were saved out of a crew of almost 2,000, those lost disappearing into the cold, dark depths of the sea. Many on board *Scharnhorst* were dead already, having been killed by the bombardment from Fraser's forces or the explosions of torpedoes. Some remained to meet a horrifying end, trapped in compartments surrounded by fire and flame, or behind bulkheads and hatches that had been buckled and warped by impact and splinter. They were forced to await death by drowning, suffocation or implosion as the wreck descended 950 feet to the bottom.

By 2100 the combined warships of Forces 1 and 2 were joined by *Sheffield*, and all were ordered to proceed independently to the Kola Inlet. Every ship arrived safely the following day, and the prisoners were transferred from the destroyers to the flagship, where they were interrogated during the passage back to base at Scapa Flow. The fleet arrived on New Year's Eve to a terrific reception from the other ships of the Home Fleet, in acknowledgement of their victory. No German officers survived and Fraser used some of the intelligence gathered by interrogation as supporting evidence in his subsequent report. Newsreel and photographic images of the time show the prisoners being led blindfold along *Duke of York's* gangway at Scapa, for transportation to a prisoner of war camp.

Success at the Battle of the North Cape was achieved through the performance of the *Duke of York* and the cruisers and destroyers that hounded and attacked the *Scharnhorst*, in compliance with Fraser's plan of action. Without her own destroyers, the *Scharnhorst* was isolated and her fate was sealed when her retreat to Altenfjord was cut off, just in time, by the four destroyers that had been released from RA 55A to reinforce Burnett's cruisers. Well executed tactics, with a measure of luck, which, in some part, was created by the experience and judgement of the British Admirals are, however, only part of the story. A significant factor was the superior capability of the British gunnery control radar, far superior to anything that the German Navy possessed, and critical to a ship's ability to shoot well at night. In human terms, the sheer physical effort and determination delivered by individual ship's companies made a major contribution to the destruction of the enemy. In *Jamaica*, for example, Sergeant Nobby Elliot and his fellow marines in X turret were, like the other guns' crews, at action stations for longer than four hours, during which time 461 rounds of 6-inch ammunition – roughly forty shells per gun – were fired. Taking into account the lack of light, lively seas, the freezing conditions and the threat of a hit from *Scharnhorst*'s main battery, the difficulty of fighting this battle cannot be overestimated. While it was true that the enemy was a single, albeit powerful, ship (a point made by Admiral Fraser in his despatch), the context and conditions surrounding this action demanded the highest standard of individual and team performance. The damage and casualties sustained during the hunt and the climax were relatively slight, and this could reasonably be attributed to accurate plotting and ship-handling that avoided enemy fire when possible, while maintaining the axis of advance in the relentless pursuit of the enemy.

On the rare occasion when Nobby spoke to the author about this battle, he made it clear just how hard this action was; confidence and morale was high but the overwhelming feeling was that the job must be done and that the *Scharnhorst* had to be sunk. He remarked that it was possible to feel pity for the survivors after the action, as all those at sea had to deal with a common, unforgiving enemy in the wild ocean that did not take sides. Nobby also had the strongest of reasons for fighting, surviving and returning home because during the course of the pursuit his wife Rose had given birth to Mary Rose, their daughter, a sister for Syd. Happily, Nobby was soon able to take some leave as *Jamaica* was sent to Rosyth to have her battle damage repaired, and she did not rejoin the Home Fleet at Scapa until 20 February 1944.

9

MORE CONVOYS, INVASION, AND THE END OF *TIRPITZ*

The destruction of the *Scharnhorst* and the temporary removal of the *Tirpitz* from the German line of battle brought the Royal Navy and its allies a three-and-a-half-month respite from the threat of the 'fleet in being'. It also seriously backfired on Admiral Doenitz and his efforts to demonstrate the solidarity of the Kriegsmarine with the overall German war effort. His poorly judged, albeit political, decision to send out the *Scharnhorst* and not recall her when the escorting destroyers were forced back by the violent weather, only served to diminish the already reduced circumstances of what remained of the surface fleet. With the Allies now firmly in the ascendancy with more merchant ships coming into service, notably the American Liberty ships, a standard design could be built and delivered in a matter of weeks. These revolutionary cargo vessels carried increased armament for protection, a feature that was seen in most of the tonnage built in wartime. The Liberty design also maximised cargo carrying space, but these welded ships tended to be inflexible and therefore prone to structural damage when operating in extreme conditions. Conditions at sea did not get any more extreme in the Second World War than on the convoys to North Russia. The resumption of regular convoys carrying vital war materiel to the advancing Russians was not something that Doenitz could afford to ignore. This time round, he deployed increased numbers of U-boats across the convoy route through the Barents Sea, adopting the by now all too familiar wolf pack tactic. Until *Tirpitz* was repaired and back in action, this was the only option. Doenitz also put pressure on the Luftwaffe to deploy more aircraft of all types – reconnaissance, fighter, bomber and torpedo bomber – in Norway. The Luftwaffe could not immediately respond because of the pressure on the German air arm on two other fronts, in support of the harassed army in the East and in defending Germany itself against the Allies' strategic bombing effort. A limited amount of aircraft remained available in Norway and it was particularly useful, when the weather permitted, in flying reconnaissance and assisting the U-boats in drawing up their patrol lines, prior to forming wolf packs when in closer contact with the convoys. Substantial reinforcements, in both aircraft and U-boats, became available later in the year, after the loss of the U-boat bases in France.

On 12 January 1944, the first loaded convoy since the success of the Battle of the North Cape set sail from Loch Ewe. JW56A comprised twenty merchant ships and a close escort of three destroyers, four corvettes, two minesweepers and a sloop. In line with the established pattern, the convoy headed for Iceland where it was due to receive its heavier ocean escort, but extremely bad weather intervened. The convoy made little progress and it lost cohesion to such an extent that the Commodore ordered all ships to seek shelter wherever they could. The convoy was eventually reassembled in Iceland but had to leave five of the Liberty ships behind, such was the damage they had endured during the storm. Two corvettes had to sail back to Scotland and JW56A finally proceeded on its voyage on 21 January, some nine days after leaving its original point of departure at Loch Ewe. With *Scharnhorst* out of the way, the Royal Navy did not provide a heavy distant covering force, but a cruiser screen consisting of HMS *Kent*, HMS *Bermuda* and HMS *Berwick*, under command of Vice Admiral Palliser, took up station to protect

JW56A and the following slower convoy JW56B, that sailed from Loch Ewe on 22 January. JW56B was made up of seventeen merchant vessels and a mixed close escort of five small ships, and had been allocated an ocean escort of six destroyers, demonstrating the increasing strength of the escort forces now being provided for the vital convoys to Russia. German intelligence reported the progress of these convoys and several U-boats were sent to form a line near Bear Island, from where they had the best chance of sighting the oncoming Allied ships, and forming a wolf pack for a concentrated attack. When JW56A was sighted on 25 January, a pack of nine U-boats converged on their prey and, during the course of the night, managed to sink two cargo ships, *Penelope Barker* and *Fort Bellingham,* with the loss of many seamen. The escorts had a busy time, chasing the many echoes they detected, and the destroyer *Obdurate* was hit and damaged but was able to carry on. Then, as dawn approached, a third and final freighter, the Liberty ship *Andrew G. Curtin*, was torpedoed and sunk.

These losses – and the confirmation that Doenitz had indeed built up his U-boat forces and was prepared to deploy them in a determined effort to cut the supply line that was feeding the Red Army's success – compelled Admiral Fraser to reinforce the escort of convoy JW56B. To arrange this, he halted the sailing of a return convoy, which action released the destroyers that had arrived in Kola with JW56A. They were swiftly despatched to the incoming JW56B and subsequently rendezvoused with the convoy on 29 January. They arrived just in time to meet a series of attacks by the fifteen U-boats in a wolf pack, sent by Doenitz, which had been led to the convoy by reconnaissance aircraft. On this occasion, the U-boats attacked both escorts and cargo ships in a furious attempt to sink as many vessels as possible, before they entered the relative safety of the Kola Inlet. One destroyer, HMS *Hardy,* suffered severe damage aft, when her stern was torpedoed, and had to be sunk by *Venus* after her surviving crew had been rescued. Thirty-five of her complement were killed as a result of the explosion. Despite all their efforts, the U-boats did not succeed in any attack upon the merchantmen and one U-boat, U-314, succumbed to a determined counter-attack by the escorts, HMS *Meteor* and HMS *Whitehall*. JW56B arrived at its destination on the morning of 1 February without any further loss, a vindication of the decision to reinforce its escort and a demonstration of the growing anti-submarine expertise of the Royal Navy. With the arrival and discharge in Russia of JW56B, a large number of merchant vessels were requiring passage and escort back to Scotland. With a similarly large number of escorts also ready to make the voyage, the decision was taken to run a single very large convoy, RA56, and this formation set sail on 3 February. After a relatively uneventful passage, which included the failure of a wolf pack to find this large target, thirty-seven merchantmen arrived safely at Loch Ewe eight days later.

On 20 February, *Jamaica* rejoined the Home Fleet at Scapa Flow having worked up after repairs at Rosyth, and prepared to join the cruiser screen that was allocated to the next loaded eastbound convoy, JW57. In planning the organisation of this convoy, Admiral Fraser carefully considered the latest changes in the tactical situation. Daylight hours were now opening up, and more Luftwaffe activity was anticipated in addition to the increasing menace of the U-boat packs. To counter these risks, Fraser decided, following the success of RA56, to make JW57 the largest convoy yet, and gave it an escort on a scale not seen before in this campaign, driven through the most inhospitable seagoing environment of the war. Working with the command at Western Approaches, the Commander-in-Chief Home Fleet obtained the services of not one but two support groups and an escort carrier, to get the convoy through and take the fight to the enemy. This was the clearest example yet of how the balance of naval power had shifted in the Atlantic, especially as shipping across that ocean was now an increasing priority, as the Western Allies prepared for the invasion of Europe. The date for this invasion, code named Operation *Overlord*, had been finally agreed between Churchill, Roosevelt and Stalin during their conference in Tehran at the end of November 1943. After much argument by the American and Russian delegates, who were insisting on the earliest possible landings, the date was moved from 1 May to 1 June, to the relief of the British architect of the Allied strategy in the West, General Brooke, the Chief of the Imperial General Staff. Brooke had wanted to delay the invasion because of the shipping position, the availability of landing craft and the time it would take to transfer divisions from Italy and then prepare them for amphibious assault. Once at the conference, however, Brooke realised that Stalin, despite his appeals for urgency in the execution of *Overlord*, seemed to be more relaxed about the Eastern Front, where the Red Army had taken the initiative. In his diary for 30 November 1943 he summed this up:

> After much argument we decided that the cross channel operation could be put off to June 1st. This did not meet all our requirements, but was arranged to fit in with proposed Russian spring offensive.[1]

The die was cast and so, during the time Admiral Fraser planned the resumption of the Arctic convoys, the destruction of the *Scharnhorst* and the larger convoy strategy, he and the Admiralty were increasingly aware that a growing proportion of the men and ships of the Home Fleet would be needed, from late spring, for participation in *Overlord*. In this context the sailing of large, heavily loaded convoys to Russia in the early months of 1944 can be seen as a sign of a strengthening commitment to Stalin and the Red Army. It was no coincidence that JW57 was accompanied by a large press corps.

JW57 sailed from Loch Ewe on 20 February with forty cargo ships and two tankers, escorted by six corvettes and the first of the support groups with four destroyers under the overall command of

Commander Tyson in *Keppel*. A second support group joined the next day, with two modern frigates, HMS *Byron* and HMS *Strule* and two old V and W class destroyers, HMS *Wanderer* and HMS *Watchman*. V and W class ships had given sterling service in both world wars, and the early experiences of the Battle of the Atlantic had resulted in the conversion of a number of these vessels to the role of Long Range Escort. Both *Wanderer* and *Watchman* were two such ships, in which parts of their machinery spaces and other internal compartments had been refitted as fuel tanks, providing sufficient endurance for escort through the air gap.

As the convoy headed for Bear Island, it was joined by the ocean escort, commanded by Vice Admiral Glennie, who flew his flag in HMS *Black Prince*, an anti-aircraft cruiser. As Fraser had stipulated, the escort carrier HMS *Chaser*, with Fairey Swordfish and Grumman Wildcat aircraft embarked, also joined, accompanied by a large destroyer force of some fourteen experienced and familiar Arctic run ships, commanded by Captain Campbell in HMS *Milne*. To complete the convoy's protection, Vice Admiral Palliser was at sea with three cruisers, *Berwick*, *Jamaica* and the Polish *Orp Dragon* providing a distant screen. Palliser's flagship, *Berwick* was a Kent class heavy cruiser with eight 8-inch guns and reinforced armour that had been added when this class was reconstructed between 1936 and 1938. *Orp Dragon*, on her first deployment since being taken over by the Polish Navy in exile only five weeks before, was equipped with five single-mounted 6-inch guns, and manned entirely by Polish sailors. Although there were Polish destroyers sailing with the Royal Navy, *Orp Dragon* was the only cruiser that operated in this manner, mainly due to the heavy lobbying of the Polish government in exile in London. Prior to the transfer, the ship, originally named HMS *Dragon*, was one of the First World War-built 'D' class light cruisers, having been commissioned in August 1918. As far as Palliser's cruisers were concerned, the passage of JW57 was completed without the need to call on their services, but meticulous research by Richard Woodman has detailed the actions that took place between the waiting U-boats and the convoy's escort. Two wolf packs were deployed and first blood was drawn by *Keppel*, which sank U-713 on 24 January, after one of the *Chaser*'s Swordfish had spotted it by radar. On 25 January, another U-boat, U-601, succumbed to an attack by a long-range Catalina aircraft, but the destroyer HMS *Mahratta* was torpedoed and sunk by U-990 with the loss of most of its crew. This tragic incident demonstrated that the U-boats were keen to knock out the escorting warships before plundering the merchant vessels, using acoustic torpedoes that were particularly attracted to the fast rotating screws of destroyers, rather than the slower paced turns of the merchant ship propellers. The German submarines were also using the schnorkel, a device that allowed them to use their faster diesel engines while submerged, albeit at a shallow depth, during the short hours of daylight. This technological innovation kept them out of sight of surface ships while maintaining touch with their intended prey. Woodman's analysis also showed the tension that existed between the escort commanders of the destroyers drawn from western approaches and Admiral Glennie's tactics. Their disquiet, but never disobedience, turned on the Admiral's deployment of the destroyers at night and of the failure to pursue U-990 after the loss of the *Mahratta*. In Woodman's words (Whinney was the commanding officer of *Wanderer*):

> Loyally assuming that 'the Admiral knows more than we do', Whinney suppressed his own and his officers' misgivings. The escorts blooded in the long struggle in the Atlantic considered their own expertise somewhat condescendingly received by the newer 'crack' destroyers of the Home Fleet.[2]

Although such disagreements were to be regretted, the passage of JW57 demonstrated the differences in doctrine and tactics that had been ground out through hard experience in two different operating environments. The arrival of carrier-borne aircraft had been a success, although conditions in an open cockpit of a Swordfish flying in these high latitudes can barely be imagined, and the U-boats' chances of avoiding detection had been seriously diminished. As far as the Russians were concerned, the valuable cargoes carried in JW57 had got through and the journalists had a propaganda field day. *Jamaica* had, in the meanwhile, returned to Scapa Flow with her squadron, and her covering services were not required for the return convoy RA57, which left the Kola Inlet on 2 March. For two days, the convoy and its large escort endured savage Arctic weather, which meant that *Chaser* could not fly off any of its aircraft, nor could the wolf packs attack. As soon as the weather eased, however, a combination of Swordfish and destroyer detected, attacked and sank U-472, although one of the empty merchant ships, *Empire Tourist*, was later torpedoed and sunk. Over the next four days the airmen of both sides played a remarkable role in reconnaissance, during weather that was hardly ideal for flying and, on the Allied side, extremely risky for operating aircraft on a rolling, pitching and frozen flight deck. The Luftwaffe kept the U-boats in the hunt but to no avail, as the Swordfish sank two of their number before the convoy steamed out of range and into Loch Ewe on 10 March.

With the approach of Arctic summer, the last outward-bound convoy of the season, JW58, was planned to ship to Russia the remaining amount of supplies that had been promised to the USSR, before this traffic was suspended and attention centred on the Home Fleet's commitment to Operation *Neptune*, the naval component of *Overlord*. There was also another consideration. From mid-January the Admiralty had continued to receive intelligence that the *Tirpitz* had recovered from the damage inflicted by the X-craft, and that by mid-March she would be in a position to threaten the Arctic convoys. The response was dramatic and twofold. Firstly, the ocean escort to JW58 was increased by the attachment of two escort carriers, HMS *Tracker* and HMS *Activity*, and two support groups from western approaches, as in the preceding convoy. Significantly, one of the latter was commanded by Captain 'Johnnie' Walker in HMS *Starling*, the Royal Navy's most effective anti-submarine commander, who had been responsible for the development of the hunting group tactics that had underwritten the navy's seizing of the initiative in the Atlantic. Secondly, large covering forces were assembled, the first to act, in the routine manner, as a distant covering screen in case the *Tirpitz* came out. The second was a force put together to carry out Operation *Tungsten*, the bombing of the *Tirpitz* in her anchorage at Altenfjord by aircraft of the Fleet Air Arm. The first covering force was commanded by Admiral Fraser in *Duke of York*, accompanied by three cruisers and the usual destroyers and its task was, in effect, to cover both the convoy and the ships dedicated to the carrying out of *Tungsten*. Assembled as a second force, with its primary task to deliver *Tungsten*, was *Anson*, commanded by Fraser's deputy, Vice Admiral Moore, along with the fleet carriers HMS *Furious* and HMS *Victorious*, and the escort carriers HMS *Emperor*, HMS *Fencer*, HMS *Pursuer* and HMS *Searcher*. The cruisers in Moore's force were *Belfast*, *Jamaica*, *Royalist* and *Sheffield*, with another screen of escorting destroyers. HMS *Royalist* was a sister ship of *Black Prince* and had only been in service for six months. She was of the modified Dido class, the modifications that were carried out arising from the seagoing experience of the first batch of the original Didos. To improve stability, the third forward superimposed turret, Q, was not fitted and, in its place, a smaller multiple anti-aircraft mounting was built. This saved weight and permitted the bridge superstructure to be moved forward and the two funnels straightened, making a distinctive silhouette when compared the earlier ships of the class. The opportunity was also taken to rearrange some of the internal compartments of the converted sub-class, so that they were all fitted out as flagships, the *Royalist* being flagship to Moore's carrier group for *Tungsten*.³ Originally, the bombing attack on *Tirpitz* was supposed to be a task for Bomber Command, but objections were raised by the Royal Air Force, which considered that Altenfjord was out of effective range of heavy bombers operating from their airfields in the United Kingdom. Other factors that were thought problematical included the unreliable weather, the strength of the numerous anti-aircraft defences on board *Tirpitz*, and the medium and light flak sited around the edges of the fjords, (*Tirpitz* was actually anchored in Kaa Fjord, an adjunct of the larger Altenfjord) that enclosed her on three sides.

Returning to the convoy JW58, it sailed from Loch Ewe on 27 March and was made up of fifty merchant vessels – with the large escort mentioned above. In addition to cargo and escort, the American cruiser *Milwaukee* joined the convoy for delivery to the Russian Navy, as part of a deal arising from the surrender of Italy six months previously. Another part of this arrangement was the subsequent transfer of the British battleship *Royal Sovereign* to the USSR. Both transfers were made by way of compensation to the USSR for not directly receiving any of the surviving warships of the Italian Navy. The passage of JW58 was another success for the Allied ships, despite the attention, after three days out, of a substantial number of Luftwaffe reconnaissance aircraft and the deployment of three large wolf packs across the predicted track of the convoy. The legendary Captain Walker struck first on 29 March when *Starling* detected, attacked and sank U961, which was not part of the wolf packs – it was too far to the west – but was on its way out into the Atlantic. When, on the following day, the first contact was made by overflying German aircraft, the convoy's strengthened air defence went into action. Between 30 March and 2 April, the escort carriers' fighters shot down five of the intruders, but this splendid effort did not prevent the first of the wolf packs from attacking on the night of 1 April.

More than fifteen U-boats attacked the convoy over the following forty-eight hours, and failed to sink a single ship. Instead they were hunted down by aircraft and escorts and three were sunk before the fully intact convoy made safe entry into the Kola Inlet on 4 April. The dramatic success of JW58 led to Luftwaffe command desisting from flying reconnaissance over the return convoy RA58, which departed Kola on 7 April with thirty-six merchant ships, escorted by the warships that had safely brought in JW58. The Luftwaffe's decision was made despite repeated urgent requests from Doenitz for more air support, and the result, rather more predictable than in the early days of the Russian convoys, was another casualty-free passage back to Loch Ewe, where RA58 arrived on 14 April. To complete this convoy season, the Admiralty rounded up all of the remaining merchant ships in Kola and provided another very large set of escorting vessels, with two escort carriers and no less than three support groups. RA59 departed Kola on 28 April and was immediately detected and attacked by waiting U-boats. One Liberty ship, *William S. Thayer*, was sunk with heavy loss of life, but the convoy escort and support groups sank three U-boats before the convoy slipped out of contact with its hunters.

Returning to the passage of JW58, and while this convoy was about twenty-four hours short of Kola Inlet, in the early hours of 3 April, Vice Admiral's Moore's task force reached the launching point for the bombing of *Tirpitz*, with the carriers turned into the wind about 120 miles from Altenfjord. The plan was that the bombers, which were Fairey Barracudas, primarily designed to carry torpedoes and which were, in effect, the monoplane replacement for the still in service Swordfish biplane, were to be launched from the two larger fleet carriers, *Furious* and *Victorious*. The fighter aircraft, consisting of American-built Hellcats, Corsairs and Wildcats, with a small number of British Seafires, were launched from the escort carriers. The fighters were deployed to provide escort and fire suppression cover for the attack, and to carry out what today would be termed Combat Air Patrol, CAP, over the task force. This was necessary as Moore's ships had limited manoeuvrability when flying off and recovering aircraft, and they were, after all, operating well within the range of enemy aircraft based on the German-controlled airfields of northern Norway. One of the more notable features of Operation *Tungsten* was the time given for the thorough preparation and training of the Barracuda bomber crews. The decision to prepare *Tungsten* had been made in December 1943, when Moore had been selected to command the attack, and it was expected that the raid would be carried out in the first half of March 1944. For training purposes, the Royal Navy had a mock-up of the *Tirpitz*, built in a loch in Scotland, the position of which was accurately defined through the use of images taken from a serious amount of photo-reconnaissance. This attention to detail, and the fact that the Barracudas were able to practise their bomb runs for at least a month before the anticipated date of the operation, gave the aircrews confidence in the operational plan. *Victorious*, however, overran the completion time of a refit and more time was therefore needed to give her aircrew the vital training required to execute this difficult attack. The postponement ensured that their training needs were met and the date of the attack was reset to 3 April. It was this readjustment that gave Admiral Fraser the opportunity to provide such heavy cover for the convoys JW58 and RA58. Quite frankly, the Commander-in-Chief had never had so many of his ships at sea 'together', another striking example of the dividends reaped from success in the Atlantic and emergency war ship building on both sides of the ocean.

The Fairey Barracudas, although primarily a torpedo bomber, were employed as dive bombers for *Tungsten*, as their torpedoes would have been stopped by the multi-layered heavy wire net defences protecting *Tirpitz*. Ten of the Barracudas had been specially adapted to carry the heaviest bombs that could be deployed on this raid, armour piercing weapons weighing 1,600lbs, which had to be dropped from a height of 3,500 feet for maximum effect. The remainder carried a mix of 500lb and 600lb bombs in various configurations of high explosive, armour and semi armour piercing capability, with a small number carrying bombs designed to produce a strong underwater blast alongside the target. These weapons had to be delivered from 2,000 feet. As both dropping heights were well within the range of *Tirpitz*'s formidable array of multi-calibre anti-aircraft batteries, the suppression role of the accompanying fighters was absolutely vital for success.

The bombers took off from their carriers in two waves, the first taking to the air at 0437, followed by the second strike force forty-eight minutes later, at 0525. All aircraft took off successfully, and the combined strength of the two equally sized waves was forty-two Barracudas and eighty fighters. The fact that the carriers were operating in complete darkness, in Arctic conditions, and undertaking an unprecedented action, made it all the more remarkable that every single aircraft designated for the raid was launched successfully. The courageous airmen who were about to attack the *Tirpitz* had been wonderfully supported by the engineers, mechanics, fitters and flight deck crews who had maintained their aircraft and warmed their engines, before setting them on the icy deck ready to fly. Before crossing the Norwegian coast, the first wave ascended to 10,000 feet and commenced their attack after dropping over the mountains, at 0528, fifty-one minutes after take-off. They achieved a good deal of surprise because, although *Tirpitz* had one anchor raised in preparation for undergoing trials, she was not yet closed up for sailing, and seems to have had insufficient warning to activate the heavy smokescreen which was her primary defence against low level bombing. The fighters swooped down and attacked the target's anti-aircraft armament, inflicting casualties among the German gunners and reducing the volume of fire that now sought to reach the diving Barracudas. The attacking bombers approached from either side of the *Tirpitz*, dividing her fire and adding further confusion to a commander and crew that had hardly any time to respond. In less than a minute, *Tirpitz* was struck by three of the 1,600lb heavy bombs, four of the 500lb and a single 600lb bomb detonated alongside, sending a severe shockwave that damaged the hull underwater. These hits, which caused some structural damage and set off fires in several compartments, were achieved for the loss of one Barracuda aircraft. As *Tirpitz's* crew dealt with casualties, damage and fire, the smokescreen, which had not fully developed at the time of the arrival of the first wave of aircraft, began to produce a thick, heavy cloud that shrouded the ship. When the second wave struck, at 0636, it was the aircraft that were more protected by this screen, as the anti-aircraft gunners struggled to sight their airborne foe. Once more, bombing success was achieved as the *Tirpitz* was hit another five times, including once by a 1,600lb weapon that failed to detonate. As in the first strike, the cost to the attackers was comparatively slight as one Barracuda and her crew were lost, but one of the fighters ditched when it had to abort its landing when returning to one of the carriers.[4]

In terms of execution, the Fleet Air Arm produced a model attack that delivered in excess of 20 tons of explosive onto a difficult and well-protected target, at minimal cost in lives and materiel. As the Royal Navy knew from bitter experience, however, German capital ships and especially the *Bismarck* and *Tirpitz*, were very heavily armoured and had a level of internal watertight subdivision that British ships, required to serve all over the globe, could only envy. Vice Admiral Moore, on receiving the news that the ship had been hit and damaged, but not crippled or sunk, wanted the aircraft in his task force to go back and strike again. It was also realised that the Luftwaffe had not intervened with the two waves of bombers and their escorts, and this was interpreted as meaning there was either a paucity of enemy air resources in northern Norway, or that the co-operation between local air and sea commands was far from efficient. The idea of an immediate second attack was soon dismissed, however, because the weather worsened at sea and both aircrew and aircraft needed time to recover from their strenuous exertions, and so the task force returned to Scapa Flow on 6 April. For *Jamaica*, this had been her first experience of operating with a carrier task force and Nobby witnessed first-hand how aircraft carriers were deployed, manoeuvred and protected when mounting a major air operation. Little did he realise, at this time, that his last wartime seagoing appointment, in the following year, would be in one of the Royal Navy's latest light fleet carriers. With the task force back at base, it was determined that another strike on *Tirpitz* was needed to complete the task. Behind this decision, however, lay a high-level disagreement between Admiral Cunningham, First Sea Lord, and Admiral Fraser, Commander-in-Chief Home Fleet. The official Royal Naval historian of the war, Stephen Roskill, later summed up the situation thus:

> Cunningham's whole instinct always was that once an enemy had been damaged a second blow should be struck as quickly as possible, before he had been allowed time to recover from the first; and on Fraser's return to Scapa he accordingly pressed him to repeat the attack as soon as possible. Cunningham's diary recounts what followed: '13 April 1944. I called up Bruce Fraser about repeat "Tungsten" and found him in a most truculent and obstinate mood. He had held a meeting with his admirals and captains and made the decision that "Tungsten" was not to be repeated. I reasoned with him and pointed out that Cs-in-Cs' decisions were not irrevocable and that the Admiralty must be allowed some voice in what operations were to be carried out.'[5]

This dispute carried on for two days after which the matter was settled, not unexpectedly, in the First Sea Lord's favour, and Vice

Admiral Moore set off on 21 April to repeat the attack on *Tirpitz*. On this occasion, however, the weather prevented an attack on Altenfjord, and the task force found and destroyed a German convoy at sea off Bodo, losing three aircraft in the process. Further raids on *Tirpitz* were carried out by the Fleet Air Arm in July and August, after it was discovered that she had been repaired in Norway and was exercising in local waters with a flotilla of destroyers, re-establishing the very real threat of the 'fleet in being', just in time for the resumption of the Russian convoys in August. By then it was clear that carrier-borne aircraft could not carry sufficient weight of munitions to hit *Tirpitz* with a mortal blow, and so the task was passed to Bomber Command and the previously reluctant Air Chief Marshal Harris. In his memoirs, Harris recalled this order and the subsequent actions taken by his heavy bomber force, but not before he made his feelings clear on the supremacy of aircraft over battleships:

> During all this period the Admiralty continued to worry about the German navy and, in particular, in the autumn of 1944, about the *Tirpitz*; our own battleships with their usual large complement of ancillary craft, were kept hanging about at home in case the Germans should decide to send the poor old lone *Tirpitz* to sea, and it was felt that some use might be found for these large units of the Royal navy in the Pacific. I was accordingly asked to intervene in this fantastic 'war' between these dinosaurs which both sides had just managed, at great expense and after vast argument, to preserve from their long overdue extinction. I was quite willing to do so, but only if this did not seriously interfere with more important operations; I gave an undertaking that we should sink the *Tirpitz* in our spare time.[6]

To be fair to the head of Bomber Command, Harris more than kept his promise, as he arranged for No. 617 (of Dambuster fame) and No. 9 squadrons to be sent to airfields in Russia where they were loaded with 12,000lb bombs and ordered to attack *Tirpitz* on their way back to their usual bases in Lincolnshire. Twenty-eight Lancasters carried out this attack on 15 September, and poor visibility resulted in one hit, on the bow, and two near misses. The weight of the forward hit caused severe damage, and *Tirpitz* was moved to Tromso, where Doenitz intended to employ her as a floating coastal battery. Even though this development appeared to permanently remove the threat of the 'fleet in being', the Admiralty pressed Harris to have another go. Using the same squadrons, the Royal Air Force attacked twice more, the first attempt thwarted, yet again, by the weather, but on 15 November 1944 the Lancasters achieved two direct hits and numerous near misses that caused the *Tirpitz* to capsize, with the loss of more than 900 of her crew.

The resumption of Russian convoys in August, following the return of the ships of the Home Fleet that had taken part in Operation *Neptune*, saw a continuation of the transformation of this campaign. The worst danger faced by the convoys was the weather, and the winter of 1944/45 provided some of the worst conditions experienced at sea throughout the entire war. This most brutal of campaigns, which pitted men and machine against the wildest forces of nature, was, in the end, a triumph for the Allied navies and the merchant ships that sailed these treacherous waters. The final statistics clearly demonstrate the strength of this victory over element and foe, but they give no indication of the human effort and suffering involved. Between December 1942 and May 1945 there were sixteen outward Arctic convoys and, after the early disasters, losses of cargo in the years 1943, 1944 and 1945 amounted to only 20,000 tons out of a laden total of 2.35 million tons, an astonishing achievement and significant contribution to the war effort of the USSR.

After *Tungsten*, *Jamaica* rejoined her squadron at Scapa Flow and spent the whole of May carrying out exercises and training in preparation for duties with Operation *Neptune*. Included in the exercises were the practice of shore bombardment in which Nobby, as gun layer, had a key role – without much by the way of previous experience. When D-Day came, however, *Jamaica* was assigned to patrol duties in the North West Approaches, to guard against any German naval encroachment from that direction. The Home Fleet, in effect, put up a blockade, supported by a huge minelaying operation undertaken by Bomber Command, to protect the 6,000 ships that Admiral Ramsay deployed to carry out and sustain the invasion. German U-boats and E-boats attempted to break through, making the very occasional attack, but the air superiority and comprehensive naval supremacy of the Allies fully protected the invasion fleet and the armies it carried into Normandy. The protective barrier was completed by the anti-submarine aircraft of Coastal Command, which searched for and sank many of the U-boats that were approaching the Channel from the Bay of Biscay. After nearly five years at war, Allied resources, co-operation and the skills gained through bitter experience had combined to bring about success in what was the largest amphibious invasion in history. With the invasion forces firmly established ashore, many of the ships in *Neptune* were dispersed, and *Jamaica* went back to Scapa Flow in the middle of June.

On 16 June, she sailed to Spitsbergen with supplies for the garrison based there, and repeated the exercise before she joined Operation *Mascot* on 14 July. This operation was one of the aforementioned series of Fleet Air Arm attacks on *Tirpitz*, following her repairs after the partial success of Operation *Tungsten*. By this time, Admiral Moore had taken over as Commander-in-Chief Home Fleet, after Fraser had been appointed to command in the Pacific, where the Royal Navy was seeking to establish itself in the climax of the Japanese war. Sailing in his flagship, *Duke of York*, Moore led a task force that consisted of the carriers *Formidable*, *Furious* and the new HMS *Indefatigable*, with cruisers HMS *Bellona*, *Kent* and *Jamaica*, and the usual complement of screening destroyers. Adopting a similar plan to *Tungsten*, the striking aircraft took off on 17 July and proceeded to the target, where they found that the Germans had early warning, and they were faced with a tremendous anti-aircraft barrage and heavy smokescreen. Losing two aircraft and failing to inflict any serious damage, the first wave returned to the carriers. In the meanwhile, the arrival of fog at sea had resulted in the termination of the planned second wave, and the ships and aircraft of Operation *Mascot* returned to Scapa Flow.

Jamaica resumed Arctic convoy duties with convoy JW59, the first to sail after *Overlord* and the summer break, leaving her anchorage on 17 August. No longer needed as part of a distant covering force, *Jamaica* joined the escorts within the convoy, where she acted a Guard Ship for the two escort carriers, HMS *Striker* and HMS *Vindex*. In another development reflecting the changed strategic and tactical situation, Rear Admiral Dalrymple-Hamilton flew his flag in *Vindex*, signifying the importance of the Fleet Air Arm in convoy protection by this stage of the war. The Admiral's other escorting forces were formidable, as JW59 had a close escort of eight – a flotilla of four Arctic veteran destroyers and an ocean support group. Finally, there was a small group of destroyers on their way to be handed over to the Russian Navy, who accompanied HMS *Royal Sovereign*, an old 'R' class battleship that was also going to the Russians (as part of the Italy deal), now renamed *Archangelsk*. The escorts took on the U-boats that attempted to intercept the convoy and many were driven off and two were sunk, although the convoy lost the frigate HMS *Kite* to a torpedo, and she went down with nearly all hands. The same escorts brought back the return convoy RA5, which departed Kola on 28 August and had a relatively peaceful passage to Scotland, interrupted only by four of the destroyers hunting down and sinking U-394 on 2 September, before safely completing the voyage at Loch Ewe on 6 September. This was *Jamaica*'s final Russian convoy but before she went in for a long refit in Portsmouth, she completed another supply run to the garrison at Spitzbergen in mid-September, the voyage marking the last time that Nobby experienced the freezing and volatile conditions of the north. On return from Spitsbergen, *Jamaica* entered Portsmouth Dockyard and commenced the refit, during the course of which X turret – the marines' turret – was removed. In its place two sets of 2-pdr pom-poms were installed, and she was fitted with the latest anti-aircraft radar, thus seriously improving her overall AA capability.[7] *Jamaica's* refit lasted until May 1945 when, following a series of successful sea trials, she accompanied the Royal Family to the Channel Islands, to mark their liberation. *Jamaica* was then despatched to join the East Indies fleet in Colombo, Ceylon (now Sri Lanka), where she arrived in October 1945, two months after the cessation of hostilities with Japan.

Sergeant Nobby Elliott left *Jamaica* on 26 November 1944 while she was undergoing her refit in Portsmouth, and had Christmas at home with Rose and their young family. It would not be long, however, before he received orders for another seagoing commission; as a 'blue water' marine it was only to be expected, even though he had already spent nearly four and a half years at sea. Nobby's gunnery skills and experience as a senior NCO were at a premium, and at a time when Britain's Armed Forces faced a severe manpower shortage, there would be no shore billet now. Since joining *Jamaica* in October 1942, Nobby and his shipmates had been involved in Operation *Torch*, eight outward- and five homeward-bound Arctic convoys, the sinking of the *Scharnhorst* and two Fleet Air Arm strikes on *Tirpitz*. The contrast between anti-aircraft action in the clear blue weather of the Mediterranean and 6-inch gunnery in the frozen wastes of the Arctic could not have been more dramatic, but the constant companion of fear and death remained every time the guns went into action. A different type of ship and a new ocean now awaited the thirty-three-year-old Royal Marine Sergeant gun layer from Devonport.

IO

MANPOWER, PACIFIC
AND VICTORY

Before moving on to Nobby's final wartime appointment, it is necessary to consider the effect of Britain's declining manpower situation and the arguments that surrounded the question of the employment of the Royal Navy in the war against Japan. With the success of Operation *Neptune*, the establishment of Western Allied Armies in France, and the increasingly safe passage of convoys across the Atlantic and Arctic Oceans, the Royal Navy looked for new employment, with participation in the Pacific seemingly being the most promising answer. In both contexts, manpower and Pacific operations, the future of the Royal Marines was, again, brought into question.

To set the background for these two important factors, it was as early as July 1944 that units in General Montgomery's 21st Army Group were suffering replacement shortages, not helped by the attrition of front-line infantry units in the Battle of Normandy. This reduction had been foreseen; it was certainly not unexpected – but Churchill and Montgomery were struggling with the fact that the United Kingdom was, by then, a junior partner in the war compared to the United States of America. This was an unavoidable fact given the scale of the ever-expanding forces and materiel supplied by the industrial

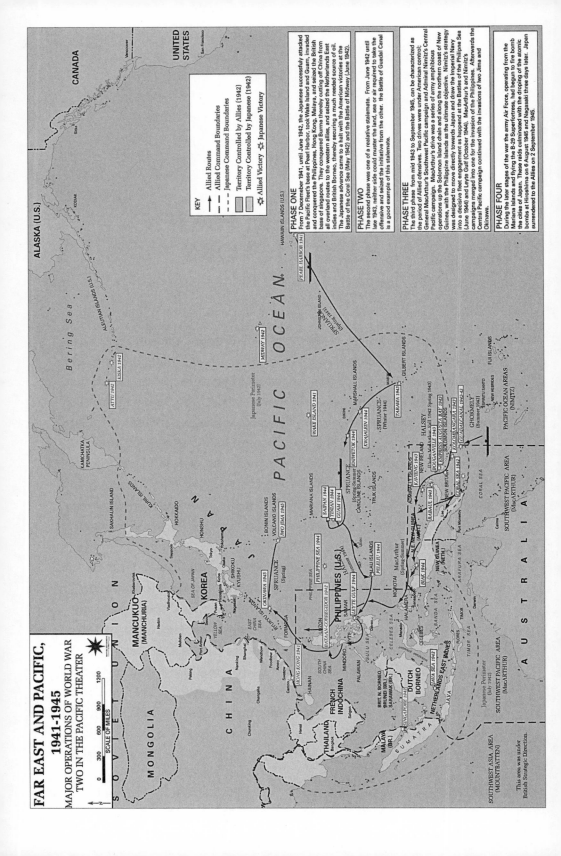

FAR EAST AND PACIFIC, 1941-1945

MAJOR OPERATIONS OF WORLD WAR TWO IN THE PACIFIC THEATER

SCALE OF MILES
0   300   600   900   1200

KEY
→ Allied Routes
--- Allied Command Boundaries
- - - Japanese Command Boundaries
Territory Controlled by Allies (1942)
Territory Controlled by Japanese (1942)
☆ Allied Victory   ☆ Japanese Victory

PHASE ONE

From 7 December 1941, until June 1942, the Japanese successfully attacked the Pacific Fleet's base at Pearl Harbor, took Wake Island and Guam, invaded and conquered the Philippines, Hong Kong, Malaya, and seized the British base of singapore. They conquered Burma thereby cutting off China from all overland routes to the western allies, and seized the Netherlands East indies and British Borneo, thereby securing a much needed source of oil. The Japanese advance came to a halt with the American victories at the Battle of the Coral Sea (May 1942) and the Battle of Midway (June 1942).

PHASE TWO

The second phase was one of a relative stalemate. From June 1942 until late 1943, neither side could muster the land, sea or air required to take the offensive and seized the initiative from the other. the Battle of Guadal Canal is a good example of this stalemate.

PHASE THREE

The third phase from mid 1943 to September 1945, can be characterized as the period of Allied offensives. Two drives were under American control: General MacArthur's Southwest Pacific campaign and Admiral Nimitz's Central Pacific campaign. MacArthur's drive was a series of army amphibious operations up the Solomon Island chain and along the northern coast of New Guinea, with the Philippine Islands as the ultimate objective. Nimitz's strategy was designed to move directly towards Japan and draw the Imperial Navy into a decisive fleet engagement as happend at the Battles of the Philippne Sea (June 1944) and Leyte Gulf (October 1944). MacArthur's and Nimitz's campaigns merged into one for the invasion of the Philippines. Afterwards the Central Pacific campaign continued with the invasions of Iwo Jima and Okinawa.

PHASE FOUR

During the later stages of the war the army Air Force, operating from the Mariana islands and flying the B-29 Superfortress, had begun to fire bomb the cities of Japan. These raids culminated with the dropping of the atomic bombs at Hiroshima on 6 August 1945 and Nagasaki three days later. Japan surrendered to the Allies on 2 September 1945.

This area was under British Strategic Direction.

might of the US. Montgomery's attitude was displayed in his plan for Operation *Market Garden*, a huge airborne invasion (*A Bridge Too Far*) that was designed to secure several key road and rail bridges in the Netherlands. Success would have taken the British Army over the Rhine and round to the Ruhr, destroying Germany's main manufacturing centre. This was unlike any plan that Montgomery had devised before, and was certainly bold, with an added British interest that success would have driven Hitler's V-weapons out of range of the UK. Eisenhower accepted the risk and supported the operation on the grounds that it would take the Allies closer to Germany.

The failure of *Market Garden* on 26 September 1944 meant that the war in Europe could not be finished before 1945, and exacerbated the manpower difficulties that Montgomery's armies faced. Churchill had concerns about the future of the British Empire, especially India, and the diminished influence in the world that Britain, in the wake of financial weakness, would experience, despite victory over Nazism and Japanese domination.

What seemed to bring the manpower question to a head with Churchill was the proposed move to the training reserve of the army's 50th Division, which Montgomery announced to its senior officers at the beginning of November 1944. This was, to all intents and purposes, disbandment, with long war service men repatriated, and the remainder sent to other units in north-west Europe, the fittest joining infantry battalions as replacements. Churchill's response to this development, which was the latest in a string of similar announcements, was swift and aggressive. On 3 December he issued a personal minute to the ministerial heads of the three armed services, Alexander, Grigg and Sinclair, and with a note to ensure that the Minister of Labour, Bevin, was to be kept informed of these proceedings. The Prime Minister's minute was topped by a sticker 'REPORT IN THREE DAYS', and underneath this demand Churchill let fly:

I am much distressed by the impending cannibalisation of the 50th Division. We cannot afford at this stage to reduce our stake in the western line of battle. We must examine all possibilities open to us. For instance, there are nearly 80,000 Royal Marines. These are no doubt needed as far as ships marked for the East are concerned, but they are not needed in anything like their present strength in vessels in non-Japanese-infected waters. The Admiralty should furnish a paper showing the exact location of all Marines, what ships they are in, what theatres these ships are marked for, how many Marines are ashore, how many are in the Training Establishments etc. I should expect at least 10,000 men to be found from this quarter alone.[1]

It is self-evident from the Prime Minister's note that he regarded the employment of Royal Marines as being mainly confined to service in ship's detachments. No mention is made of the role of the Royal Marine Commandos, who were employed in what was an essentially infantry capacity but, to be fair, they were not of a significant number. It was not just in the Royal Marines that Churchill probed for the additional front line soldiers that the Army required. In this minute he went on to ask the Admiralty for recruitment and training figures for the Royal Navy, as he considered that 5,000 of these recruits, including a good proportion of their instructors, could be sent to the Army. Neither did the Royal Air Force escape the attention of the Prime Minister, although he did recognise 'that the Air are more closely engaged than the Navy at the present time', but this did not stop him for asking for more troops from the RAF Regiment to be moved over to the Army. Churchill's final plea was for a review of the Army's own establishment, concentrating on the various staffs and training units that had grown exponentially since the beginning of the war. His desire was that the able-bodied in these roles be replaced by older men and by those recovering from wounds, and he made his reasoning in characteristically blunt and clear terms:

> It is a painful reflection that probably not one in 4–5 men who wear the King's uniform ever hear a bullet whistle, or are likely to hear one. The vast majority run no more risk than the civil population in the south of England. It is my unpleasant duty to dwell on these facts. One set of men are sent back again and again to the front, while the great majority are kept out of all fighting to their regret.[2]

This was a theme that the Prime Minister warmed to throughout the war, chiding the Chiefs of Staffs as to the proportion of administrative and support servicemen to those in the firing line. Churchill's comments about the same men being used at the front time after time, was particularly relevant to the 50th Division, which had fought with the BEF in France, then the western desert, Sicily and Italy before being repatriated for training for *Overlord*. Landing on Gold Beach on D-Day, the Division fought through the Battle of Normandy before taking part in *Market Garden* as part of the ground relief force in XXX Corps. Montgomery, who had witnessed a mutiny within the Division when some of the troops thought they had been deceived into landing at Salerno, was well aware that it had become tired, hardly surprising given the amount of active service seen by its brigades and battalions. Churchill's chiding did not stop with the Army, for another of his *bêtes noires* was the failure of the Fleet Air Arm to justify its increasing resources of ships and men in the middle months of 1943. In one minute to Alexander, the

First Lord of the Admiralty, the Prime Minister expressed his frustration by writing that it was

> ...a rather pregnant fact that it had lost only thirty killed out of a strength of 45,000 in the three months ending 30th April 1943.[3]

Wise heads prevailed at the Admiralty and the First Lord did not take this bait, as the time was swiftly approaching when escort carriers made a more than sound return on the country's investment, helping to tip the balance in the Battle of the Atlantic. It is also possible to detect the seeds of Operation *Tungsten* here, which demonstrated the capability of the new, large, fleet carriers operating with their escort counterparts.

Churchill's request for a report in three days on the question of what he regarded as surplus Royal Marine manpower, elicited a detailed reply. On 5 December, the Commandant General, Royal Marines, Major-General Sir Thomas Hunton, wrote to the First Lord of the Admiralty, Alexander, with a table giving a breakdown on the employment of members of his Corps, and headed by the following remarks:

> The present effective strength of the Corps is 67,655 (*Author's note: Not the 80,000 claimed by Churchill*). It is assumed that 12,000 will be lost on re-allocation during the 12 months following the defeat of GERMANY, leaving 55,655 available. The Corps' commitments for the war against JAPAN require 59,842. Thus the Royal Marines will be short by approximately 4,000 men.[4]

What is interesting about the original document is that the figures giving the present strength, the remainder after the defeat of Germany and the commitment for Japan, are all pencilled amendments to the original, typed numbers. In the first case, the effective strength has been increased, as the result of this amendment from 64,791 the post victory figure increased by 2,864 and the Japan figure increased by 2,887. While these figures may or may not be of significance, the short time available to produce this report, and the speed of the staff work involved, is evidenced by the last minute amendments, and is a reminder of the pressure Churchill maintained on his advisers. What is more significant is Churchill's assumption of 80,000 apparently being reduced, at the head of the report to 67,655. Further reading of Major-General Hunton's remarks offers an explanation as he excluded 6,700 Royal Marine Engineers, on the grounds that they were tradesmen and therefore unsuitable for transfer to the infantry. Hunton also exempted from the total the 6,841 Royal Marines employed by the Royal Navy, in naval establishments and naval air stations, presumably on guard and security duty. The reasoning behind this exemption was that Hunter considered that the feasibility of lowering these numbers was the responsibility of the naval staff, and not the Commandant General Royal Marines (CGRM). Hunton's exemptions totalled 13,541, so Churchill's overall estimate of 80,000 was quite accurate, and perhaps the CGRM's conclusion of a shortage of '4,000 men' should be read as a point for negotiation rather than fact. Hunton's breakdown of the employment of the Corps provides excellent evidence as to how the Royal Marines had diversified and expanded from the 13,000 regulars and reservists that existed in 1938. Here is a summary of the report's figures, covering the most significant commitments:

Minor Landing Craft and Support Craft	13875
Headquarter Divisions and Depots	10519
Fleet – serving as shipboard detachments and including bands	7838
Special Service Group (RM Commandos and 30 Assault Unit)	6926

Duty in RN Establishments and Air Stations	7084
Training Groups (Royal Marines in training)	6799
Serving with Allied Naval Commander Expeditionary Force	4023
(Earmarked for reduction before the end of the war with Germany)	

There were approximately a further 10,000 Royal Marines accounted for in Hunton's report, undertaking a variety of tasks including a siege regiment in Dover, garrisons and miscellaneous base and guarding duties.[5] The figure that stands out most prominently in this summary is the number of Royal Marines serving in landing craft and support craft roles, nearly double those serving at sea in the Corps' most traditional occupation, and a complete reversal of the situation at the outbreak of war in 1939. With the invasions of Sicily, Italy and Normandy, and various smaller scale landings in South East Asia, amphibious operations had become a vital means of attacking enemies on their own ground. After Normandy, British strategy looked to South East Asia and the Pacific, where amphibious capability was a pre-requisite in any strategy to remove the Japanese from their conquests, and eventually attack their homeland. In their traditional role, the number of marines serving at sea had hardly increased since 1939, because most of the ships built for the navy in the intervening period were smaller escort types, such as corvettes, destroyers, frigates and sloops, with no room or reason for a marine detachment on board. At this point, it is worth reiterating that no new battleships or fleet aircraft carriers had been completed since 1942, and no cruisers were built after 1941. The numbers of marines serving in headquarters and establishments (not including those under the direct control of the Royal Navy, as argued by Hunton) amounted to 9,217, which was one of the Prime Minister's most persistent concerns. The Royal Marine

Commandos, noted here as part of the Special Service Group, were viewed, alongside the landing craft capability, as the future of the Corps, arising out of the work of combined operations and the spirit of the Madden Report. In this report, Hunton described the disposition of RM Commando forces:

> S.S. [*Special Services*] Group is composed of four brigades. 1st S.S. Brigade (two R. M. Commandos) is training in U.K. and awaiting passage to the Far East 2nd S.S. Brigade (two R.M. Commandos) is serving with Land Forces, Adriatic. 3rd S.S. Brigade (two R.M. commandos) is in Burma and 4th S.S. Brigade (three R.M. Commandos) is serving with 21st Army Group.[6]

An RM Commando (like Parachute units) was about two-thirds the size of an army infantry battalion and was organised in rifle troops as opposed to companies, which explains the relatively small number employed in this capacity. As can be seen, Hunton's commandos were serving, in December 1944, in north-west Europe, the Mediterranean and Burma, with one brigade earmarked for the Far East or Pacific theatre. Hunton, when serving as Adjutant General Royal Marines in early 1943, played a pivotal part in the reorganisation and the future survival of the Corps. At this time, and apart from the service at sea of the 'blue water' Royal Marine detachments, there were thousands of marines in the RM Division and the two MNBDOs that had been built up soon after the war started, and these were playing very little part in the active prosecution of the war. It was realised that this state of affairs and misuse of manpower could not be tolerated, especially as plans were being made for the invasion of France and taking the land war to Germany. As head of Combined Operations, Admiral Mountbatten insisted that the RM Division and its battalions be converted to the commando role, and threatened disbandment if this was not carried out. Almost coincidentally, the then First Sea Lord, Admiral of the Fleet Dudley Pound, then looked to the Royal Marines to provide the thousands of landing craft crew that would be needed in *Overlord* and other amphibious operations. It was Hunton who pushed the reorganisation through and made it work, but it was not straightforward, as Julian Thompson explained:

> The AGRM, Major General Hunton, must take much of the credit for pushing this decision along, against the entrenched views of some of the more traditional, old-style Marine officers of the time, who saw no need to change the Marine way of doing things which had been good enough for the last 279 years. This small reactionary element could not, or would not, see that times had changed, and it was simply not good enough for over half the Corps to have no prospect of taking part in the war because there was no employment for them while they clung to outmoded organisations and practices. It was a case of adapt or die.[7]

Having used the report to the First Lord of the Admiralty to take stock, as it were, of the operational status of the Royal Marines in December 1944 and explain the basis of its future, it is appropriate to consider how it was used to provide the Prime Minister with the answer – or at least part of the answer – he was looking for. After commenting on the dispositions and numbers he had compiled, General Hutton proposed that, if future commitments for the Japan war were kept low, the Corps could offer 'about 5,650 officers and men' for service in Europe, consisting of a RM Brigade of 4,500 with the remainder joining the 'common pool'. But this was not a straightforward offer as the effect of carrying this out would mean that:

a) No R.M. Detachments would be available for H. M. Ships not serving in Eastern waters.
b) No Marines will be available for training in the Beach Organisation until after the war with Germany.

c) The 5th RM Anti-Aircraft Brigade must revert to Admiralty
control from the War Office.[8]

The Admiralty realised that this proposal of about 50 per cent of
what Churchill had asked for, with its caveats, would not assuage
the Prime Minister, and amended the CGRM's offer by adding
another brigade and leaving the 5th Anti-Aircraft brigade with
the army, raising the number of Royal Marines to be 'loaned' to
the army to 11,868. It was this number that was approved by the
War Cabinet on Thursday, 21 December 1944, when manpower
planning for 1945 was agreed:

> The Committee recommended the transfer of 20,000 men
> from the Royal Navy (11,868 of whom would be in formed
> units of the Royal Marines) and 20,000 men from the Royal
> Air Force, a large proportion of whom should be of high
> medical category.[9]

In concluding this section on manpower and future roles for the
Royal Marines, the Admiralty memoranda that made sure that
the term 'in formed units' was used in the final decision, provided
evidence of the often bitter rivalry between the armed services. With
personnel fighting and dying in the air, on land and at sea over vast
areas of the globe, it seems almost distasteful that, after five years of
war, this remained the case. Between the wars, territorial fights over,
for example, the Fleet Air Arm, against a very restricted economic
background can be, however misguided, at least understood. At
the end of 1944, before the war was even over, it appears that the
services were already fighting each other for post-war preference.
In this particular example, 'in formed units' meant that the Royal
Marines being sent 'on loan' to the army would retain their identity
and esprit de corps, in an attempt to ensure the preservation of the
Royal Marine Commando role. In one note, the CGRM made the

following observation, initialled in agreement by the First Lord of the Admiralty, that needs no further comment:

> The Army's attitude seems to me to be part of the usual War Office policy of trying to use the Marines, a first class force of fighting men, for the purpose of doing odd jobs and if we provide the Two Brigades for the Western front, which are now under consideration, I have no doubt that the Army will seize the opportunity of trying to earmark one of these Brigades, or possibly both, for occupational duties in Germany, using the Army troops which are thus released for the roles which the Marines are counting on fulfilling in the Eastern Theatre.[10]

For the Royal Marines, therefore, the Corps commitment to 1945 consisted of three elements, the detachments on board the larger naval vessels, the RM Commandos in several theatres of war, and in the provision of crews for landing and support craft for amphibious and combined operations. From the above paragraphs, it is clear the Royal Navy had been planning to participate in the Far East and Pacific campaigns, and these plans included the role of Royal Marine shipboard detachments, as Sergeant Nobby Elliott was about to find out. But this clear-cut commitment to joining the dominant US Navy in the closing stages of the Pacific war was not arrived at without argument. Roosevelt, Churchill and the Combined Chiefs of Staff first discussed the question of the war against Japan at the Sextant Conference, held in Cairo from 22 to 26 November 1943. At this conference the British Chiefs of Staff made it clear that they wished to confine the existing British Eastern Fleet, based in Colombo, to operations in South East Asia only, so making the Pacific theatre the main area of operations against Japan. To ensure British naval participation in this campaign, it was proposed to establish a British Pacific Fleet, with the most modern capital ships available, with its own fleet train for maintenance and supply, operating from bases in Melbourne and Sydney. Given the scope of the Pacific theatre, the size of the fleet train required to maintain the British Pacific Fleet on an independent basis, and the time it would take to find the shipping resources, this proposal looked impracticable over the short term. In the Pacific, the US Navy had generated and perfected a huge fleet train, consisting of tankers, supply ships, repair and maintenance vessels, utility carriers for aircraft, stores and replacements, with general transports, hospital ships, depot ships and salvage craft enabling the fighting fleets to operate at sea for months at a time. At this stage of the war, where was Britain going to acquire the ships to support its own Pacific Fleet, albeit one of more modest proportions? As Cunningham noted:

At the Admiralty in the autumn and winter of 1944 we had also to overcome the very natural resistance of the Minister of War Transport to letting us have all the ships we needed for the Fleet train in the Pacific. Shipping was woefully short, and the number of vessels we required was certainly imposing, far exceeding anything that had ever been thought necessary.[11]

The calculations that were made in the Admiralty, 'far exceeding anything that had ever been thought necessary', had been worked out in the preceding spring, when it was judged that about ninety-five ships, capable of carrying around one million tons of cargo, would be needed to supply and sustain the operation of a Pacific Fleet Train. This was an impossible demand, as Britain, according to a minute from Churchill to the Admiralty in April 1944, needed an 'absolute minimum of twenty-four million tons of imports this year and next, to sustain its war effort at home, even with a strict ration in place for the entire civilian population.'[12]

In the end, the Admiralty could not override the absolute priority given to shipping that was needed for Britain's survival and home-based war effort, and had to settle for a third of the tonnage its calculations had called for. To be fair to Admiral Cunningham, however, he had been used to working with very restricted resources in the Mediterranean and was himself sceptical as to the lavishness of the scale of the Pacific Fleet Train, while realising that if the Royal Navy was to operate on an equivalent scale to the US Navy, then 'lavish' was indeed appropriate. With the scaling back of the train, it seems most improbable that the Royal Navy would have been able to operate in the vast spaces of the Pacific without at least a good measure of reliance upon the massive logistic capability of the US Fleet Train and its island bases such as Manus. Nevertheless, it has to be recognised that this ambitious proposal was designed to alleviate fears that the United States Navy would be required to heavily support the British Pacific Fleet, and thereby reinforce the prejudice against the Royal Navy held by the Anglophobe US Admiral Ernest King, Commander-in-Chief United States Fleet and Chief of Naval Operations. However, King was not the only person with reservations about this proposal, for Churchill had his eye on the Royal Navy concentrating its forces in the Eastern Fleet in co-operation with South East Asia Command. This appealed strongly to Churchill's imperial beliefs in that it would strengthen a British-controlled theatre and restore Britain's prestige in the countries that were to be liberated from the Japanese, as well as in maintaining influence in India. In this sense, success in South East Asia Command would be a British victory, whereas participation in the Pacific, where the Royal Navy would be absolutely dwarfed by the huge and increasing size of the US Pacific Fleet, would see Britain viewed as a very junior and almost irrelevant partner. In his inimitable style, the Prime Minister argued and harried the British Chiefs of Staff and, after a series of compromises were thrown out in the spring of 1944, he finally gave way to the professional judgement of the heads of the armed services. Churchill had always acknowledged that even if the offer of a British Pacific Fleet was made, there was no guarantee the Americans would accept it, and there was nothing to suggest they needed any assistance in the Pacific theatre, even without taking into account the well-known objections and views of Admiral King. The matter was finally settled at Octagon, the Second Quebec conference, which was held in that city between 12 and 16 September 1944. The minutes of the first plenary session, 13 September 1944, with the President, the Prime Minister and the Combined Chiefs of Staff include the following:

THE PRIME MINISTER
...There were certain elements inimical to Anglo-American good relations which were putting it about that Great Britain would take no share in the war against Japan once Germany had been defeated. Far from shirking this task, the British Empire was ardent to play the greatest possible part. We had every reason for doing so. Japan was as much the bitter enemy of the British Empire as of the United States. British territory had been captured in battle and grievous losses had been suffered. The offer he, the Prime Minister, now wished to make, was for the British Main Fleet to take part in the major operations against Japan under United States Supreme Command...THE PRESIDENT intervened to say that the British Fleet was no sooner offered than accepted.[13]

As soon as the conference was over, the Admiralty commenced work on the command, composition and deployment of the fleet. These arrangements were presented to Churchill by the First Lord of the Admiralty in a paper dated 25 October 1944. In order to create the new British Pacific Fleet, the Admiralty proposed that the Commander-in-Chief of the Eastern Fleet, Admiral Fraser (of

Scharnhorst fame) be appointed Commander-in-Chief Pacific Fleet and proceed to Sydney from Colombo with the major units of the Eastern Fleet, which would form the nucleus of the Pacific force. In place of the reduced Eastern Fleet, an East Indies station was created, under the command of Admiral Fraser's erstwhile deputy in Colombo, Vice Admiral Power. Churchill approved these appointments and dispositions. The strength of the British Pacific Fleet was spelt out as follows, commencing with the nucleus drawn from the Eastern Fleet, due in to Sydney before the end of the year:

    1 Fast battleship
    4 Fleet Carriers
    6 Cruisers
    21 Destroyers and a number of escorts

The strength of the British Pacific Fleet will be built up as rapidly as possible and, by July 1945, the Fleet should consist of:

    5 Fast Battleships [including the French *Richelieu*]
    6 Fleet carriers
    4 Light Fleet carriers
    16 Cruisers
    40 Fleet Destroyers
    90 Escorts
    These units will be supported by a Fleet train, minesweepers and ancillary craft to maintain its lines of communications from Eastern Australia and to defend its advanced bases.[14]

By fast battleships, the Admiralty meant the KGV Class 14-inch ships, and the four Fleet carriers represented two-thirds of the Fleet carriers at the Royal Navy's disposal. As for the Light Fleet carriers, there were to be only five in service by the time the war against Japan ended. It took until March 1945 for the new British Fleet to assemble most of its fleet supply train and the fleet it could support – two battleships, four fleet carriers, five cruisers and eleven destroyers – placed under the command of Admiral Nimitz as Task Force 57. As an indication of the size of this modern force when compared to its American counterpart, Task Force 58, Task Force 57 was less than half its size and TF58 had a strike capability in excess of the Royal Navy. The Royal Navy had won the war in the Atlantic but had lost its global pre-eminence – a high price to pay for victory but completely logical in terms of an economy and a productive capability that had been driven into the ground in the struggle to stand up to and defeat fascism. One significant point worth remembering here was that in the Pacific, there was no Allied Supreme Commander – the theatre was completely American, divided into Pacific Oceans Area and Southwest Pacific Area Commands, held by Admiral Nimitz and General Macarthur respectively, an arrangement resulting from a political decision by President Roosevelt, rather than one dictated by the exigencies of war.

The size of the command and the need to maintain cordial working relationships at the highest level, with both Nimitz and Macarthur, required Admiral Fraser to lead the British Pacific Fleet from a base in Sydney, while his deputy, Vice Admiral Rawlings, commanded Task Force 57 at sea. By being based in Australia, Churchill and the British Chiefs of Staffs hoped that the governments of Australia and New Zealand would see this as a renewed commitment to the two dominions. Both countries had already contributed a great deal of their manpower and resources to the Allied cause in the Middle East and Europe, as well as fighting the Japanese in the South West Pacific. Following the British defeats in Hong Kong and Singapore, and the taking of the Philippines by the Japanese, Australia had wasted no time in placing its forces in the Pacific under the virtual command of General MacArthur, and the British government was very conscious of this fact and its implications for the Commonwealth after the war. It was no surprise, therefore, that Churchill promptly informed the Australian Prime Minister, John Curtin, of Fraser's appointment, in a communication dated 8 November 1944:

He [*Fraser*] hopes to arrive in Australia, with some of his staff, in the near future, to meet you and your ministers and to discuss the arrangement for the maintenance of his fleet... After discussions in Australia, it is intended that he should proceed to Pearl Harbour for talks with Admiral Nimitz... Vice Admiral, Administration, should be stationed at Melbourne ... and he and his staff would work in close association with the Australians Commonwealth Navy Board and would make arrangements with them for the Fleet's requirements to be met.[15]

The Prime Minister also sent Curtin details of the strength of the fleet, as described above, but was careful to advise the Chiefs of Staff that details of command and organisation were not to be publicised until the approval of the United States had been received. Within three weeks, however, on 28 November, Admiral King, on behalf of the United States Navy, gave his agreement to these arrangements and confirmed that the British Pacific Fleet would be required to operate wherever the operational situation demanded, and would come under the command of either MacArthur or Nimitz according to the location of the tasks it was set. With King's approval, however reluctant, when the British Pacific Fleet joined forces with Nimitz's Task Forces, co-operation and support were readily given, particularly at lower level, thereby alleviating the shortcomings of the British Fleet Train. The operation of the British Fleet Train also had a lot to learn from the Americans. Taking the example of refuelling at sea, British ships carried this out line ahead, floating the flexible pipeline between tanker and receiver, whereas the US Navy carried out this evolution with the ships abreast, using cranes and derricks. Not only did this permit for safer and faster transfer, it also meant that multiple hoses could be used, thereby saving time.

With the command, organisation and broad deployment of the British Pacific Fleet (BPF) agreed and fixed, it is now appropriate to look a little more closely at its composition, especially with regard to the capital ships that represented the leading edge of the Royal Navy in 1945. This is not to state that the eighty-plus destroyers, frigates, sloops and corvettes, plus fifteen cruisers, nine escort carriers and approximately thirty submarines that were eventually committed to the BPF were of less importance. Indeed, the larger units of the Task Force could not have operated without them, but the capital ships, battleships fleet and light fleet carriers represented the main investment in resources and were the most modern vessels available in the Royal Navy. For example, all four

The battleship *Howe* became the flagship of Admiral Sir Bruce Fraser, the newly appointed Commander-in-Chief of the British Pacific Fleet for the final stages of the war against Japan.

of the remaining KGV class battleships (after the loss of the *Prince of Wales* in 1941), were deployed to the BPF and HMS *King George V* and HMS *Howe* took part in operations in the Pacific. HMS *Duke of York* and HMS *Anson* arrived too late for action, but were present at the subsequent surrender of Japanese forces in Tokyo Bay and Hong Kong respectively. In an ideal situation these ships, with their heavy armour and large complements, needed to be adapted to tropical conditions, with special attention placed on crew habitation and the effect of the very high levels of heat and humidity on machinery and maintenance. Although British ships were designed for global operation, a prolonged period of steaming at sea, away from shore bases, placed new demands on ships and men. The fact was, however, that there was no time to make anything but the most rudimentary adjustments, and life below decks existed in a stifling, sweltering and unwholesome atmosphere. For the fleet carriers, with their armoured flight decks, the situation was even worse. Under the deck, which absorbed the sun's heat during the day, lay a honeycomb of flats, cabins, messes and compartments, which simply baked. However, the heavy armour gave some protection against kamikaze attacks and was a 'luxury' that the United States carriers, with their wooden decks, did not enjoy. As mentioned earlier, the Royal Navy by this time had ceased production of expensive battleships and fleet carriers, with the exception of HMS *Vanguard*, which was considerably larger than the KGVs with eight 15-inch guns as its main armament. Despite Churchill's best efforts to have her completed and commissioned before the end of the war, this was not possible, and so the Royal Navy's last battleship went into service in 1946, and was decommissioned and scrapped just fourteen years later in 1960. The fleet carriers that joined the British Pacific Fleet were HMS *Formidable* and HMS *Illustrious,* which carried fifty-one aircraft, HMS *Implacable*, HMS *Indefatigable*, and HMS *Indomitable*, with a capacity for more than sixty aircraft, and

HMS *Victorious* with fifty-two. All these carriers saw action in the Pacific and both *Illustrious* and *Victorious* survived hits by kamikaze pilots, which failed to put them immediately out of action. Further carrier support was furnished by the 11th Aircraft Carrier Squadron, which consisted of four Colossus class light fleet carriers, HMS *Colossus*, HMS *Glory*, HMS *Venerable* and HMS *Vengeance*. Each of these ships carried forty aircraft, half of which were Corsair fighters and the remainder Barracuda bombers. All four were completed and commissioned in late 1944 or early 1945 and sent to the Pacific after working up. They arrived too late to participate in any action, but spent time in the Pacific reoccupying Hong Kong, Singapore and other former Japanese-held territories, before being used as transports for the recovery of prisoners of war and the repatriation of Allied servicemen. As fleet carriers were very expensive (with their high speed and armoured decks), the commissioning of the light fleet type was a utilitarian attempt to boost naval aviation resources at a time when the aircraft carrier was clearly beginning to supersede the battleship as the main capital unit of the fleet. They were constructed at private shipyards used to mercantile standards of production, without heavy armour and with engines that operated at a speed of 25 knots – several knots less than their big 'sisters'. They provided a larger and stronger air capability than the escort carriers, which had been speedily built on merchant ship hulls in the United States and hurried into service to combat the U-boat threat in the West.

It was to one of the light fleet carriers, HMS *Glory*, that Sergeant Nobby Elliott was drafted, in what was to be the last seagoing appointment of his long service. Nobby joined *Glory* at the Harland &Wolff shipyard in Belfast on 16 February 1945, one of a large marine detachment of about company strength of more than 100 men, including a band. *Glory* displaced 13,190 tons, was 695 feet in length with a beam of 80 feet and a draught of just more than 23 feet. She carried a crew, including Fleet Air Arm, of

HMS *Glory* pictured in 1946.

1,300 and had a top speed of 25 knots, delivered by two shafts powered by turbines generating 40,000 horsepower. Aside from her aircraft, *Glory's* armament consisted of twenty-four 2-pdr pom-poms, in six quadruple mountings, arranged around the perimeter of the flight deck for anti-aircraft defence. A proportion of these were manned by the Royal Marines, under the command of Captain Gosling RM, and the marine detachment was also available for boarding and shore parties, landings, prisoner escort and a variety of duties that were expected to arise in the Pacific war and its aftermath.[16] *Glory* had been formally commissioned in January and, after Nobby joined, she undertook a full working up programme with the Home Fleet, a process designed to bring crew and ship up to a high level of operational effectiveness. Experienced senior NCOs like Nobby would have played a key role in delivering the required standard of efficiency and teamwork. In April, the Barracudas of 829 Naval Air Squadron and the Corsairs of 1815 Naval Air Squadron were embarked, and *Glory* spent the rest of the month completing air trials and exercising her air wing. On 14 May, *Glory* left Greenock, on the Clyde, after refuelling and storing ship, and sailed out to Malta, which became the base for an extended period of exercises with the Mediterranean Fleet. These exercises were completed in early July and *Glory* passed through the Suez Canal on her way to the naval base at Trincomalee, on the north-east coast of Ceylon, where she arrived on 16 July 1945. The final leg of her voyage to Australia consisted of a long passage across the Indian Ocean, during which *Glory* and her crew received the tumultuous news of the dropping of the atom bombs on Hiroshima and Nagasaki, followed by the Emperor of Japan's public announcement of the unconditional surrender of the Japanese Empire and people.

This unprecedented broadcast, notable in translation for not mentioning on a single occasion the word 'defeat', was made on 15 August 1945, the very day that *Glory* arrived in Australia's Sydney harbour. The author recalls Nobby talking about the feeling of relief that swept through the ship, quickly followed by the realisation that perhaps the Emperor's edict would not be obeyed by all Japanese forces scattered throughout the Pacific. Most of all, however, he and his fellow marines thought of the huge distance between Australia and home, and wondered how long it would be before they returned to their loved ones. One of Nobby's shipmates was the Cornish poet Charles Causley, then serving as Chief Petty Officer Coder in the signals department. Causley had joined the Royal Navy as a 'Hostilities Only' rating in 1940 and served until demobilisation in 1946. He frequently complained of seasickness and how the old salts ribbed him for it, but he wrote with affection about his time in *Glory*, beginning with a poem about the ship in Belfast:

> I was born on an Irish sea of eggs and porter,
> I was born in Belfast, in the MacNiece country,
> A child of Harland & Wolff in the iron forest,
> My childbed a steel cradle slung from a gantry.

I remember the Queen's Road trams swarming with workers,
    The lovely northern voices, the faces of the women,
    The plane trees by the City Hall: an *Alexanderplatz*,
And the sailors coming off shore with silk stockings and linen.

    I remember the jokes about sabotage and Dublin,
    The noisy jungle of cranes and sheerlegs, the clangour,
The draft in February of a thousand matelots from Devonport,
    Surveying anxiously my enormous flight deck and hangar.

I remember the long vista of ships under the quiet mountain,
The signals from Belfast Castle, the usual panic and sea-fever,
    Before I slid superbly out on the green lough,
    Leaving the tiny cheering figures on the jetty for ever.

    Turning my face from home to the Southern Cross,
    A map of crackling stars and the albatross.[17]

Causley also wrote how the size of the aircraft carrier, compared
to the small ships he spent most of his time in, meant that he was
always getting lost and confused. As for arriving in Sydney on the
day of victory, however, Causley describes how, in a short story
entitled *Tug Wilson and the Dove of Peace*, in the afternoon of
that first day he had a run ashore with his friend Tug, and listened
to a radio blaring from a shop:

Suddenly the music stopped and I heard a voice, an English
voice. A little crowd gathered around the shop floor, and the
voice went on speaking: I was too far away to hear what. But
the crowd grew bigger, and I could hear the voices of the people
in the back. 'Attlee,' they were saying, 'that's who it is: Clem
Attlee.' Then a pause, and another voice: an Australian voice.
It sounded vaguely like Joe Chifley, the Aussie Prime Minister...

I could hear ship's sirens blowing in the harbour: then bells ringing... ... 'THE WAR IS OVER', they cried, 'IT'S OVER!'[18]

As soon as the euphoria of the moment had passed and the celebrations concluded, the carriers of the 11th Squadron were given their orders to assist in implementing the containment and surrender of Japanese forces. At the request of the Australian government, *Glory* was given the task of proceeding to a point off Rabaul, on the north-east tip of New Britain, so that the local Australian commander, Lieutenant General Sturdee, could accept the surrender of 139,000 Japanese army and navy personnel based in New Britain, the Solomon Islands, Bismarck Archipelago and New Guinea. For this purpose, *Glory* rode in St George's Channel, between the islands of New Britain and New Ireland, and embarked the Japanese Lieutenant General Imamara and Vice Admiral Kusaka. Before the surrender documents were signed on the flight deck, *Glory*'s crew mustered as witnesses, and the Royal Marines provided armed guards, while the Corsairs of her fighter wing patrolled the skies above. Victory was complete, and Nobby rated this as one of his finest moments; it was certainly a bitter sweet moment that he cherished for the rest of his life.[19]

The war may have been over as far as the fighting was concerned, but Nobby and *Glory* were needed to assist with the collection of prisoners of war and their repatriation. For this purpose, the hangar deck was converted into accommodation for 1,000 personnel and additional medical facilities and staff were embarked. Between the end of September and the summer of 1946, *Glory* made three trips to collect British PoWs who had been assembled in Manila from camps in the Pacific. The prisoners were nursed and treated on board as *Glory* carried them across the ocean to the Canadian port of Esquimalt, at the southern tip of Vancouver Island. After reception here, and once they were deemed fit for overland travel, they were taken by rail to the east coast for the final leg of their

Royal Marines of HMS *Glory* in the Sydney victory parade.

The Japanese surrender aboard HMS *Glory*.

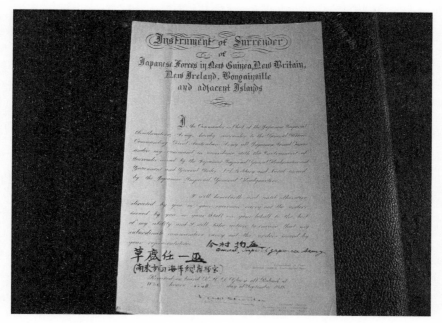

The surrender document.

Royal Marines band aboard HMS *Glory*.

journey to the United Kingdom. Nobby never spoke to the author in any detail about the plight and condition of the prisoners of war, but it was clear that he had found the experience disturbing. When this duty was complete, *Glory* remained with the BPF, and on 1 February 1947 Nobby was promoted to Colour Sergeant, becoming the most senior NCO in the marine detachment and designated, within the Corps, Sergeant Major. *Glory* spent a further eight months in the Far East, and it is from this period that the author has a copy of a letter home from Nobby to his family in Devonport. No apologies are made for reproducing it in full here as, in addition to the touching personal details, it illustrates the dangers and risks of operating aircraft at sea, even in times of peace. The letter is headed 'Sgts. Mess HMS Glory' and dated 'Wednesday 17 June', (the day seems to be incorrect, possibly due to time difference):

My own darling devoted wife and sweetheart, hoping my darling that this letter will find you and the children in the best of health as it leave [*sic*] me fine and always thinking of you. We shall not be getting our mail until we get into Sydney tomorrow morning so I am just waiting for tomorrow to come. We have been at sea since Monday doing flying exercises and it has been a very unlucky period for us. Yesterday one of our planes was coming in to land, when it suddenly banked over and crashed into the sea. It sank in a couple of minutes and the pilot did not have a chance to get out. Today the aircraft were revving up to take off and one of the fellows holding the chocks by the wheels of a plane walked into the propeller as it was spinning around and he was killed instantly. We are burying him tomorrow morning at sea. It certainly has been two black days for us. The last time was at Jervis Bay when we lost about four pilots. Tomorrow, Thursday, we arrive in Sydney and remain until Saturday when we leave for Adelaide on the west [*sic*] coast of Australia. The weather is fine but there is a chilly nip in the wind, especially in the evenings. I am fine dearest and quite busy these days with new faces joining and old ones leaving. It is surprising the number of people taking their discharge out here and getting married too. I suppose it's a case of 'Love at first sight.' Anyhow it is a land of opportunity for the trier. We have had several of the marines married since we have been in this time. I am always thinking of you darling and love you with all my heart and soul. I hope the weather is nice and you can get out as much as possible. Mary loves it, I know and I hope Sid is being good too. Take care of yourself my sweet. All my love and heaps of kisses… Always. Bert. Lots of love to Mary and Sid from Daddy.[20]

It is a matter of regret that earlier correspondence has not survived, but this touching and matter-of-fact letter does at least manage to convey the absolute importance to morale of the exchange of mail in a world where there was no other practical means of personal communication.

Glory eventually returned to Devonport, where she arrived at the end of November, before being paid off and subsequently moved to the reserve fleet, joining a multitude of surplus vessels that a war-stricken economy could no longer afford. Colour Sergeant Nobby Elliott went home on 1 December 1947, after a final commission at sea that had lasted what must have seemed like a very long two years and nine months, the longest period of foreign service in his twenty-one years and four months in the Corps. Out of these twenty-one years, Nobby had spent twelve years and eight months afloat, more than half of his total service to date. The needs of the Royal Navy, and the exigencies of war, had required him to serve on three ships between the outbreak of war and the surrender of Japan. This meant that he had served five years of the Second World War afloat on active service, a remarkable length of time in the front line. The need for his experience and skills resonates with the remarks of Churchill when he remarked that 'One set of men are sent back again and again to the front, while the great majority are kept out of all fighting to their regret.' Churchill was writing about the Army but for the 'blue water' Royal Marines serving the guns of the Royal Navy, it was ever thus.

Following his final departure from *Glory* in January 1948, when he was drafted to service ashore, Nobby received this fulsome testimonial from his Commanding Officer, Captain Gosling RM:

H.M.S. Glory
Devonport
10.5.48

PLY/X100 CLR./SGT. A.T. ELLIOTT R.M.

The above named N.C.O. has served as my Sergeant-Major for the last three years, to my entire satisfaction. He is industrious, loyal and conscientious, with a complete understanding of men, tempering his strictness with sympathetic tact.
In civil employment I consider his value will be greatest in those tasks in which hard work, initiative and loyalty are required.
During the past four months I have missed, most keenly, his cheerful efficiency and hope that one day we shall meet again.

Signed L. V. Gosling Capt. R.M., O.C. Detachment.[21]

Sergeant-Major Elliot proceeded from *Glory* to take up his final appointment in the Royal Marines, that of Recruiting Sergeant Major, Plymouth. In this position Nobby would march, in full uniform, from his family quarters in Ernesettle down to the Royal Navy and Royal Marines recruiting office in the still-shattered city centre. Every day this reminded him of the devastation caused to his home city by the Luftwaffe air raids; raids that had seen Rose and the children take shelter, like thousands of others living in this great naval city, in the surrounding hills. There was, after all, no point in taking the children to the Watts family in blitzed London, where members of Rose's family, including the author's father, had been bombed out twice from the houses they lived in, next to the Thames embankment in south-west London. Nobby completed the recruiting assignment, and his pensionable service, on Armistice Day, 11 November 1950, the day before his thirty-ninth birthday. He had served, as man and boy, twenty-four years, two months and fifteen days in the Corps of which he was so proud. For his dedicated service, Nobby was awarded three Good Conduct Badges, the Long Service and Good Conduct Medal, Coronation

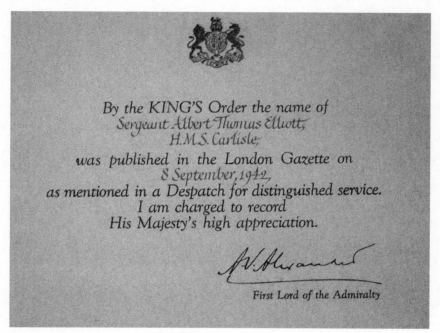

By the KING'S Order the name of
Sergeant Albert Thomas Elliott,
H.M.S. Carlisle,
was published in the London Gazette on
8 September, 1942,
as mentioned in a Despatch for distinguished service.
I am charged to record
His Majesty's high appreciation.

First Lord of the Admiralty

Mentioned in Despatches, 8 September 1942.

Medal, 1939–45 Star, Atlantic Star, Burma Star with Pacific Clasp and War Medal. On his medal ribbons he proudly wore the bronze single oak leaf insignia of the Mention in Despatches he had received when on *Carlisle* in the Mediterranean.[22]

Discharge papers, 26 September 1950.

11

CONCLUSIONS

The sea is a very unforgiving environment, and seafarers are only too aware of its overwhelming size and ability to change, sometimes over a short period of time. Being at the mercy of the weather, day in and day out, teaches all mariners a respect for the forces of nature that lie beyond human control and influence. The author experienced this when sailing in cargo ships, especially during long voyages across the Pacific where, for three weeks, there would be few, if any, sightings of land or other vessels. What is difficult to imagine, however, and what this book has sought to describe is how, in time of war, seamen (and marines) went beyond these bounds of respect, and undertook the most hazardous of voyages while fighting for their lives against an equally committed human opponent. For the men of the 'merchant navy' many of which were poorly treated by their often temporary employers, the losses of men and ships in 1939–45 were on an unprecedented scale. Theirs was an international sacrifice, with crews of neutral nationality and of the British Commonwealth (India in particular) continuing to sign on after experiencing the horrendous passage of convoys across the Atlantic, Mediterranean and through the Arctic Circle to Russia, such was the all-embracing nature of the Second World War. As a civilian service, where discipline relied, as far as British ships were concerned, upon the flimsy provisions of the Merchant Shipping Acts and not the Articles of War enforced in His Majesty's Ships, it remains a source of admiration that they fought through to the end. There were many who did it just to earn a living and to support their families, and some sailed in merchant ships because they simply could not abide the idea of service discipline curbing what they valued as their own free spirit. But still they went on, carrying out an unseen duty whatever the immediate and personal motive, until the war was finished and victory won. The British merchant fleet was largely rebuilt after the war and expanded until it reached its largest size, in terms of tonnage, in the mid-1970s. Since then, changes in global economies and the expansion of world trade, which has given rise to a considerable increase in bulk shipping and containerisation, have moved the operation of vessels from Europe to South East Asia and the Far East. Nowadays, the Indian sub-continent, China, the Philippines and Indonesia provide the lion's share of officers and ratings to ships of most flags. One of the consequences of this is that the general public in Britain and the West have lost awareness of merchant ships and the place of seafarers in their lives. They were anonymous in 1940 too.

For the Royal Navy, the Second World War saw it reach a peak in terms of the number of sailors and ships that were employed to engage an enemy that seriously threatened, for more than three and a half years, to starve the United Kingdom into submission. The Royal Navy entered the war ill-prepared and unfit to deal with the challenges the Third Reich presented, with inter-war economies and naval treaties denying the senior service the wherewithal to fulfil its worldwide responsibilities. It is hoped that the events described in this book have clearly shown the extent and overworked nature of the Royal Navy's many duties in the war. It has been seen how outstanding commanders, such as Cunningham, Fraser, Ramsay, Somerville and Tovey, and innovative leaders like Sherbrooke, Vian and Walker, to name but a few, skilfully handled their limited and overstretched resources to resist and then destroy the Kriegsmarine. Their leadership, however, would have come to nought if it was not for the fact that a relatively small number of experienced professional officers and NCOs, including reservists and recalled pensioners, absorbed the arrival of tens of thousands of RNVR officers and 'Hostilities Only' ratings. There is no substitute for experience at sea, and the Royal Navy's most significant achievement, after early disasters, was in converting so many 'amateurs' into an anti-submarine force that eventually succeeded in winning the Battle of the Atlantic. With the war won and with the treasure of the United Kingdom all but spent, the Royal Navy, at its peak in 1945, began a long, slow decline as economic reality, the rise of the United States Navy and the Cold War replaced the certainties of the past.

Paradoxically, the reverse has happened to the Royal Marines because, even though their numbers were drastically reduced after demobilisation, the Corps had replaced its traditional role with two specialisms that were ideally suited to the post-war world, offering flexibility and a more economic method of projecting power. During the war, the continuation of the ship detachment role was very necessary, if only to keep the guns firing in the heavy units of the fleet, and this study has demonstrated how hard-worked the 'blue water' marines were in the Second World War. Although Royal Marine detachments remained on many larger warships until the demise of the cruiser in the 1960s, the commando role found fresh employment in Korea, with the United Nations, Malaya and Borneo, combining amphibious capability with a special forces' expertise that exactly met the changing patterns of engagement. The Royal Navy contributed to this by lobbying for, and obtaining, commando carriers such as HMS *Albion* and HMS *Bulwark*, converted from their original function as light fleet carriers and later, the specialist assault ships HMS *Fearless* and HMS *Intrepid*.

All four of these ships have been replaced by modern vessels in service today, and it is Royal Marines who crew the specialist assault and landing craft, while the inheritors of the Cockles, the Special Boat Service, provide the Royal Navy with a counterpart to the Army's Special Air Service – this despite attempts during several defence reviews to bring the requirement for the Royal Marines into question. The decision by Admiral Mountbatten to force the Royal Marines to adopt the commando role 'or die', and the requirement from the Admiralty for a vastly increased number of landing craft crew, effectively ensured the post-war survival of the Corps. That these changes were implemented so effectively is to the credit of the CGRM, General Hunton, who reaffirmed that Royal Marines were, in essence, soldiers who served on sea and land, hence their long standing motto *Per Mare Per Terram*, a point made forcefully by Hunton to the Admiralty at the end of the war.[1] Such was the change and the overwhelming strength of the arguments in its favour that, Major General Julian Thompson was later able to write:

It was the Second World War which saw the genesis of the Royal Marines as Elite Troops.[2]

In piecing together the story of the Royal Marines and the war at sea 1939–45, it became clearly evident that the remarkable doggedness and will of Winston Churchill played a more important role than his ability to deliver carefully crafted speeches to encourage the nation. The constant minutes, memorandums and even haranguing of the Chiefs of Staff, displayed a level of energetic commitment to the cause that pushed the professionals to the limit. There is no doubt that he was a difficult man to work for, with unusual late working hours that added to the Chiefs of Staffs burden, but he carried this through for five and a half years, the first three years of which provided the country with one disaster or evacuation after another. By keeping everyone on their toes, however, he ensured that strategic decisions were taken for the right reasons, and after every angle had been investigated and argued almost to destruction. Paradoxically, Churchill's own strategic ideas, often floated without being thought through, were conceived and argued for in a manner that he would have found difficult to accept from a subordinate. Nevertheless, as strong, capable and determined leaders such as Brooke and Cunningham were prepared to take on the Prime Minister, these flights of fantasy were rejected, sometimes at personal cost to the individual. Despite this, Churchill did not, in the scope of this book and on the basis of the documents read, once overrule his professional advisers. By standing up to Hitler in 1940, the course of war was set and no one can deny the essential victory that, for the second time in a generation, was gained by, to paraphrase Churchill, the people's sacrifice, blood, sweat and tears.

The overall conclusion that the author has reached about the war at sea in 1939–45, is that it involved not just the longest battle of the war, the Battle of the Atlantic, which was the most vital action for the protection and survival of the United Kingdom, but also an ever-expanding commitment to action in several very different and widespread areas, in support of allies, army and air force. In fact, Allied strategy, the principal architect of which was General Brooke, was predicated upon – and indeed thoroughly dependent on – the allocation of shipping resources. In the end this meant robbing Peter to pay Paul, as ships and supplies were juggled to meet emergencies as well as to provide for operations connected to longer-term strategies. All the timetables for the campaigns in the Middle East, Sicily, Italy, Normandy and the Far East had to be set against the availability of shipping and landing craft and, as far as the USSR was concerned, the need to maintain supplies to the Red Army was of the utmost importance in the defeat of the German forces in the East. The scarcity of shipping determined that a logical, pragmatic, one-step-at-a-time approach was the only way to implement grand strategy, regardless of political and post-war considerations. Through the prism of shipping, it is possible to understand the interconnectedness of this most complex, difficult and risky enterprise – the waging of war on a global scale.

Finally, the debt that the United Kingdom owes to its heritage of seafarers, from home and abroad and in whatever uniform, in the struggle for the preservation of freedom cannot be exaggerated. This book is dedicated to all those who served at sea and especially to the ordinary but very special seamen who never made the final voyage home.

12

EPILOGUE

The fate of Nobby's first wartime ship, *Carlisle*, has already been described in an earlier chapter. But what of the *Jamaica* and *Glory*? It will be recalled that Nobby left *Jamaica* as she was undertaking an extensive refit in Portsmouth, after which she conveyed the Royal Family to the Channel Islands, before sailing east to join the East Indies station. *Jamaica* remained there, as Flagship, 4th Cruiser Squadron, until returning to the United Kingdom where she had a further refit, in Devonport, which lasted all of 1948. Sent to the America and West Indies station in January 1949, she was summoned from there to Hong Kong, to reinforce the fleet after the Yangtze incident involving HMS *Amethyst* in April. Remaining in the Far East, *Jamaica* was one of the first warships to engage in the Korean War, in June 1950, undertaking a series of shore bombardments against Communist artillery batteries. On 8 July, during one such exchange she suffered the first British casualties of the war, when one rating and six soldiers were killed and others wounded. Her next engagement was the covering of the landings at Inchon on 15 September 1950, where she was the first Allied ship to be credited with the shooting down of an enemy aircraft in this campaign. Two days later, *Jamaica* was attacked by aircraft and another crew member was killed and three wounded. Over the next four years *Jamaica* spent time in refit in the United

Kingdom and in the reserve fleet, before joining the Mediterranean Fleet in Malta, from where she participated in Operation Musketeer, the invasion of Suez, being the last ship to leave Port Said when Britain withdrew in December 1956. *Jamaica* was finally paid off on 2 September 1957 and was eventually sent for scrap on 20 December 1960. She'd had a busy post-war career that saw further action and frequent updating, reflecting the changing times of both the country the Royal Navy.[1]

HMS *Glory* was taken from reserve and also participated in the Korean War, where she was involved from 2 July 1950 until 19 May 1953. During this period she had two diversions, the first being to Sydney for refit in October 1951, and the second being for a strike against Malay terrorists on 27 October 1952. After a further refit in Portsmouth, *Glory* joined the Mediterranean Fleet, remaining until March 1954. Between August and September, she was used to ferry aircraft to the Far East, and her last employment was as a base ship, in January 1955, for helicopters assisting snow-bound communities in Scotland. *Glory* was sold for scrap in 1961.[2]

When Sergeant Major Nobby Elliott took his pension from the Royal Marines in November 1950, he joined the Dockyard Police in Devonport, following an established tradition, and served as a constable for the next twenty-five years, until finally retiring at the state pension age of 65 in November 1976. This position kept him in touch with his former colleagues and shipmates, and continued his involvement with the Royal Navy. On 12 August 1969 Nobby received the following:

COMMENDATION BY THE CHIEF CONSTABLE, ADMIRALTY CONSTABULARY

Constable W.752 ELLIOTT, HM Dockyard, Devonport and Constable W.751 GARDNER, RNAD Ernesettle (lately HM Dockyard, Devonport), are commended for cool and policeman like action in dealing with a man who threatened them with a knife and who was subsequently arrested and convicted of being in possession of an offensive weapon and of using threatening and abusive words and behaviour.

Signed F. O. Seward, Chief Constable.[3]

Even at the age of 57, it appears that it was hard to keep a good man down.

Nobby spent his retirement quietly with Rose in Stoke, Devonport, having remained loyal to his roots throughout his life. Nobby and Rose were typical of their generation and upbringing in that they lived simply and just got on with life, even through the years of separation during the war. Nobby enjoyed nearly sixteen years of retirement and died in 1992, followed by Rose in 1994.

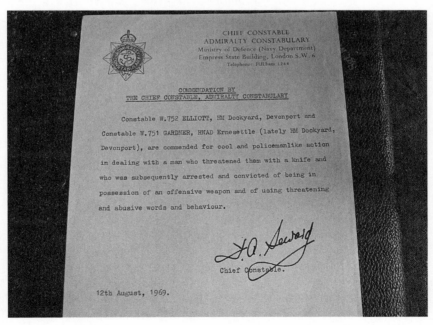

The Commendation.

NOTES

Chapter One

1. The National Archives ADM 286/137 Complements of HM Ships 1 October 1923.
2. Ladd, James D., *The Royal Marines 1919–1980*, (London: Jane's 1980) pp. 24–25.
3. *London Gazette*, No. 29751, 15 September 1916.
4. The National Archives ADM 201 Correspondence of the Royal Marines Office.
5. The National Archives ADM 234/940 Instructions for Royal Marine Divisions.
6. The National Archives ADM 1/8645/182 Order in Council 30 July 1923.
7. Ibid.
8. The National Archives ADM 116/2241 Officers' Pay in 1924 – Revision of Rates.
9. Ibid.
10. *London Gazette*, July 1920, Royal Navy substantive pay lists.
11. *Hansard*, HC Deb 30 July 1925 vol. 187 cc671 – 3W671W, written answer stating average rates of wages of time workers in certain industries.

Chapter Two

1. Certificate of Service Albert Thomas Elliott.
2. Certificate of Service William Moses Smerdon Elliott.
3. The legend is based on author's conversations with his great aunt, the late Miss Doris Pullinger, sister-in-law of Nobby and the last surviving member of that generation in the family.

4. Marriage Certificate, Devonport district, Vol. 5B, p. 979.
5. Royal Naval Museum Library, Ship information, HMS *Carnarvon*.
6. Ibid. HMS *Godetia*.
7. Certificate of Service Albert Thomas Elliott.
8. Royal Naval Museum Library, Ship Information, HMS *Erebus*.
9. Ibid. HMS *Frobisher*.
10. The National Archives ADM193/19 Royal Marine Training Manual 1932.
11. Ibid. Section 2.
12. Barnett, Corelli, *Engage the Enemy More Closely – The Royal Navy in the Second World War* (London: Hodder & Stoughton 1991) p.24.
13. The National Archives ADM/116/2746 London Naval Conference, 1930. Memorandum by the Chief of the Naval Staff, 17 January 1930.
14. Ibid.
15. The National Archives Cabinet Papers CAB/23/78 Cabinet meeting 14 March 1934.

Chapter Three
1. Royal Naval Museum Library, Ship information, HMS *Malaya*.
2. Royal Naval Museum Library, Ship information, HMS *Capetown*.
3. Whitley, M. J., *Cruisers of World War Two: An International Encyclopaedia* (London: Brockhampton Press 1999) p.73.
4. Royal Naval Museum Library, Ship Information, HMS *Rodney*.
5. Certificate of Service, Albert Thomas Elliott.
6. The National Archives CAB 16/112 DRC 37 Defence Policy and Requirement Committee minutes.
7. The National Archives CAB 16/412 DPR 129 Admiralty report to DPRC October 1936.
8. There was controversy over how swiftly the *Prince of Wales* lost power to its armament because of the aerial bombardment and flooding. For further details see: Middlebrook, M., & Mahoney, P., *Battleship* (London: Allen Lane 1977).
9. The National Archives ADM 53/105595 HMS *Royal Oak* Ship's Log November 1937.
10. Royal Naval Museum Library, Ship Information, HMS *Royal Oak*.

Chapter Four
1. The National Archives CAB 21/522 Correspondence James/Ismay 26 January 1938.

2. The National Archives CAB 21/1264 Conscription: National Service (Armed Forces) Act 1939.
3. The National Archives ADM 1/22955 Promotion to Sergeant.
4. The National Archives ADM 1/10312 Service Dependants Allowance.
5. Royal Naval Museum Library, Ship Information, HMS *Carlisle*.
6. Royal Naval Museum Library, Ship Information, HMS *Dido*.
7. Royal Naval Museum Library, Ship Information, HMS *Cairo*.
8. Royal Naval Museum Library, Ship Information, HMS *Calcutta*.
9. Royal Naval Museum Library, Ship Information, HMS *Colombo*.
10. The National Archives ADM 358/3139 HMS *Carlisle* Bomb Attack.
11. Royal Naval Museum Library, Ship Information, HMSs *Carlisle*, *Curacoa* and *Afridi*. Also see Whitley, p.69.
12. Hamilton, Nigel, *Monty, The Making of a General 1887–1942* (London: Coronet 1984) p.270.
13. Ibid.
14. Quoted in Connell, John, *Wavell, Scholar and Soldier* (London: Collins 1964) p.200.
15. Cunningham, Admiral of the Fleet, *A Sailor's Odyssey* (London: Hutchinson 1951) p.239.
16. For the best exposition of this argument, *see* Barnett, pp.212–213.
17. Rohwer, Jurgen, *Chronology of the War at Sea 1939–45* (London: Chatham 2005) p.36.
18. Cunningham, p.265.
19. Ibid., p.309.

Chapter Five

1. Edwards, Bernard, *The Merchant Navy Goes to War* (London: Hale 1990) Chapter 1.
2. Beckman, Morris, *Flying the Red Duster* (Stroud: Spellmount 2011) pp. 27–28.
3. Ibid. p. 133.
4. HMS *Rawalpindi* was a converted P&O liner that was sunk by the German battlecruisers *Scharnhorst* and *Gneisenau* north of the Faeroes on 23 November 1939.
5. Author's conversations with John Marshall, November 2005.
6. Letter to author from John Marshall, 30 October 2005.
7. Auckland War Memorial Museum, MS-98-1, Letter to crew of HMS *Carlisle*, signed by Lieutenant Mackenzie and Captains Boyce, Morris, Jacobs and Lawse.
8. Cunningham, p.357.

9. Ibid. p.363.
10. Ibid. p.363.
11. The National Archives, ADM/320 Naval Staff History, Battle of Crete, 1960 updated version of Battle Summary No.4.
12. The National Archives ADM 53/113833, HMS *Carlisle* Log May 1941.
13. The National Archives ADM 358/3139 HMS *Carlisle* damage.
14. The National Archives ADM 267/82 Damage Reports No. 21 HMS *Carlisle*.
15. The National Archives ADM 53/113833, HMS *Carlisle* Log May 1941.
16. The National Archives ADM 358/3139 Reports from Lieutenant-Commander H. B. G. Holmes, in command HMS *Carlisle*, 3 June 1941.
17. The National Archives, ADM/320 Battle Summary No. 4, Captain William Powlett.
18. The National Archives, ADM 358/3139 Appendix No. II.
19. Connell, p.472.
20. Cunningham, p.440.
21. The National Archives, ADM1/20017 Despatches on the Battle of Sirte 22 March 1942.
22. Ibid.
23. Account drawn from despatches from Admiral Harwood, who took over from Cunningham after the latter's departure for Washington in April 1942, and Admiral Vian.
24. Cunningham, p.460.
25. The National Archives, ADM1/20017 Despatches on the Battle of Sirte 22 March 1942.
26. See *London Gazette*, 8 September 1942.

Chapter Six

1. Barnett, p.67
2. Royal Naval Museum Library, Ship Information, HMS *Jamaica*.
3. See the plans in Roberts, John, *British Warships of the Second World War* (Barnsley: Seaforth 2017).
4. For a fully detailed account of PQ17, and comprehensive coverage of all the Arctic convoys, see Woodman, Richard, *Arctic Convoys 1941–1945* (London: Murray 1994).
5. HMS *Belfast*, now moored in the Thames as part of the Imperial War Museum, has turrets, shell rooms and magazines that are very similar to those on *Jamaica*. It is also possible to see the 4-inch open mounted secondary armament, similar to *Carlisle*'s main.
6. Danchev, A., and Todman, D., (eds), *War Diaries 1939–1945, Field Marshal Lord Allanbrooke* (London: Weidenfeld & Nicholson 2001), p.284.
7. Ibid. p.320.

8. Cunningham, p.502.
9. Ship's details from Haines, G., and Cdr Coward, B. R., *Battleship, Cruiser, Destroyer* (Leicester: Bookmart:1995)
10. The National Archives, ADM 234/369. Despatches on the Battle of Barents Sea. Also quoted in Barnett, p.279.

Chapter Seven

1. Woodman, p.328.
2. The latest research has been written up in great and revealing detail in Ashdown, Paddy, *A Brilliant Little Operation: The Cockleshell Heroes and the Most Courageous Raid of WW2* (London: Aurum 2012). This quotation is from The National Archives DEFE 2/271 Combined Operations Directory and is also found in Ashdown, p.346.
3. For a full account of the development of the Royal Marines, effectively avoiding disbandment see Thomson, Julian, *The Royal Marines: From Sea Soldiers to a Special Force* (London: Pan 2001).
4. Readers are referred to Episode 10: Wolf Pack of the renowned television series *The World at War* (Thames Television 1973). Of particular note are the face-to-face interviews, thirty years after the events described above, with Gretton, Sherwood and Doenitz.

Chapter Eight

1. Danchev, A. and Todman, D., p.316.
2. Ibid. p.450.
3. *Daily Telegraph*, August 1991, Obituary of Rear-Admiral Rupert Wainwright.
4. The National Archives, CAB 106/332, Admiral Fraser's despatch on the sinking of the *Scharnhorst*, written 28 January 1944. Reprinted in the *London Gazette*, 5 August 1947, p.3703.
5. Busch, F-O, *The Sinking of the Scharnhorst: The German Account* (Bristol: Cerberus 2004) p.50.
6. Ibid. p.3704.
7. Cunningham, pp.590–91
8. *Daily Telegraph*, May 1995, Obituary of Captain E. H. Thomas. Captain Thomas was awarded a bar to his DSC for this fine piece of navigation.
9. A arcs are opened so as to expose an enemy to a full broadside, rather than just the guns of the fore or after turrets.
10. Busch, p.117.
11. *Daily Telegraph*, August 1991, Obituary of Rear-Admiral Rupert Wainwright.
12. The National Archives, CAB 106/332, Admiral Fraser's despatch, p.3708.

13. *Daily Telegraph*, October 1994, Obituary of Captain Paul Chevasse.
14. Busch, p.136.
15. The National Archives, CAB 106/332, Admiral Fraser's despatch, p.3710.

Chapter Nine
1. Danchev, A. and Todman, D., p.486.
2. Woodman, p.384.
3. Whitley, p.118.
4. For a detailed description of Operation *Tungsten* see Kemp, P., *CONVOY! Drama in Arctic Waters* (London: Cassell 2000) pp.109–202.
5. Roskill, S., *Churchill and the Admirals* (Barnsley: Pen & Sword 2004) pp.237–238.
6. Harris, Sir Arthur, *Bomber Offensive* (London: Collins 1947) p.255.
7. Readers should note that this explains the appearance of HMS *Exeter*, played by HMS *Jamaica*, in the feature film, *Battle of the River Plate* (Powell and Pressburger: 1956).

Chapter Ten
1. The National Archives ADM116/5346 Prime Minister's Personal Minute No. 1176.
2. Ibid.
3. ADM 205/56 Churchill to Alexander 23 July 1943. Also reproduced in Roskill, p 232.
4. The National Archives ADM116/5346 RM 465/13/44 G. (SD).
5. Ibid.
6. Ibid.
7. Thompson, pp.300–301.
8. The National Archives ADM116/5346 RM 465/13/44 G. (SD).
9. The National Archives ADM116/5346 Conclusions of War Cabinet meeting 173 (44).
10. The National Archives ADM116/5346. Note to First Lord.
11. Cunningham, p.614.
12. Barnett, p.879.
13. The National Archives PREMIER 3/329/4 Octagon Conference minutes.
14. The National Archives PREMIER 3/164/3 First Lord to Prime Minister Command and Redeployment of the Fleet in Far Eastern Waters.
15. The National Archives PREMIER 3/164/3 Churchill to Curtin.
16. Royal Naval Museum Library, Ship Information, HMS *Glory*.

17. Causley, Charles, *Collected Poems 1951–1975* (London: Macmillan 1975), 'HMS Glory'.
18. Causley, Charles, *Hands to Dance* (a collection of stories.) (London: Carroll Nicholson 1951) 'Tug Wilson and the Dove of Peace.'
19. A film of the surrender on board HMS *Glory* is available on YouTube and at the Australian War Memorial, Canberra.
20. Private Papers Albert Thomas Elliott, letter home from HMS *Glory,* June 1947.
21. Private Papers Albert Thomas Elliott, Testimonial from Captain Gosling RM. 10 May 1948.
22. Certificate of Discharge, Colour Sergeant Elliott, Royal Marines.

Chapter Eleven
1. Ladd, p.264.
2. Thompson, p.2.

Chapter Twelve
1. Royal Naval Museum Library, Ship Information, HMS *Jamaica.*
2. Royal Naval Museum Library, Ship Information, HMS *Glory.*
3. Private Papers Albert Thomas Elliott, Commendation from Chief Constable, Admiralty Police August 1969.

BIBLIOGRAPHY

Primary Sources

The National Archives

The National Archives ADM 286/137 Complements of HM Ships 1 October 1923.

The National Archives ADM 201 Correspondence of the Royal Marines Office.

The National Archives ADM 234/940 Instructions for Royal Marine Divisions.

The National Archives ADM 1/8645/182 Order in Council 30 July 1923.

The National Archives ADM 116/2241 Officers' Pay in 1924 – Revision of Rates.

The National Archives ADM193/19 Royal Marine Training Manual 1932.

The National Archives ADM/116/2746 London Naval Conference, 1930. Memorandum by the Chief of the Naval Staff, 17 January 1930.

The National Archives Cabinet Papers CAB/23/78 Cabinet meeting 14 March 1934.

The National Archives CAB 16/112 DRC 37 Defence Policy and Requirement Committee minutes.

The National Archives CAB 16/412 DPR 129 Admiralty report to DPRC October 1936.

The National Archives ADM 53/105595 HMS *Royal Oak* Ship's Log November 1937. HMS *Royal Oak*.

The National Archives CAB 21/522 Correspondence James/Ismay 26 January 1938.

The National Archives CAB 21/1264 Conscription: National Service (Armed Forces) Act 1939.

The National Archives ADM 1/22955 Royal Marines, promotion to Sergeant.

The National Archives ADM 1/10312 Service Dependants Allowance.

The National Archives, ADM/320 Naval Staff History, Battle of Crete, 1960 updated version of Battle Summary No.4.

The National Archives ADM 53/113833, HMS *Carlisle* Log May 1941.

The National Archives ADM 267/82 Damage Reports No. 21 *HMS Carlisle.*

The National Archives ADM 358/3139 Reports from Lieutenant-Commander H. B. G. Holmes, in command HMS *Carlisle*, 3 June 1941.

The National Archives, ADM 358/3139 Appendix No. II.

The National Archives, ADM/320 Battle Summary No. 4, Captain William Powlett.

The National Archives, ADM1/20017 Despatches on The Battle of Sirte 22 March 1942.

The National Archives, ADM 234/369. Despatches on the Battle of Barents Sea.

The National Archives, CAB 106/332, Despatch on the sinking of the *Scharnhorst.*

The National Archives ADM116/5346 Prime Minister's Personal Minute No. 1176.

The National Archives ADM 205/56 Churchill to Alexander 23 July 1943.

The National Archives PREMIER 3/329/4 Octagon Conference minutes.

The National Archives PREMIER 3/164/3 First Lord to Prime Minister Command and Redeployment of the Fleet in Far Eastern Waters.

The National Archives PREMIER 3/164/3 Churchill to Curtin.

London Gazette

London Gazette, No. 29751, 15 September 1916. Major Francis Harvey VC RM.

London Gazette, July 1920, Royal Navy substantive pay lists.

London Gazette, 8 September 1942. Sergeant Albert Thomas Elliott RM, Ply. X 100, Mentioned in Despatches.

Royal Naval Museum Library, Portsmouth. Ship information

HMS *Afridi.*

HMS *Cairo.*

HMS *Calcutta.*

HMS *Capetown.*

HMS *Carlisle.*

HMS *Carnarvon.*

HMS *Colombo.*

HMS *Curacoa.*

HMS *Dido.*

HMS *Erebus.*

HMS *Frobisher.*

HMS *Glory.*

HMS *Godetia.*

HMS *Malaya.*

HMS *Rodney.*

Miscellaneous

Auckland War Memorial Museum, MS-98-1, Letter to crew of HMS *Carlisle*, signed by Lieutenant Mackenzie and Captains Boyce, Morris, Jacobs and Lawse.

Albert Thomas Elliott – private papers.

Author's conversations with John Marshall, November 2005.

Letter to author from John Marshall, 30 October 2005.

Hansard, HC Deb 30 July 1925 vol. 187 cc671 – 3W671W, written answer stating average rates of wages of time workers in certain industries.

Marriage Certificate, Devonport district, Vol. 5B, p. 979. Albert Elliott & Rose Watts.

Royal Marines Certificate of Service Albert Thomas Elliott.

Royal Navy Certificate of Service William Moses Smerdon Elliott.

Secondary Sources

Newspapers

Daily Telegraph, August 1991, Obituary of Rear-Admiral Rupert Wainwright.

Daily Telegraph, May 1995, Obituary of Captain E. H. Thomas.

Daily Telegraph, August 1991, Obituary of Rear-Admiral Rupert Wainwright.

Television Programme

The World at War (Thames Television, 1973) episode 10: Wolf Pack.

Books

Ashdown, Paddy, *A Brilliant Little Operation: The Cockleshell Heroes and the Most Courageous Raid of WW2* (London: Aurum 2012).

Barnett, Corelli, *Engage the Enemy More Closely: The Royal Navy in the Second World War* (London: Hodder & Stoughton 1991).

Beckman, Morris, *Flying the Red Duster: The Battle of the Atlantic 1940* (Stroud: Spellmount 2011).

Bennett, G. H. and R., *Survivors: British Merchant Seamen in the Second World War* (London: Hambledon 1991).

Busch, F-O, *The Sinking of the Scharnhorst: The German Account* (Bristol: Cerberus 2004).

Connell, John, *Wavell: Scholar and Soldier* (London: Collins 1964).

Cunningham, Admiral of the Fleet, *A Sailor's Odyssey*, (London: Hutchinson 1951).

Danchev, A., and Todman, D., (eds), *War Diaries 1939–1945, Field Marshal Lord Alanbrooke* (London: Weidenfeld & Nicholson 2001).

Dimbleby, Jonathan, *The Battle of the Atlantic: How the Allies won the War* (London: Viking 2015).

Edwards, Bernard, *The Merchant Navy Goes to War* (London: Hale 1990).

Edwards, Kenneth, *Operation Neptune: The Normandy Landings, 1944* (London: Fonthill 2013).

Evans, Richard, J., *The Third Reich at War* (London: Allen Lane 2008).

Greene, Jack, and Massignani, Alessandro, *The Naval War in the Mediterranean 1940–1943* (London: Chatham 1998).

Haines, G., and Cdr Coward, B.R., *Battleship, Cruiser, Destroyer* (Leicester: Bookmart 1995).

Hamilton, Nigel, *Monty: The Making of a General 1887–1942* (London: Coronet 1984)

Harris, Sir Arthur, *Bomber Offensive* (London: Collins 1947).

Ireland, Bernard, *Cruisers* (London: Hamlyn 1981).

Kemp, P., *CONVOY! Drama in Arctic Waters* (London: Cassell 2000).

Ladd, James D., *The Royal Marines 1919–1980* (London: Jane's 1980).

Lavery, Bryan, *Churchill's Navy* (London: Conway 2006).

Middlebrook, M., & Mahoney, P., *Battleship* (London: Allen Lane 1977).

Roberts, John, *British Warships of the Second World War* (Barnsley: Seaforth 2017).

Moulton, J. L., *The Norwegian Campaign of 1940: A Study of Warfare in Three Dimensions* (London: Eyre and Spottiswode 1966)

Pope, Dudley, *73 North: The Battle of the Barents Sea 1942* (London: Chatham 2000).

Prysor, Glyn, *Citizen Sailors* (London: Penguin 2012).

Rohwer, Jurgen, *Chronology of the War at Sea 1939–45* (London: Chatham 2005).

Roskill, S., *Churchill and the Admirals* (Barnsley: Pen & Sword 2004).

Roskill, S., *War at Sea 1939–1945 Vols 1–3* (London: HMSA 1954–61).

Thomson, Julian, *The Royal Marines: From Sea Soldiers to a Special Force* (London: Pan 2001).

Vian, P., Admiral Sir, *Action this Day: A War Memoir* (London: Muller 1960).

Whitley, M.J., *Cruisers of World War Two: An International Encyclopaedia* (London: Brockhampton Press 1999).

Williams, Andrew, *The Battle of the Atlantic* (London: BBC 2002).

Winton, John, *The Death of the Scharnhorst* (London: Antony Bird 1984).

Woodman, Richard, *Arctic Convoys 1941–1945* (London: Murray 1994).

Woodman, Richard, *Malta Convoys 1940– 1943* (London: Murray 2000).

INDEX

Abbeville 55
Adelaide 266
Aden 37, 47, 63–5
Admiralty Fire Control
   Table 11
Aegean Sea 29, 84, 90,103
Afrika Korps 73, 97, 118
Aisthorpe, Skipper 133
Akureyri 160
Alexander, First Lord of the
   Admiralty, A.V. 201,
   203, 204, 245, 248
Alexander, General Sir
   Harold 119, 154
Alexandria 28, 53, 61,
   64–5, 72, 74, 76–2, 85–7,
   89, 91, 94–9, 101–2, 104
Algiers 120–4
Altenfjord 128, 136, 140,
   156, 164–65, 169, 177,
   187–99, 194
Amphibious warfare 59, 121
Andalnes 56–7
Anglo-American
   relations 213
Anglo-French Supreme War
   Council 55
Anglo-German Naval
   Agreement 34
Anti-aircraft armament 36,
   40, 191, 220
Anti-aircraft cruisers 51,
   57–8, 68, 72, 80, 184
Archangel 112, 119, 157,
   160
Arctic Convoys 107, 119,
   135, 140, 155, 157, 183,
   186, 195, 197–9
Argyll & Sutherland
   Highlanders 83
Army School of Infantry 29
Atlantic Fleet 20, 36, 39
Attlee, Clement 222

Auchinleck, General
   Sir Claude 93, 99,
   118–119, 153
Australia 68, 108, 214–6,
   221, 227
Axis warships
   Admiral Scheer 113
   Axum 52
   Bismarck 38, 44, 69–70,
      192
   Dresden 24
   Friedrich Eckholdt 133
   Gneisenau (WW1) 24
   Gneisenau (WW2) 45,
      125
   Graf Spee 109, 128
   Hipper 125, 128–33, 136,
      147
   Littorio 100
   Lutzow 125, 128–34, 136,
      140, 155, 157
   Prinz Eugen 70, 125
   Richard Beitzen 133
   Scharnhorst (WW1) 24
   Scharnhorst (WW2) 125,
      135, 140, 155–80, 183,
      198, 214
   Tirpitz 113, 125, 135,
      140, 153, 155–7, 179–81,
      183, 185–98
   U-47 45
   U-255 137
   U-258 149
   U-314 182
   U-354 127
   U-394 197
   U-472 186
   U-601 185
   U-713 185
   U-954 150
   U-990 185
   Vitorria Veneto 74
Azores 141

Babjohns, Marine 85
Baltic Sea 54, 56
Bamford, Captain
   Edward 14
Barcelona 142
Bardia 73
Barrow in Furness 146–7
Battle of Barents Sea 133,
   147
Battle of Britain 65
Battle of Cape Matapan 74
Battle of Coronel 23
Battle of Crete 52, 75–7,
   79, 82–4, 90
Battle of El Alamein 119,
   154
Battle of Jutland 12
Battle of Mers el Kabir 64
Battle of the North
   Cape 164–77
Battle of River Plate 108–9
Battle of Sirte (First) 95
Battle of Sirte (Second) 100,
   104
Battle of Taranto 73
Battle of the Atlantic 73,
   105, 110, 147, 151, 184,
   204, 233, 235
Bear Island 126–7, 137,
   160, 162, 181, 184
Benghazi 52, 95–7
Berbera 64
Bergen 56
Bevin, Minister of Labour,
   Ernest 201
Bey, Rear Admiral 163–71
Bismarck Archipelago 223
Bletchley Park 74, 148–9
Bordeaux 142–3, 145
British Army Units
   8th Army 95, 97, 99, 118,
      119
   Leicester Regiment 83

Sickleforce 56
Special Air Service 142
XIII Corps 73
British Somaliland 64
Brooke, General Sir
Alan 118–9, 153, 183,
235
Bulgaria 72
Burnett, Rear Admiral
Robert 114–6, 125–6,
129–33, 137, 157,160,
162, 164–9, 177

Calabria 65
Cameron, Lieut. 155–7
Campbell, Captain 184
Canada 75, 107
Cape Horn 24
Cape Town 51
Casablanca 120–2
Causley, CPO
Charles 221–2
Ceylon (Sri Lanka) 64, 198,
221
Chamberlain, Neville 55–6
Chatham 14, 17, 50, 52
Chavasse, Lieut. Cmdr.
Paul 175
Chelsea 37
Chifley, Joe 221
China 29, 32, 37–8, 50,
232
Churchill, Sir Winston 30,
54–6, 62, 72, 79, 81, 93,
110–11, 113, 118–20,
142, 152–53, 155, 183,
199, 201–5, 209–16, 218,
228, 234–5
Clyde 45, 50, 143, 220
Cockles 142–5, 234
Cold War 233
Colombo 64, 198, 210,
214
Combined Operations 142,
145–6, 207, 210
Convoy GA15 78
Convoy HX237 149–50
Convoy JW51A 125–7
Convoy JW51B 125,
127–32, 134, 136
Convoy JW52 136–7
Convoy JW53 136–7

Convoy JW54A 158
Convoy JW54B 158
Convoy JW55B 160,
162–4, 167
Convoy JW56A 180–1
Convoy JW56B 181–2
Convoy JW57 182–6
Convoy JW58 186–90
Convoy JW59 197
Convoy MW10 98, 102,
104
Convoy MW6 68, 72, 74–5
Convoy MW7A 79–80
Convoy MW7B 79–80
Convoy MW8A 96–7
Convoy MW8B 96
Convoy MW9 98
Convoy ONS5 149–50
Convoy PQ17 113, 115–6,
134, 153
Convoy PQ18 112, 114–5
Convoy RA51 136
Convoy RA52 137, 140
Convoy RA54A 157–8
Convoy RA54B 158
Convoy RA55A 160, 162,
167
Convoy RA56 182
Convoy RA57 186
Convoy RA58 189–90
Convoy RA59 189
Convoy SC129 149–51
Convoy WS8 79–81
Conway, Marine 143
Cork and Kerry, Admiral of
the Fleet Lord 59
Cowes week 38
Cradock, Rear Admiral
Percy 23
Cunningham, Admiral of the
Fleet Sir Andrew 61–2,
64–5, 72–5, 77–8, 80–3,
90–1, 93–9, 103, 120–1,
123–4, 153–4, 161, 168,
193, 211–2, 232, 235
Curtin, John 216
Cyrenaica 35, 95–7, 99
Czechoslovakia 45, 109

Dalrymple-Hamilton, Rear
Admiral 197
Darlan, Admiral 123–4

De Gaulle, General 93, 124
Deal 25, 28–9, 35, 47
Denmark 56
Denmark Strait 44, 140
Derna 97
Devonport 7, 22, 26, 38–9,
43–4, 50–1, 53, 61, 222,
226–8, 237–9
Dieppe 121, 146
Djibouti 63–4
Doenitz, Admiral Karl 110,
135, 140, 148–51, 162–3,
179–81, 189, 195
Dunkirk 52, 78, 120

Eastney 45, 50, 142
Eisenhower, General Dwight
D 120, 123, 201
Ellery, Marine 143
Elliott, Albert Thomas
'Nobby' 7–8, 20–1,
35, 43, 75–6, 86, 93–4,
103–4, 116, 123, 140,
152, 198, 210, 219,
227–8, 238 et passim
Elliott, née Caplin, Mary
Maria 21
Elliott, née Martin, Lillian 22
Elliott, née Watts, Rose 8,
37, 229
Elliott, Petty Officer William
Moses Smerdon 21
English Channel 118
Enigma 74, 148
Esquimalt 223
Ewart, Marine 143

Fairey Barracuda 189–92,
219–20
Fairey Swordfish 59, 184
Falkland Islands 23, 42
Faroe Islands 112
Finch, Sergeant Norman 14
Finland 58
Fisher, Marine 143
Focke-Wulf Condor 115
France 10, 14, 16, 30–1,
34, 53, 55–6, 61, 64, 105,
123–4, 127, 143, 151,
163, 180, 199, 203, 207
Fraser, Admiral Sir
Bruce 114, 116, 153–5,

157–62, 164–70, 172–4, 176–8, 181–4, 187, 190, 193, 213–7, 232
Free French 93
French Navy 64, 214
Freyberg, General 79, 82

Geddes, Sir Alexander 15
Germany 15, 34, 45, 49, 54–5, 62, 64, 72, 106, 111, 117, 140, 157, 163, 180, 201, 204, 206–8, 210, 213
Gibraltar 23, 44, 52, 62, 79–81, 120–2, 124, 144
Gironde 142–4
Glennie, Rear Admiral 83, 184–5
Godde, Acting CPO 176
Godfroy, Vice Admiral 64
Godwin-Austen, Major General 64
Golokov, Admiral 159
Gort, Field Marshal Lord 60
Gosling, Capt. LV, RM 220, 228
Greece 52, 72–9, 82, 92, 99
Greenock 220
Gretton, Commander Peter 149
Grigg, Secretary of State for War, P.J. 201
Grumman Hellcat 189
Gulf of Aden 63

Haakon VII, King of Norway 44
Halifax, Nova Scotia 24, 110, 149
Hampton, Captain 78, 87
Harris, Air Chief Marshal Sir Arthur 194–5
Harvey, Major Francis 14
Harwood, Admiral Sir Henry 103, 108, 153
Hasler, Major 142–6
Henty-Creer, Lieut. 155
Heraklion 82–3, 91
Hewitt, Admiral 121
Hintze, Captain 178
Hiroshima 221

Hitler, Adolf 34, 56, 92, 105, 109, 124, 127–8, 134–5, 154, 201, 235
Hong Kong 37–8, 215, 218–9 237
Horton, Admiral Sir Max 149–50
Hudspeth, Lieut. 155–6
Hungary 72
Hunton, General Sir Thomas, RM 204–8, 234
Hutchinson, Captain 101

Inchon 237
Indian Ocean 32, 53, 63, 108
Invergordon 19–20, 39
Ismay, Sir Hastings 47
Italian East Africa 62–3
Italian Navy 65, 72, 74, 78, 91, 188

James, Vice Admiral Second Sea Lord 47
Japan 16, 23, 30–1, 198–9, 204–5, 208, 210, 213, 215, 217, 227

Kaa Fjord 156, 188
Khartoum 63
King, Rear Admiral 83
Kola Inlet 127, 129–30, 136, 159–60, 167, 177, 181, 186, 189
Korean War 237, 238
Kriegsmarine 56, 127, 162–3, 179, 233
Kristiansand 56
Kummetz, Admiral 128–35

Laver, Corporal 143
Leach, Admiral Sir Henry 42
Leach, Captain John 42
Lebanon 93
Liberty Ships 179–81, 189
Libya 61, 63–4, 73, 94
Loch Ewe 39, 115–6, 125, 136–7, 157–8, 180–3, 186, 188–9, 197
London Treaty 31, 39–40, 112

Longmore, Air Chief Marshal Sir Arthur 82, 93
Lulea 54
Lumsden, Major Frederick 14
Lympstone 47

Macarthur, General 215–6
Macdonald, Ramsay 20, 44
Mackinnon, Lieut. 143
Madagascar 53
Madden, Admiral Sir Charles 16–7, 28–9, 31–3, 146, 207
Maleme 82, 90
Malta 28, 52, 54, 61–2, 65, 72–3, 75, 79, 94–102, 115, 220, 238
Manila 223
Manus 212
Marshall, Marine John 75–6
Mason, Captain Dudley 52
Maud, Queen of Norway 4
Mehdya 122
Melhuish, Commodore 130
Merchant Navy 66, 78, 103, 105–6, 110, 231
Merchant ships, British, (unless stated otherwise)
Ajax 96
Andrew G. Curtin (USA) 181
City of Calcutta 96
City of Lincoln 72
City of Manchester 72
Clan Campbell 98–9, 102
Clan Chattan 98
Clan Ferguson 72, 96
Empire Archer 130
Empire Song 80
Fort Bellingham 181
New Zealand Star 80
Ohio 52
Pampas 99, 102
Penelope Barker 181
Perthshire 72
Professor Woermann (ex Germany) 23
Queen Mary 13, 58
Rowallan Castle 98
Talabot 99, 102

Thermopylae 96–7
William S. Thayer
 (USA) 189
Mills, Marine 143
Moffat, Marine 143
Molde 57
Montevideo 109
Montgomery, Field Marshal
 Bernard 59–60, 119,
 199, 201, 203
Moore, Vice Admiral Sir
 Henry 158, 187,
 189–90, 192, 194, 198
Morocco 118, 120, 122
Mountbatten, Admiral Sir
 Louis 142, 146, 207,
 234
Murmansk 29, 112, 127,
 140, 159–60
Mussolini, Benito 61

Nagasaki 221
Namsos 57–8
Narvik 54–6, 59
Neame, Captain 96
New Britain 223
New Guinea 223
New Ireland 223
New Zealand 29, 32, 68,
 108, 215
Nimitz, Admiral
 Chester 215–6
North Africa 62, 73, 76,
 93, 118–9, 123–4, 154
North Cape 128–9, 157,
 171, 175, 177, 180
North Russia 112, 119,
 125, 179
North Sea 33, 39, 45, 54, 56
Norway 44, 54, 55–7,
 60–1, 113, 115, 125,
 127–8, 135, 140, 155,
 163, 180, 190, 192, 194

Octagon Conference 213
Operation *Barbarossa* 92
Operation *Demon* 76–78
Operation *Dynamo* 52, 120
Operation *Exporter* 93
Operation *Frankton* 141,
 144–6
Operation *Husky* 53, 103

Operation *Ironclad* 53
Operation *Lustre* 72, 75,
 78
Operation *Market
 Garden* 92, 201
Operation *Mascot* 196–97
Operation *Musketeer* 238
Operation *Neptune* 186,
 195, 199
Operation *Pedestal* 52, 115
Operation *Regenbogen*
 128–30
Operation *Source* 155, 157
Operation *Tiger* 79, 81
Operation *Torch* 38,
 118–22, 124, 154, 198
Operation *Tungsten* 187–8
Operation *Varsity* 92
Operation *Wilfred* 55
Operation *Overlord* 38,
 183, 186, 197, 203, 208
Oran 120–2, 124
Oslo 44, 56

Palliser, Vice Admiral 180,
 184
Parker, Lance-Corporal
 Walter 14
Patton, General George 121
Pearl Harbor 94, 105, 111,
 216
Persia (Iran) 155
Phillips, Vice Admiral Sir
 Thomas 42
Philippines 215, 232
Place, Lieut. 155–7
Plymouth 24–5, 28, 35–6,
 38, 105, 117, 147, 228
Poland 109
Port Said 89, 238
Port Stanley 23–4
Port Sudan 63
Portsmouth 17, 26, 35, 37,
 44–5, 59, 142, 152, 198,
 237, 238
Pound, Admiral of the Fleet
 Sir Dudley 61–2, 124,
 152–3, 207
Powlett, Captain
 William 88
Prien, Gunther, U-boat
 Captain 45

Rabaul 223
Raeder, Admiral 128, 135
Raikes, Lieut. 143
Ramsay, Admiral Sir
 Bertram 120, 124, 196,
 232
RDF 85, 88–9
Red Army 111–2, 127,
 183, 235
Rommel, Field Marshal
 Edwin 73, 111, 118–20
Roosevelt, President Franklin
 Delano 105–6, 118,
 155, 183, 210, 216
Rosyth 178, 182
Royal Marines
 Detachment 142
 Mobile Naval Base Defence
 Organisation 79
Royal Marine Band 11,
 26–7, 36, 59
Royal Marine Brigade 17,
 46, 79, 207–10
Royal Marine Bugler 11–2,
 20, 25–6, 69, 75–6, 98
Royal Marine
 Commandos 7, 146,
 202, 207, 210
Royal Marine Division 17,
 28–9, 146
Royal Marines Boom Patrol
 Special Boat Service 142,
 234
Royal Navy, Commonwealth
 & Allied warships
 Achates 129–33
 Achilles 109
 Activity 187
 Afridi 58
 Ajax 72, 83, 91, 94,
  108–9
 Albion 233
 Amethyst 237
 Anson 40, 114, 158,
  187, 218
 Apollo 44
 Arethusa 57
 Ark Royal 80
 Auckland 64, 78
 Aurora 96, 122–3
 Avenger 114–5
 Avon Vale 102

Index

Barham 35, 72
Beagle 125
Bellona 196
Bermuda 180
Berwick 180, 184
Bison (French) 58
Biter 151
Black Prince 184, 187
Blake 22
Bonaventure 72, 75
Breconshire 94–5, 98–9, 101–2
Broke 122
Bulwark 233
Byron 184
Cairo 52
Capetown 36–8, 50
Carlisle 37, 50–4, 56–8, 61, 63–5, 72, 75-8, 80–90, 93–104, 117, 230, 237
Carnarvon 22–4
Ceres 64
Chaser 184–6
Cleopatra 99–100
Colombo 53
Colossus 219
Coventry 53, 65, 72, 77, 80, 94
Cumberland 137
Curacoa 57–8
Decoy 78, 98
Defender 78
Delhi 122
Devonshire 58
Diamond 77
Dido 51, 80, 83, 91, 96, 98–9
Dragon 184
Duke of York 40, 114, 159, 161, 165, 168–77, 187, 196, 218
Duncan 150
Emperor 187
Erebus 26
Euryalus 94, 96, 98–100
Exeter 109
Fearless 233
Fencer 187
Fiji 83, 88–9
Formidable 72, 158, 196, 218

Foxhound 96
Frobisher 26–8
Furious 187, 189, 196
Galatea 57, 94
Glenearn 77
Glengyle 77, 83
Glenroy 84
Glory 219–21, 223–8, 237–8
Gloucester 72, 83, 88
Godetia 24
Good Hope 23
Grenade 58
Greyhound 86, 88
Gurkha 96
Hardy 181
Hartland 123
Hasty 83, 99
Havock 96, 99–102
Hereward 83
Hero 99–101
Hobart 64, 94
Hotspur 96
Howe 40, 217–8
Hyderabad 130
Illustrious 65, 74, 218–9
Imperial 58
Implacable 218
Indefatigable (Battlecruiser) 13
Indefatigable (Aircraft Carrier) 196, 218
Indomitable 41, 218
Intrepid 233
Invincible 13, 24
Jamaica 112, 114, 116–7, 122–5, 129, 132–3, 136, 140–2, 146–7, 152, 154, 157–9, 161, 170–8, 182, 184, 186–7, 193, 195–8, 237–8
Kandahar 78, 83, 95
Kashmir 88
Kelly 88
Kelvin 96, 99
Kent 157, 180, 196
Keppel 184–5
Kimberley 64, 83
King George V 40, 125, 136, 218
Kingston 83, 99, 101
Kipling 96, 99

Kite 197
Largs 122
Leda 116
Legion 96, 99, 101–2
Lion 13
Lively 99–101
Liverpool 89
Mahratta 185
Malaya 35–6
Malcolm 122
Maori 96
Matchless 125, 167, 176
Mauritius 42
Meteor 182
Milne 184
Milwaukee (USA) 188
Monmouth 23
Musketeer 167–8
Naiad 83–4, 94, 96, 98
Nelson 30, 38, 40
Neptune 94–5
Nigeria 52
Norfolk 137, 157, 160, 162, 166–9, 171, 174, 176
Northern Gem 133
Nubian 83
Obdurate 129–32, 181
Obedient 129, 131–2
Onslow 129–31
Opportune 125, 167
Orion 72, 77, 83, 91
Orp Dragon (Polish) 184
Orwell 129, 131–2
Pathfinder 52
Penelope 95, 99–102, 181
Perth 78, 83
Phoebe 80
Prince of Wales 40–2, 70, 96, 111, 218
Pursuer 187
Queen Elizabeth 80, 95
Queen Mary 13
Ramillies 43
Renown 43, 80
Repulse 41, 43, 96, 111
Resolution 43
Revenge 43
Rodney 30, 38–40, 123
Royal Oak 43–5, 50, 109
Royal Sovereign 43, 188, 197

Royalist 187
Saumarez 159, 171,
  173–4
Savage 159, 171, 173
Scorpion 159, 171, 173,
  176
Searcher 187
Sheffield 125, 132–3,
  137, 160, 166, 168–9,
  177, 187
Sikh 99–100
Somali 116
Starling 140, 187
Stord (Norwegian) 159,
  171. 173, 176
Striker 197
Strule 184
Sussex 141
Tracker 187
Tuna 143–4
Valiant 35,72, 95
Vanguard 218
Venerable 219
Vengeance 219
Venus 181
Victorious 187, 189–90,
  219
Vindex 197
Virago 167
Vivid 21, 24
Wager 70
Walney 123
Wanderer 184–5
Warspite 35, 72, 80
Watchman 184
Whitehall 182
Wryneck 77
X Craft5 155–7
York 72, 75
Zulu 99
Rumania 72
Ryder, General 122

Salonica 76–7
Sardinia 120
Scapa Flow 22, 29, 39, 45,
  54, 58, 61, 109, 114, 116,
  125, 141, 146, 152, 158,
  175, 177, 182, 186, 193,
  195–7

Schnorkel 185
Sextant Conference 210
Sheard, Corporal 143–4
Sherbrooke,
  Captain 129–31, 233
Sherwood, Lieut.
  Cmdr. 150
Sicily 53, 80, 103, 118,
  120–1, 124, 140, 154,
  203, 206, 235
Sidi Barrani 73
Sinclair, Air Minister,
  Archibald 201
Singapore 37, 42, 96, 111,
  215, 219
Slapton Sands 59–60
Solomon Islands 223
Somerville, Admiral Sir
  James 80, 223
Spain 56, 144
Sparks, Marine 142–4
Special Operations
  Executive 142, 145
Spitsbergen 116, 196, 198
Stalin, Joseph 117, 119,
  155, 183
Stalingrad 127, 154
Stoddart, Rear Admiral, 23
Stuka 58, 85–88, 91
Sturdee, Lieut. General 223
Sturdee, Vice Admiral Sir
  Doveton 23–4
Suda Bay 75–9, 82
Suez 37, 61–2, 71, 75, 79,
  94, 154, 221, 238
Sweden 54–5
Sydney 211, 214–5, 221–2,
  224, 226, 238
Syria 92–3, 120

Tedder, Air Chief Marshal Sir
  Arthur 93, 99
Thomas, Captain
  E.H. 169–70
Tobruk 73, 94, 97–9
Toulon 124
Tovey, Admiral Sir
  John 114, 125, 133,
  136, 153, 232

Transmitting Station 11,
  27, 36, 61, 117, 147, 171
Trincomalee 221
Trondheim 56–7
Tsing Tao 23
Tunis 120–1, 124
Tunisia 154
Tyson, Commander 184

United States of
  America 15, 25, 30–1,
  33–4, 105–7, 110–11,
  114, 117, 120–1, 148,
  151, 154–5, 199, 213,
  216, 219
United States Navy 111,
  140, 158, 212, 216, 233.
US Rangers 123

Vancouver Island 223
Vian, Admiral Sir Philip 58,
  94–6, 99–101, 161, 233
Vichy 64, 93 118, 120–4
Vladivostok 155
Von Spee, Vice Admiral
  23–4
Vought Corsair 189,
  219–20, 223

Walker, Captain
  Johnnie 140, 187–88,
  233
Wallace, Sergeant 133
Washington 103, 117, 120,
  152
Washington Treaty 15–6,
  20, 30–1, 40
Wavell, General Sir
  Archibald 60, 65, 73,
  79, 82, 90, 92–3, 153
Wehrmacht 111
Weston, Major General 79
White Sea 115
Wilson, General Sir
  Maitland 76
Wolf packs 110, 140, 148,
  180–2, 185–6, 188